D1598808

Mother Imagery

in the Novels of Afro-Caribbean Women

Mother Imagery
in the Novels of Afro-Caribbean Women

Simone A. James Alexander

University of Missouri Press

Columbia and London

Library of Congress Cataloging-in-Publication Data

Alexander, Simone A. James, 1967–
    Mother imagery in the novels of Afro-Caribbean women /
Simone A. James Alexander.
        p.   cm.
    Includes bibliographical references (p.   ) and index.
    ISBN 0-8262-1309-X (alk. paper)
    1. Carribbean fiction (English)—Women authors—History
and criticism.   2. Women and literature—Caribbean Area—
History—20th century.   3. Women and literature—United
States—History—20th century.   4. American fiction—Afro-
American authors—History and criticism.   5. American fiction—
Women authors—History and criticism.   6. Marshall, Paule,
1929—Criticism and interpretation.   7. Kincaid, Jamaica—
Criticism and interpretation.   8. Condé, Maryse—Criticism
and interpretation.   9. Mothers and daughters in literature.
10. Motherhood in literature.   11. Mothers in literature.   12.
Home in literature.
    I. Title.
    PR9205.4.A48   2001
    813'5093520431—dc21

                                                        00-061985

⊗ This paper meets the requirements of the
American National Standard for Permanence of Paper
for Printed Library Materials, Z39.48, 1984.

Text design: Elizabeth K. Young
Jacket design: Vickie Kersey DuBois
Typesetter: BOOKCOMP, Inc.
Printer and binder: Thomson-Shore, Inc.
Typefaces: Comic Sans, Palatino

For permissions, see p. 215

To my mother
and to all unsung Caribbean mothers
who made this project possible.

Contents

Acknowledgments

I acknowledge and express deep appreciation to the many wonderful people whose encouragement and support made the writing of this manuscript possible. First, I would like to thank the University of Missouri Press, which welcomed and accepted my proposal for the publication of this book. I especially thank the editor-in-chief, Beverly Jarrett, who was my initial contact, and Jane Lago, who has exhibited tremendous patience in guiding me through the initial stages. I also thank Karen Caplinger, the marketing manager, and Annette Wenda, the copyeditor, for her insight and wonderful suggestions.

My thanks to faculty at Rutgers University, New Brunswick, namely, Abena Busia, Reneé Larrier, Josephine Diamond, and Gerard Aching, who has since joined the faculty at New York University, for their careful reading, patience, guidance, and insight during the early stages of this manuscript. Sincere thanks also to Nancy and Candace of the English Department at Rutgers. I am also very grateful to Maryse Condé for her kindness and openness and for granting me an interview. I am also very appreciative of her continued support.

I thank the Dean of English and Humanities of Pratt Institute, Toni Oliviero, for her generous support and encouragement. I am indebted to Ken Boxley and Tess Magsaysay of the Ken Boxley Scholarship Foundation, who provided me with a fellowship without which this project would not have been possible. I thank the Graduate School at Rutgers University for a Study Abroad Fellowship that enabled me to pursue research in Jamaica at the University of the West Indies, Mona. I extend special thanks to Barbara Sirman and Dean Harvey Waterman. I also thank Elizabeth Wilson of the University of the West Indies, who greatly encouraged me in my endeavors, and Jean Small, who greatly contributed to my pleasant stay in Jamaica.

Sincere thanks to my friends Paula, for her encouragement and support and for playing an important role during the earliest phases of this project, and Shondel, who has offered meaningful suggestions, valuable advice, and support. I would also like to thank my lifelong friend Alana, who was an inspiration during my research in Jamaica.

Thanks also to my husband, Aubrey, for his patience, unconditional love, and unwavering support. I would like to express special thanks to my family and relatives who supported me during the undertaking of this project. Finally, I thank my greatest inspiration, my new baby, Amani Jalil.

Mother Imagery

in the Novels of Afro-Caribbean Women

Introduction Reclaiming Identities

Afro-Caribbean Women Writers Writing the Self

Although recent scholarship has attempted to give voice to women's writings, notably those of Western women, Caribbean women writers and their writings have received little critical attention, and as such their works have seldom been given the serious scholarly attention or sustained critical scrutiny they deserve. In conformity with this lack, comparatively little has been published about Afro-Caribbean women writers. Despite this oversight or minimal acknowledgment of their works, it would be misleading to suggest that Caribbean women writers have not gained some level of recognition over the last decade. Among the writers who have gained national and international recognition are Paule Marshall and Maryse Condé.[1]

The three Caribbean women writers who are at the forefront and arguably occupy center stage of Caribbean writings in the Western Hemisphere are Paule Marshall, Maryse Condé, and Jamaica Kincaid.[2] Although geographically situated in the West, these women establish a direct and distinct connection with the Caribbean as they write "home."[3] It is rather ironic that though situated in the "master's house," the women are empowered and heroically assert

1. Paule Marshall's most recent novel, *Daughters* (1992), was selected by *Booklist* as the best novel of the year. Maryse Condé was the recipient of the prestigious French award Le Grand Prix Litteraire de la Femme, and the first woman to be honored as a Puterbaugh Fellow by the University of Oklahoma. Grace Nichols's *I Is a Long Memoried Woman* won the Commonwealth Poetry Prize in 1983. Zee Edgell's first novel, *Beka Lamb* (1982), won the 1982 Fawcett Society Book Prize.

2. This assertion is not intended to undermine or overlook the great works by other Caribbean women authors, but these three women are often found on college curricula and are taught more often in U.S. colleges and universities. They are also frequently the subjects of ongoing debates at conferences.

3. All three authors reside permanently in the United States but have maintained connections with their respective homes, Kincaid with Antigua, Marshall with her adopted home, Barbados (she is a first-generation immigrant of Barbadian parentage), and Condé with Guadeloupe, either through their writings or

1

themselves writing against the "master" narrative. Accentuating their heroism, this study not only validates the authors as great writers, but also argues that their works deserve greater critical attention because of the unique perspective: these women share blackness, femaleness, and Caribbeanness as they give "voice to their experiences and join in the attempt of women throughout the world, particularly in the African diaspora," to redefine themselves. The literary works of these women novelists seek to give expression to voices that have not always been heard as loudly and as clearly as they should have been. Adhering to Selwyn Cudjoe's acknowledgment that "the rise of women's writings in the Caribbean cannot be viewed in isolation, [because] it is a part of a much larger expression of women's realities that is taking place in the postcolonial world and civil rights era in the United States," this study simultaneously celebrates through critique Caribbean women's literary accomplishments, and acknowledges that the writings of these women, which are grounded within the black diaspora, are a part of a larger current of writing that is taking place worldwide.[4]

In spite of the fact that Caribbean women's writing is in dialogue with mainstream European culture and writings, the Caribbean, similar to the uniqueness of the three women, is intrinsically distinct and should be noted for that fact. Addressing the West Indian situation, Lemuel Johnson quotes Alain Brossat, who sums up the "predicament of the West Indian" in the following words: "The uniqueness of the West Indian situation is precisely the absence of a pre-colonial homeland."[5] Although that kind of absence is a unique phenomenon, it is also complicated, made more so because of the absence also of a postcolonial homeland, in the case of the French colonies, namely, Guadeloupe and Martinique. These complications are underscored when one speaks of or, rather, seeks a homeland elsewhere than his or her place of origin.

---

by enacting physical journeys. Therefore, it is no coincidence that the Caribbean is almost always, especially in the case of Marshall and Kincaid, the source and topic of their literary works and discussions.

4. Selwyn R. Cudjoe, ed., *Caribbean Women Writers: Essays from the First International Conference*, 5, 6.

5. Lemuel Johnson, "Sisters of Anarcha: Speculum in a New World? Caribbean Literature and a Feminist Hermeneutics," 243.

In search of Caribbeanness or what I often refer to as Caribbean sensibility, I have been engaged in ongoing dialogues and debates with African Caribbeanists.[6] As such, this discussion is the fruit of interviews and conversations I have had with notable Caribbean writers-scholars, including Edward Kamau Brathwaite, Maryse Condé, and Elizabeth Wilson. Significantly enlightening was my interview with Maryse Condé because it triggered my exploration of the multifaceted relationship she has with her mother.[7] This is an eclectic relationship that Condé shares with other Caribbean women writers, specifically Jamaica Kincaid and Paule Marshall. Apart from having complex relationships with their mothers, biological as well as surrogate, these women also have complex, ambiguous relationships with their various "home" spaces: the Caribbean, Africa, France, England, or the United States. These complexities, which I argue are embedded in the triangular relationship among the mother, the motherland(s) to include both Africa and the Caribbean, and the mother country, are addressed and detailed in the ensuing discussion.

The terms *mother country* and *motherland* are used synonymously and often interchangeably in many works to refer to the existing dominant political and economic forces. One such work is Susheila Nasta's *Motherlands*. As the title of her book suggests, it refers collectively to the motherland and the mother country. When not referred to collectively, Nasta uses the term synonymously: "colonial motherland or mothercountry [*sic*]." Apart from her synonymous use of the terms *motherland* and *mother country*, Nasta, in the broadest sense, employs the term *motherland(s)*. Apart from Africa and the Caribbean,

---

6. I use the terms *Caribbeanness* and *Caribbean sensibility* to refer to works that are Caribbean or West Indian in content, tone, and sensibility, works that address and incorporate the Caribbean (islands) as a means of establishing a distinct identity that can be uniquely classified as an African Caribbean identity. Apart from locales, this sensibility depends heavily upon the incorporation and emphasis on vernacular theory, or what Edward Kamau Brathwaite appropriately refers to as "nation language." Although Condé writes in "standard" French, her later works, such as *The Tree of Life* and *Crossing the Mangrove*, are informed by African Caribbean oral histories. *The Tree of Life* is a proverbial title, and *Crossing the Mangrove* is built around a Caribbean wake. By *African Caribbeanists*, I mean scholars and critics-writers whose focus of study is the Caribbean.

7. Maryse Condé, interview by author, New York, July 9, 1997.

Nasta's "Motherlands" extend to South Asia. Although her discussion is important to my project, my use of the term *motherlands* does not include Asia; instead, it is grounded in specific locales—the Caribbean and Africa—and black aesthetics and cultures, namely, black diasporan cultures and practices. When referred to simultaneously, I refer to the Caribbean and Africa as Motherlands, with either a capitalized *M* or a lowercased *m*. When referred to separately, the singular, noncapitalized *m* as in motherland or mother('s)land refers to the Caribbean and the capitalized Motherland to Africa. Hence, I employ a distinctive use of the terms, incorporating a dual usage of the terms *Motherlands* or *mother('s)land* in this study. In the chosen texts, I argue that the mother('s)land, the Caribbean, functions as an extension of the Motherland, Africa. Paule Marshall, among other writers, endorses this theory, for in *Praisesong for the Widow* the Caribbean is figured as the site of spiritual revivals where broken souls are mended and where spiritual renewal and rejuvenation can be achieved.[8] Spiritually broken and disembodied, the protagonist, Avey Johnson, miraculously finds herself on the island of Carriacou, where she acquires spiritual "wholeness."

Although *mother country* is used interchangeably when speaking of the dominant colonial powers, it is also used specifically to refer to England, France, or the United States. However, it can be argued that the latter is the existing dominant force, having reversed roles with England, epitomizing the colonial power and functioning as the mother country. Carole Boyce Davies contends that the United States' interest as an imperial power has long been established, but it was overlooked because of the European colonial powers', England's and France's, dominance of the world. Addressing this disregard, Davies asserts: "[T]he writers tied to the British and/or French colonial agony model missed the articulation of United States interests in the Caribbean as more consolidated than was the visible political apparatus of the European colonial powers." Davies interprets President Bush's "visit to Martinique and his discussion with Mitterrand

8. Susheila Nasta, ed., *Motherlands: Black Women's Writing from Africa, the Caribbean, and South Asia,* xix. In her novel *Tar Baby*, Toni Morrison also figures the Caribbean as a homesite. The healing process between mother and daughter takes place on the Caribbean island Haiti in Edwidge Danticat's *Breath, Eyes, Memory.*

[as a] tactic acknowledgment that, in the face of French colonialism, the US master remained present, assertive and dominant."[9] This domineering presence and assertiveness of the "imperial master," the United States, is aptly addressed by Jamaica Kincaid in her book *A Small Place*. Offering a harsh critique of the present condition in her homeland, Antigua, Kincaid addresses the double colonization, formerly by England and presently by the United States, of the island and its people. Kincaid's juxtaposition of England and the United States (she offers a parallel critique of the two countries in her book) is of utmost significance, for it illuminates similar colonizing principles that unite the mother countries, England as former and the United States as present, as imperial powers.

First and foremost, as mother countries, England and the United States are united in their separatist ideologies. Kincaid observes that in spite of England's occupation of the island, in spite of the fact that "everywhere they went they turned it into England; and everybody they met they turned English," the inhabitants were scorned, and in actuality "no place could ever really be England, and nobody who did not look exactly like them would ever be English." Making a similar analogy of the United States, Davies interrogates the term *African American*, which she claims has synonymous identification with black Americans of African decent. Addressing the monolithic nature of this identity, Davies pinpoints the strategic exclusion of other "Third World" peoples, namely, Asians, Arabs, and Latinos. Commenting further on this exclusion, Davies contends that "in the United States the historical convergence between 'race' and 'nationality' has kept separate, for the most part, all the possibilities of organizing around related agendas and has operated in terms of

9. Because of its history as the great colonial power of Europe, its occupation-cum-colonization of the English-speaking world, including the Caribbean, England is often referred to as the mother country. This title is also conferred upon her as a result of mercantilism, monopoly, and regulation of a nation's economy and state power. Operating within this continuum, I argue that France and the United States can also be classified as mother countries. While the Caribbean French islands of Guadeloupe and Martinique are still extant colonies of France, the present political policies of the United States mirror the colonizing principles that governed these and the English-speaking Caribbean islands, meaning domination, subtle exploitation, and submission. Carole Boyce Davies, *Black Women, Writings, and Identity: Migrations of the Subject*, 25.

polarizations of various races. It has also either sublimated racial differences or reified them in essential ways." The polarization of races in turn imposes a monolithic identity on those polarized. This monolithic identity is manifested in the term *African American*, where "American has become synonymous with United States imperialistic identity," an identity that according to Davies "could correctly refer to the African peoples of the Americas: North America, the Caribbean and South America."[10] Not only is the polarization of various races a common theme of U.S. imperialism, but a common feature of imperialism is also polarization within a specific race. Kincaid addresses the polarization within a race as she questions the adopted ideologies of the presiding government of Antigua, which by mirroring the colonials, in a similar manner, sets itself apart from the ordinary (colonized) people.

The United States' colonization of the island of Antigua comes in the form of tourism. Kincaid views this new form of colonization, otherwise known as neocolonialism, as the worst enemy of the people. For though the tourist industry purports to modernize and provide economic stability to the people, it actually creates greater polarization among them. Kincaid observes of tourism in Antigua that those allowed to venture near the tourist industries are servants, a privileged status in the given situation. While the American tourist can journey to the Caribbean to find solace, the reverse is not true for the Caribbean person who journeys to the mother country, the United States. This fact is illuminated in Kincaid's novel *Lucy*, in which the main character on her first day in America is confronted with the coldness of the place, which she later finds is synonymous with the coldness of the people. The reverse journey to the United States is one not of pleasure but of economics. The mother country, the United States, unlike the motherland, Antigua, does not provide the peace and tranquility the U.S. tourists experience. Hence, the mother country is not the hospitable place the term implies. Reemphasizing Isabel Carrera Suárez's observation, the irony in journeying to the mother

10. Jamaica Kincaid, *A Small Place*, 24. Although Kincaid specifically speaks of colonization of the island of Antigua, I expand this discussion to include all the English-speaking countries in the region that have been part of the British Empire. Davies, *Black Women*, 9.

country is "the exchange of a [motherland] for a supposed [mother country] in the hope of improving a life made difficult in great part by the exploitation of that [mother country] itself."[11] Having left the motherland for the mother country, then, it becomes obvious that the relationship between the two is noticeably different. This so-called exchange bears the imprint of entrapment. The mother in mother-land is symbolic of the land, the body, the connecting bridge; mother country, because of its unknown vastness and unattainable nature, epitomized by the country, speaks of alienation and estrangement. Hence, the mother is the cord that (dis)unites the motherland and the mother country.

Adopting the notion of "othermother" of such writers as Gloria Wade-Gayles and Rosalie Riegle Troester, my usage of the term *mother* encompasses mother as biological and as "other."[12] The "othermother" that these writers refer to is the substitute mother who takes on and takes over the nurturing role from the biological in times of need or crisis, becoming a pillar of strength and support for the estranged daughter. The othermother is a positive influence for the daughter and therefore encompasses a nurturing, supporting image. Apart from being an othermother, that is, a surrogate other, I extend "otherness" to the biological mother, meaning she is often seen as an "other" mother, an enemy to her daughter, particularly when she appears to advocate colonial habits and mannerisms. As an apparent advocate of colonial habits, she enters the enemy zone for her complicity with the mother country. While the biological mother encompasses both a nurturing and a suffocating image, the other in (m)other country is linked to a suffocating image, though it purports to be a nurturer.

Addressing the question of the significance of mother(s)land(s), Susheila Nasta argues, "[C]learly mothers and motherlands have provided a potent symbolic force in the writings of . . . women."

11. Isabel Carrera Suárez, "Absent Mother(land)s: Joan Riley's Fiction," 300.
12. Gloria Wade-Gayles introduces the concept of the "othermother" who substitutes the biological or blood mother ("The Truths of Our Mothers' Lives: Mother-Daughter Relationships in Black Women's Fiction"). This othermother theory is also duly represented by Rosalie Riegle Troester in "Turbulence and Tenderness: Mothers, Daughters, and 'Othermothers' in Paule Marshall's *Brown Girl, Brownstones.*"

Acknowledging Nasta's observation, the potent symbolic force is the mother, who in passing on the generational narratives to her daughter functions as female precursor, thereby transferring the authority of authorship to her daughter. Nasta further asserts that the employment of the mothers-motherlands themes is twofold: first, its main purpose is to "demythologize the illusion of the colonial 'motherland' or 'mothercountry,'" and second, it is a "movement to rediscover, recreate and give birth to the genesis of new forms and new languages of expression." On one level, the real political conflicts between the motherland and the mother country are given expression or, rather, are exposed within the personal mother-daughter relationship. It is through the daughter that this conflict-ridden relationship is channeled and the notion of an ideal colonial mother or mother country is debunked. This illusion becomes more transparent when the daughter journeys to the mother country. "Demythologizing the illusion of the colonial mothercountry," the daughter is able to combat this mythic notion, allowing what Nasta refers to as the re-creation and "genesis of new forms and new languages of expression."[13] In short, the daughter asserts herself and in so doing illuminates the personal and political relationships with the mother, the motherlands, and the mother country.

My critical approach to this trichotomous relationship rests heavily on Condé's own personal relationship with her mother, motherland, and mother country. My incorporation of Condé's relationship as a precursor to this discussion does not in the least suggest that the relationships Caribbean peoples have with their distinct motherlands are homogeneous; rather, it is employed as a means of highlighting links, despite social, cultural, and political differences—and geographical locations—among Afro-Caribbean women and their writings. Her relationship also illuminates and serves as an explanation of the relationships that Caribbean peoples in general have with their respective motherlands.

Like many Caribbean women writers who have complex relationships with their respective mothers and motherlands, Condé's relationship with her mother's land, Guadeloupe, and her Motherland, Africa, is fraught with alienation and ambivalence. Condé argues

13. Nasta, *Motherlands*, xix.

that these traits are the results of misconception, misunderstanding, and the prematurity of the Pan-Africanist movement espoused by Marcus Garvey, and later Padmore and others.[14] Questioning the ideology of the Pan-Africanist intellectuals, Condé disputes "the idea perpetuated by Négritude that all Blacks are the same." In Condé's opinion this is a homogeneous and somewhat racist, stereotypical conception, once practiced by the colonials and now seemingly perpetuated by the Pan-Africanist movement, that lumped all blacks together, based exclusively on skin color or appearance or both. Condé adamantly negates this notion of sameness among blacks as she exclaims, "every Black society is different." Necessarily, the universal principle of unity and sameness among all blacks was founded within a particular theoretical and ideological framework and, as such, seriously overlooked the repercussive tendencies of slavery, epitomized in the Middle Passage and the process of colonization, another subtle form of slavery, and the devastating effects that this bondage or any other form of enslavement had and still has on the human psyche. This overlooking of important facts was a "big mistake and caused a lot of sufferings in the minds of West Indians and African-Americans as well."[15] The sufferings experienced as a result of slavery and colonization, and to a great extent the disillusionment experienced by the rejection of their African brothers and sisters, are detailed and adequately recorded in Condé's first two novels, *Heremakhonon* and *A Season in Rihata*.

14. It is worthy of mention that having lived away from her home and people for numerous years Condé has since "made peace with her island," meaning she has reconciled with her mother's land, Guadeloupe, where she spends immeasurable time refamiliarizing herself with the island and the island's people and culture.

The theorists of the Pan-Africanist and Négritude movement are too numerous to mention. However, in this instance, one can cite Marcus Garvey, who is considered the founding father of the Universal Negro Improvement and Conservation Association and African Communities League, also known as the Universal Negro Improvement Association (UNIA); Leopold Senghor, whose name is synonymous with Négritude; Padmore; and Aimé Césaire. Under the direction of Garvey, this movement sought to build in Africa a black-governed nation.

15. Maryse Condé, "Pan-Africanism, Feminism, and Culture," 60. Refer to this article for a complete discussion on the theme of Pan-Africanism and the Pan-Africanist movement as viewed and interpreted by Condé.

Although Condé's novels are not autobiographical (in the strict sense of the word), her personal experiences shape her protagonists. Disillusioned, like her protagonists, Marie-Hélène in *A Season in Rihata* and Veronica in *Heremakhonon*, with her mother's land, Guadeloupe, Condé migrated to Africa, where she lived for several years. Instead of finding the homeland she sought, she was faced with further alienation and disappointment. In an interview with Mohamed B. Taleb-Khyar, Condé confesses, "When I was living in Africa I was just a French West Indian living in the motherland. . . . I discovered that Africa was not my homeland. . . . Africa helped me to discover that I am not an African. I lived in Africa and I was so terribly unhappy. . . . I understood that I did not really belong there. I am not an African. I am West Indian and I belong to the West Indies. Africa helped me to see exactly who I am."[16] Condé has come under harsh criticism for her revealing statement, though she maintains that her confession is not her "looking down upon Africa."

Indeed, Condé is openly voicing her disillusionment and disappointment with the "proponents of Négritude" that promised diasporan blacks a homeland in the Motherland and total assimilation and identification with their long-lost African brothers and sisters. Condé further voices her disappointment in the following words: "We were led to believe that Africa was an ideal home. When we discovered it was not, we suffered. Without Négritude, we would not have experienced the degree of disillusionment that we did. The issue of 'likeness' or 'similarity' is erroneous."[17]

This absence of an ideal homeland intensifies the imagining and the inventing of home spaces or homelands, thus leading to the construction of imagined homelands or "imagined communities." A term coined by Benedict Anderson, *imagined community* is used to define a nation as imaginary. Anderson's concept of "imagined community" is exclusively and politically oriented and founded on capitalist conceptions evidenced by his equating and conflating his communities with nations. Although Anderson's actions seemingly have global, universal connotations, he simultaneously resists the idea that there is in fact a "real" community based on a histori-

16. Maryse Condé, "An Interview with Maryse Condé and Rita Dove," 355–56.
17. Condé, "Pan-Africanism, Feminism, and Culture," 60.

cal past, instead arguing that what we think of as the past "imagined" concept, put together selectively from fragments, ‿‿‿‿ on our present ideological needs. In accordance with his conviction, Anderson proposed the following definition of a nation as "an imagined political community—and imagined as both inherently limited and sovereign."[18] Although my discussion is somewhat borne out of his political, capitalist ideas, my incorporation and adaptation of his "imagined communities" deviate from his prescriptive political definition of home spaces and focus on the cultural and spiritual aspects of what constitute the imagined. Accordingly, embedded in my term *imagined homelands* are the cultural and spiritual values of community that constitute both the "real" and the "imagined." Anderson regards the real and the imagined as oppositional concepts; when not oppositional, the imagined evidently substitutes the "real." Rejecting the limitations placed on the real and the imagined, I regard these concepts as enhancing. Anderson also negates the idea of an existing historical past and argues that the past is always imagined, selective, and fragmented. Although I agree that the past can be imagined and fragmented, I view Anderson's referral to the past as a concept as a further negation of its reality. This negation also seems to suggest that his community is more imaginary, meaning it is unreal or nonexistent, than imagined. Although the notion of an ideal community is arguably unrealistic, I maintain that a community can be both real and imagined. It is real because it is imagined. Although my concept of community or homelands is more material, it does not overlook or undermine the political, and continuous, based on a specific, even if "imagined" or reconstructed, historical past. Rejecting the strictly political, I contend that the sovereign nature of nations limits and restricts communal kinship among peoples, establishing hierarchical structures and relationships among them. A nation also speaks of territorial boundaries and is based on sameness: same ethnicity and, often, same language.

In spite of the fact that Anderson denounces the separatist values of the Garvey era by his rejection of and questioning of the notion of a

---

18. Benjamin Anderson, *Imagined Communities: Reflection on the Origin and Spread of Nationalism*, 15. The term *imagined homelands* is borne out of Anderson's "imagined community."

"real" community, his (political) usage of the term *nation* is seemingly linked with or borne out of Garvey's aim to build a so-called black-governed nation. Repudiating purity and separatist values advocated by the Garveyian movement, Anderson claims that his point of departure is his viewing of "nation-ness, as well as nationalism, [as] cultural artefacts of a particular kind."[19] In spite of its apparent potentials, his community is repeatedly defined by mainstream political ideologies, and not by cultural artifacts as he contends. I propose an imagined homeland, although distinct, founded on difference and multiplicity. Far from being exclusionary and separatist, this imagined homeland illuminates kinship, continuity, and communal relations between black diasporic peoples and their fellow members from the Motherland. Regardless of the political context, my imagined homeland, despite specific localities, is a social yet universal group that shares a common cultural and historical heritage. Hence, I emphasize the cultural and spiritual aspects of communities and communal relationships, vital components that constitute both the "real" and the imagined, as they link diasporan Africans with continental Africans. Far from being imaginary, my community, though imagined, is "real."

Despite the imaginary implications of his community, Anderson still contends that kinship exists among those people who constitute his imaginary community. Similar to Anderson's nationalistic idea, the members of my imagined homelands secretly acknowledge their kinship with their fellow members. A nation, as Anderson sees it, "is imagined because the members of the smallest nation will never know most of their fellow members, meet them, or even hear of them, yet in the minds of each lives the image of their communion." Dissimilar to Anderson's unknown, which is premised singularly on the literal, my imagined homeland also encompasses the known. Although it is true that one imagines the unknown and often the nonexistent, therefore demonstrating "the confidence of community in anonymity," one can also imagine even amid the known the "non-anonymous."[20]

A perfect example of this communion, imagining amid the known, is seen in Condé's *Heremakhonon*. Before her departure for the Moth-

19. Ibid., 4.
20. Ibid., 15, 40.

erland, Africa, Veronica Mercier perceives Africa as the savior of the black diaspora and convinces herself that Africa will restore lost souls. Even though her presence in the Motherland contradicts her imaginary reconstruction of it, she still continues to believe that Africa's sole task is to unite the black diaspora.[21] Veronica goes in search of her imaginary community only to shatter this "confidence of community in anonymity," supporting Anderson's idea of the community "imagined as both inherently limited and sovereign." Anderson contends that the nation is "imagined as limited because even the largest of them, encompassing perhaps a billion living human beings, has finite, if elastic, boundaries, beyond which lie other nations. No nation imagines itself coterminous with mankind." Despite the shattering of the "confidence of community in anonymity" and the finiteness of community, there still exists in the minds of people a kinship, however dismal, with their fellow members of the community. Although nations set up boundaries that exclude mankind, the overriding principle of communities is comradeship. I am not suggesting that communities are devoid of boundaries, but they are not means of creating distance between peoples. Although various communities comprise social groups sharing common characteristics or interests, they perceive themselves as distinct in some respect from the larger communities or societies within which they exist. It is this distinction that is dangerously overlooked and that Condé gives voice to in noting, "[E]ach island has an identity of its own, even if we cannot divorce our problems from theirs." In her revealing observation, Maryse Condé comments that the notions of nationalism and Pan-Africanism "must be redefined in the context of present realities." Allocating Africa as the ideal homeland and delegating Africa the singular task of uniting all Mother Africa's lost children both limits it and gives it dominion over other communities. This limitation on one hand, and empowerment on the other, works against the unifying principles of kinship and communal relations on which communities are founded. Condé further hints at the foolhardiness of conceiving Africa as the ideal homeland of or for all

---

21. Veronica seeks an "ideal" homeland, which is nonexistent and therefore imaginary. In a similar manner, I think that Anderson seeks an ideal historical past devoid of fragmentation. I disagree with his idea that we selectively reconstruct our past—many of us are not that privileged.

blacks when she notes that "it is difficult to achieve unity within the Caribbean, even among people who share a common history and language. . . . So how can we talk of Pan-Africanism . . . ?"[22] Similar to Anderson, who disputes the infiniteness and unlimitedness of nations, Condé dispels the notion of "absolute" unity within the Caribbean. The imagining of a national group or community simultaneously affirms one's inclusion in and separation from the body of this community. This vision of a community can be assessed as a process of self-creation, which stands in contrast, on one hand, to the Bakhtinian notion that it is ultimately the community that defines us and, on the other, to the African principles of community and kinship.[23] However, in Condé's novel *Heremakhonon*, this imagining outside the community does not in the least promote self-creation. It actually hinders growth and communal relations. Void of spiritual essence, the community falls short of it goals, further hindering the individual's growth.

The spirit of communal relationships is revived in Condé's other novel *I, Tituba, Black Witch of Salem*. In contrast to *Heremakhonon*, this notion of the community and kinship is ritualistically celebrated in *Tituba*. Therefore, the notions of home and space are less imagined because the titular protagonist, Tituba, is at home with herself in the mother('s)land, Barbados. Home becomes a concretized, fixed location and not an imaginary homeland or motherland.

The process of imagining, then, becomes associated with the creation or celebration of a national culture rather than with the invention of an ideal homeland. In contrast to Négritude and Pan-Africanism founded exclusively on the basis of race or color or both, this new concept that advocates culture is called "Créolité." This new literary movement founded in the French West Indies

22. Anderson, *Imagined Communities*, 15–16; Condé, "Pan-Africanism, Feminism, and Culture," 57, 60, 57.

23. On one hand, I am operating within the Bakhtinian notion of community as he works it out in "Response to a Question from the Novy Mir Editorial Staff" (see Mikhail Bakhtin, *Speech Genres and Other Late Essays*). On the other hand, I am referring to the African principles of community and kinship as employed by such theorists as Karla Holloway, John Mbiti, and Peter Paris. Bakhtin's notion of the community is culturally oriented. Extending on the cultural, the African principles of community and kinship address the spiritual nature and essence of communities.

under the governance of the author Patrick Chamoiseau promotes the local and oral cultures and traditions. Nonetheless, it does not endorse exclusion; rather, it calls for an intermeshing of other cultures. Language is also an important factor in the advancement of the local cultures, and therefore, in the spirit of Créolité, the local language, Creole, substitutes the French (colonial) language. Commenting on Chamoiseau's conception of Créolité, Condé declares, "Chamoiseau's work does not even mention Négritude. Instead, he is an advocate of Créolité. . . . [T]he new concept of Créolité does not refer to race or color. It refers only to culture." Despite Condé's assertion, the race or color of a people determinedly speaks of their cultural background. Though Chamoiseau may not have mentioned explicitly the race or color of the Creoles, it can be argued that these concepts are embedded in his definition. Moreover, he talks about the Antilles, a specific locale where the term *Créolité* is arguably loaded with racial and color connotations. Inasmuch as Condé's adaptation of "Créolité" refers to a specific region of the Caribbean, the Antilles, and "is a syncretic culture which meshes French, Blacks from Africa, East Indians from India, and other Asians into a new culture," my usage of the term that functions as a substitute for Négritude and Pan-Africanism extends beyond the Antilles to include the English-speaking Caribbean. Perhaps this inclusion defies the odds, for Françoise Lionnet contends that because "there is no real equivalent for the word 'métis' in English," one can "infer that for all English-speaking peoples the very concept of race is different from that of the French . . . speakers." She later adds that "certain categories, such as créole and métis, are not part of any visible racial difference for the average English speaker." Though *Créole* and *métis* may be used interchangeably by English speakers because of a lack of "visible racial difference," it is significant that these terms also have cultural and literary connotations attached to them. Apart from referring to people of mixed blood or heritage, *métis* and *Créole* illuminate the weaving together of various cultures and the blending of the oral with the written. Although I agree that the concept of race is different for not only English- and French-speaking (Caribbean) people but also every individual, I too support and promote the idea of similarities within the specific concepts: race and color among

diverse, heterogeneous group. Their very differences ac-
their similarities. Hence, my usage of *Créolité* is not only
˗˗˗˗˗˗ ˗pecific but race and gender specific as well. To borrow
Lionnet's words, this adaptation demythologizes "essentialist glo-
rifications of unitary origins, be they racial, sexual, geographic, or
cultural."[24]

Similar to Condé, I claim that the culture of the Caribbean is
unique and specific. Culture is a means of preserving self and, by
extension, a homeland or motherland. Addressing various cultures
and cultural phenomena, Amilcar Cabral asserts, "[T]he value of
culture is a factor of resistance of foreign domination." This resistance
is appropriately addressed in Paule Marshall's novel *Praisesong for
the Widow*. The heroines of the novel represented by the Carriacouan
folks refuse to let outside forces destroy their "ideal" homeland of
Carriacou.[25] They preserve their unique African culture by living it.
When posed the question "How can one define West Indian culture?"
Condé responds: "[C]ulture is not an entity to be defined; a culture
is something to be lived. So the people of the Caribbean do not have
to define exactly what they are, who they are, what constitutes their
culture. They just have to live as West Indians." Thus, by invoking
their culture and their past through African dance rituals, the Carriacouan residents live as African Caribbeans. In so doing, they refuse
domination, refuse "neutraliz[ation]" and the "paraly[sis]" of their
African cultural heritage.[26] Celebration of cultural heritage ensures
the continuity of history, and acceptance of one's culture facilitates
the knowing and acceptance of the self. The undying relationship
they have with their culture speaks of the relationship they have
with their motherland, Carriacou.

In contrast, the relationship that Maryse Condé has with her
motherlands, Guadeloupe and Africa, is conditioned and mediated

24. Condé, "Pan-Africanism, Feminism, and Culture" 60; Françoise Lionnet,
Autobiographical Voices: Race, Gender, Self-Portraiture, 13–14, 9.
25. Amilcar Cabral, "National Liberation and Culture," 53. I use the term
folk not in a derogative manner but to illuminate the invocation and revalidation of folk aesthetics and values that were once deemed inconsequential and
insignificant.
26. Condé, "Pan-Africanism, Feminism, and Culture," 61; Cabral, "National
Liberation and Culture," 53.

by colonial intervention. The same can be said for the relationships both Jamaica Kincaid and Paule Marshall have with their respective motherlands. Stripped literally and figuratively of their original Motherland, Africa, and their mother tongues, Caribbean or, rather, diasporic peoples have had to reinvent themselves for themselves. In perpetuating the destructive nature and agenda of slavery, colonization has negatively affected not only the "adopted and adapted" (Caribbean) culture but also the place (geographic) and Caribbean peoples alike.

This negative effect of colonization in all its complexities is explored in Kincaid's most recent fictional work, *The Autobiography of My Mother*. The protagonist, Xuela Claudette Richardson, lives a life devoid of love and meaningful relationships. Her intense hatred extends not only to people but to her homeland, Dominica, as well. This hatred for the land is misplaced and misdirected because of the absence of a mother. This conflation of the mother and the land, echoing Moira Ferguson, is a "double articulation of motherhood as both colonial and biological." As Ferguson recognizes, Morris and Dunn conclude that "to implement this double negotiation Kincaid foregrounds a complicated matrix of mother images that encompasses not only her island home and its unique culture [but also] . . . the body of tropes, talismans and female bonding that is a woman's heritage through her own and othermothers. The land and one's mothers, then, are co-joined." Adopting Morris and Dunn's "complex duality," Ferguson operates within this dichotomy. This fact is underscored by the title of her book, *Jamaica Kincaid: Where the Land Meets the Body*. The land, of course, symbolizes the island, and the body represents the mother. Though Ferguson's dichotomy enhances this study, it limits my discussion to the Caribbean islands, the locale where Kincaid's novels *Annie John* and *Autobiography* are staged.[27] In light of this, this study expands on and de-

27. Moira Ferguson, *Colonialism and Gender Relations from Mary Wollstonecraft to Jamaica Kincaid: East Caribbean Connections*, 1–2. Ferguson's discussion in *Jamaica Kincaid: Where the Land Meets the Body* includes Kincaid's *At the Bottom of the River, A Small Place, Annie John*, and *Lucy*. However, her discussion does not include Kincaid's latest novel, *The Autobiography of My Mother*, because at the time Ferguson wrote her book in 1994, *Autobiography* (1996) was not yet published. Although *Lucy* is set in the metropolitan city of New York, and

viates from Ferguson's dichotomous relationship between mother and land. I argue that the relationship is one not just between the mother and the mother's land, and by extension the Motherland, but also includes the mother country. Therefore, this relationship is a trichotomous one that, first, illuminates the notion of a triad or a triangular relationship and, second, underscores the tensions within this triangular relationship. Thus, my usage of trichotomy is twofold: apart from the notion of a triad, it accentuates a triangular relationship fraught with conflict, and potentially separable into three distinct parts: mother, motherlands, mother country. In accordance with my theorizing, the novels discussed are marked by the tensions between the mother and the birthplace, the colonizing territory (to which some of the main protagonists subsequently migrate), and the (mythical) existence of a "true" motherland, Africa.

The mother is the principal component of this triangular relationship and is supposed to maintain the trichotomy. This support is evident in the mother-daughter relationship, for the mother passes on the generational or maternal narratives (or both) to her daughter, thereby providing and validating a viable female culture. Privy to the generational narratives, the daughter is appropriately armed and is expected to negotiate her identity. This negotiation is heavily dependent upon the relationship she has with her mother and conditions her relationship with the motherland and the mother country. Often, acceptance of the daughter by the mother leads to the daughter's acceptance and adoption of the motherland. Hence, the daughter's relationship with her mother predetermines her relationships with the motherland and, to a lesser extent, with the mother country. Nonetheless, far from being a period marked by serenity, the daughter, in negotiating her identity, is confronted with seemingly insurmountable tensions among her mother, her mother's land, and the colonizing mother country. In her attempt to identify with the mother and thereafter the motherland and the mother country, she faces the possibility of being disembodied and stripped of selfhood. This disembodiment is first

---

Ferguson acknowledges that it is "a new site" (the full title of her chapter on *Lucy* is "Lucy: A New Site"), she does not make much of it.

and foremost epitomized by the mother country. As a result of its colonizing principles, the mother country figuratively disembodies the colonized individual, leaving him or her soulless. This (dis)possession of the soul can be classified as what Erna Brodber calls the process of "zombification," which describes a state wherein one is brutally stripped of knowledge of his or her original world and left as an empty shell or flesh, capable only of receiving orders from someone else and unquestioningly carrying them out.[28]

Daughters experience zombification not singularly by the mother country but also (subconsciously) by their mothers, whose love becomes suffocating as they mature into adulthood. As a result of this inhibiting environment in which the mother is transformed into an "other," the daughter seeks her individual identity. Often this decision to "break away" is seen as a traitorous act by the mother, who feels that her impositions cater to the well-being of her daughter. Nasta contends that this so-called traitorous act not only takes place on a personal level between mother and daughter but also has political connotations. "In countries with a history of colonialism, women's quest for emancipation, self-identity and fulfillment can be seen to represent a traitorous act, a betrayal not simply of traditional codes of practices and belief but of the wider struggle for liberation and nationalism." Interpreting the need for selfhood and identity as treachery speaks to the intoxicating effects of colonization on the female psyches. The daughter in turn sees the mother as a betrayer of her trust. As "other," she is often equated and conflated with the colonizer. Commenting on Kincaid's works, Ferguson contends, "[T]he relationships between Kincaid's female protagonists and their biological mothers are crucially formative yet always mediated by intimations of life as colonized subjects."[29] Unquestionably, the mother-daughter relationship is formative; however, this relationship is not just a simple matter of mediation. Instead, it can be classified as a colonized relationship between the colonizer and the colonized in which the (powerful) mother fits the profile of a colonizer and the (powerless) daughter is the colonized. Kincaid confirms this in an

28. Erna Brodber, *Myal*, 107.
29. Nasta, *Motherlands*, xv; Ferguson, *Jamaica Kincaid*, 1.

interview with Ferguson herself. She confesses:

> In my first two books, I used to think I was writing about my mother and myself. Later I began to see that I was writing about the relationship between the powerful and the powerless. That's become an obsessive theme, and I think that it will be a theme for as long as I write. And then it came clear to me when I was writing an essay that became "On Seeing England for the First Time" that I was writing about the mother—that mother I was writing about was really Mother Country. It's like an egg; it's a perfect whole. It's all fused some way or other.[30]

Although the mother becomes one with the mother country, further enhancing her power, the daughter remains fractured, disabling her to become part of this "perfect whole." Because of the inscriptions of colonial cultures upon her by her parents and in turn the society, the daughter perceives this relationship as a colonized one. Instead of a nurturing parent, she sees a suffocating "other." We are confronted with this colonizing "other" from the first few pages of Condé's *Heremakhonon*. Alluding that her father reminds her of a Mandingo marabout, Veronica thereafter refers to him in like manner. Although the term has African ancestral connotations, one cannot help but notice the Mandingo's propensity for things colonial and his perpetration of colonial habits and ways of life. Veronica notes, "My father the Mandingo marabout used to say that appearances were everything. For form's sake. How many times we heard that. He drummed into us dignity, heads up, correct dress and manners. . . . Even on the beaches we were not allowed to walk barefoot, to feel the warm sand. We were hardly out of the water when our maid, Mabo Julie, was running toward us with our sandals in her hands."[31] The relationship that Veronica has with her mother is no less strained, and she also sees her mother as a perpetrator of colonial values and habits and condemns her in a harsher manner than she does her father for accepting the laws of the fatherland. This harsh criticism that Veronica evinces upon her mother signals the estrangement between mother and daughter.

Like the mother-daughter relationship, colonization in the islands can also be regarded as "crucially formative," for it fashions

---

30. Jamaica Kincaid, "A Lot of Memory: An Interview with Jamaica Kincaid," 176.

31. Maryse Condé, *Heremakhonon*, 4, 83.

and molds, though often negatively, the individual's mind. Kincaid harshly critiques this negative molding in *A Small Place*. Even after the colonials have left Antigua, one is of the impression that they are still on the island, for the local government alarmingly mirrors them. Similarly, Mrs. John of Kincaid's *Annie John* and the Mandingo marabout are both products of colonialism; hence, they are constantly referenced and conflated with the colonials. Although the daughter's first encounter is with her biological mother, the Caribbean nation is given birth by colonialism.

In noting that the relationships between daughters and mothers are "mediated by intimations of life as colonized subjects," Ferguson concludes that the relationship between the land and one's mother is "always fraught with fear, alienation, and ambivalence, is always about separation." First, I heartily agree with Ferguson's conclusions only as long as the mother and daughter do not see "eye to eye," if the daughter severs ties with her mother('s)land. In Simone Schwarz-Bart's *Bridge of Beyond*, the mothers are more or less affirming mothers, and the heroine, Télumée, is at home with herself on the island of Guadeloupe because of the nurturing relationships she has with her grand/mothers.[32] Second, this relationship suffers severance only upon the daughter's entrance into womanhood, a period that the mother interprets as a relinquishing of "innocence." The daughter's prepubescent years are defined by comfort and bonding with the mother. This is clearly illuminated in *Annie John*, when Annie lovingly recalls and recounts childhood memories of time spent with her mother on the island of Antigua. These loving memories are later contrasted with intense hatred that Annie feels for her mother and that she eventually carries with her to the mother country, England. Blinded by anger because of the mother's apparent complicity with the colonial mother country, the daughter does not recognize the source for potential alienation as she journeys to the mother country. Notably, Annie leaves for the mother country in her teenage years, attesting to the fact that separation from the mother('s)land often, and perhaps always, occurs during the daughter's pubescent years.

---

32. Ferguson, *Jamaica Kincaid*, 2. Télumée's relationship with her mother is plagued with ambivalence, and she is eventually abandoned by her mother and left in the care of her grandmother, who fills the void by nurturing her and providing her with the necessary tools for acquiring her sense of self.

Similarly, Marshall's Selina Boyce of *Brown Girl, Brownstones* leaves her hometown, Brooklyn, for Barbados during her teenage years, and Condé's Tituba leaves her homeland with her lover and eventual husband, John Indian, at approximately the same age. These departures for the others' land by daughters are quests for selfhood, initiated and exacerbated by a lack of self and spiritual consciousness and connectedness.

Nevertheless, the relationships daughters have with their mothers remain pivotal in the daughters' identity formation. For the most part, the texts discussed are written from the perspective of daughters, bestowed the authority of authorship by their mothers. Although this authority is underscored by many women theorists, including Nasta, equal importance and significance should be given to the themes of motherhood and mother-daughter relationships because they are significantly intertwined with the bestowal of authorship and are often the key to daughters' success or failure. The mother-daughter relationship is a recurring theme in the works of many Afro-Caribbean women writers, and Condé, Marshall, and Kincaid—beginning with Kincaid's *Annie John*—are no exceptions. After leaving her mother and her mother's land in desperation and anger, Annie John does not find peace (within herself) in the mother country. Her restlessness is transferred to Lucy, the heroine of Kincaid's second novel with the same title, which, though it is not a sequel to *Annie John*, continues the themes of the mother-daughter separation and the alienation that follows. Annie is said to leave for England, and *Lucy* opens with Lucy in the United States. Lucy's concrete presence there once again speaks to the role reversal of mother country between England and the United States, complicating an already complex mother-daughter relationship defined by extremities and intensities: love and hatred, intimacy and estrangement.

This study is divided into five chapters. In the first chapter, "Resisting Zombification: (Re)Writing/Righting the Literary Canon," I argue that the act of resisting provides a clearing ground or space, a mother's land, for Afro-Caribbean women writers and writings. The potentially silenced and marginalized women are rendered voices in the novels of Jamaica Kincaid, Maryse Condé, and Paule Marshall. The writers give their protagonists voices through their own personal experiences; therefore, in rewriting their histories, a new tradition is born, a "womanist" tradition is given birth. As both mothers and daughters, these women are empowered to tell their own, their mothers', and in turn their daughters' stories. I trace this act of resistance and self-assertion in Jamaica Kincaid's *Annie John* (1986) and *Autobiography of My Mother* (1996), Paule Marshall's *Brown Girl, Brownstones* (1959) and *Praisesong for the Widow* (1983), and Maryse Condé's *Heremakhonon* (1985) and *I, Tituba, Black Witch of Salem* (1992). I argue that these texts give birth to or, rather, invent a woman-centered ideology and literary genre, "fictional autobiographies" or narratives, as I interchangeably refer to them.[33] The use of the adjective *fictional* with *autobiographies* is to accentuate the nonconventional, nonrestrictive use of the term *autobiography* in the works of these women novelists. Though *I, Tituba, Black Witch of Salem* and *Praisesong for the Widow* are not autobiographical (in the strict sense), the authors have had to re-create and reconstruct the lives of the characters, artistically injecting and invoking their personal narratives, histories, and lived experiences. This personal invocation gives the works a (quasi-)autobiographical component. It is also noteworthy that Tituba is not a fictionalized individual (though she is "fictionalized" in European historical accounts), but a historical one. Hence, one can argue that Condé simultaneously wrote her biography and an autobiography. The women whose lives these women novelists create are the embodiments of themselves yet not them. Their "fictional autobiographies" differ from the customary conventional autobiography in that they do not constitute the simple retelling of one's life story, but are a complex mixture of dreams, myths, and histories.[34] The retelling and preservation of these dreams, myths, histories, and memories by daughters are conspicuously facilitated by women, mothers, nurturers, and "othermothers."

33. I also incorporate portions of other novels of these three women to accentuate this act of resistance: Paule Marshall's *Chosen Place, the Timeless People,* Maryse Condé's *Season in Rihata,* and Jamaica Kincaid's *Lucy.*

34. This complex mixture of dreams, myth, and histories is Audre Lorde's definition for her "biomythography," a coinage she employs to describe her own autobiographical narrative. Nevertheless, Lorde is the real-life protagonist of her autobiographical piece, *Zami: A New Spelling of My Name,* unlike Kincaid, Condé, and Marshall.

This specific female bonding, channeled through the mother-daughter relationship, is explored in the second chapter, "I Am Me, I Am You: The Intricate Mother-Daughter Dyadic Relationship," as developed in Kincaid's *Annie John* and *Autobiography of My Mother*. I argue that in spite of an ambiguous mother-daughter relationship classified equally by intense love and intense hatred, this relationship provides a space for female bonding outside the ramifications of colonial paternalism. These relationships (this "conventional" mother-daughter relationship is noticeably absent in *The Autobiography of My Mother*) are frequently conjured in the kitchen or in other so-called female spaces, thus highlighting the importance of the mother('s)land. This female space is aptly claimed by Kincaid, who categorizes not only her writing but also her daily existence as "arranging the world" from the kitchen table. She proudly asserts, "If I actually ran the world, I'd do it from the kitchen."[35] Rather than subscribe to the age-old definition of the kitchen as a place of restriction and confinement, this domestic space is celebrated by Kincaid as a place of freedom and unmeasured creativity. Marshall coined a wonderful phrase adequately encompassing the domestic world and the poetic (oral storytelling) world of the "kitchen women," honoring them with the prestigious title of "Mother Poets." In "The Making of a Writer," Marshall speaks about the self-empowerment that women attain in the kitchen, a space within which they concoct and compose their language, poetry.

Kincaid's repeated and somewhat exhaustive references and returns to the themes of mother, mothering, and motherhood serve only to validate the powerful presence of the mother. She is all-encompassing, omnipresent, and omniscient. Her lurking presence becomes threatening, therefore transforming her into a stepparent. Applying Gilbert and Gubar's concept of the wicked stepmother to illuminate this adopted colonizing image of the mother, I argue that the transformations that the mothers go through from loving parents to wicked stepparents or stepmothers are the same as that experienced by the Wicked Queen Stepmother. Reconstructing the fable "Snow White and the Seven Dwarfs," Gubar and Gilbert detail the plot of the Wicked Queen Stepmother to kill her stepdaughter, Snow

---

35. Jamaica Kincaid, "An Interview with Jamaica Kincaid," by Donna Perry, 503.

White, contending that her actions are influenced by the patriarchy. I conclude that daughters' sole concern is not only the colonizing images their mothers appear to adopt, seemingly conspiring with the mother country, but also the daughters' fear of becoming their mothers and by association adopting this colonizing image and presence. This fear culminates in the daughter suffering from an "illness" known as "matrophobia," which, according to Adrienne Rich, "is the fear not of one's mother or of motherhood but of becoming one's mother."[36] This fear is tangible and manifests in Annie John, who spends incalculable time convincing herself that she is not her mother or like her. Amid this fear, the daughter is faced with the task of finding self, of becoming and creating a space where she is at home with herself. The search for self is "complete" when one has a sense of "home," when one has made peace with the mother and the mother's land. However, I contend that this acquisition of "wholeness" is achieved only with the help and nurturing presence of a mother who is defined by her spiritual mooring. The absence, literal or figurative, of a mother sends a daughter in search of another mother(land). This desperate quest for "wholeness" and home space forces and forges an imaginary re-creation of home, giving one a false sense and a false hope of the self. This theme is addressed in the third chapter.

In "Imagined Homelands: Engendering a Mythic Return 'Home,'" I examine Condé's *Heremakhonon*, the text of which I argue facilitates the engendering of this mythic, nostalgic return "home" to Africa, to an imaginary community or homeland, and *Tituba*, a text that in contrast demythologizes and dispels this mythic, imaginary creation of a home space. This demythologizing is possible because of the acceptance of the mother('s)land and eventual self-acceptance.

Self-acceptance often entails resistance of being labeled, defined, and marginalized by the other. Resistance of an imposed identity and creation of a new identity bear the stamps of self-validation and self-preservation. I argue that in the process of self-assertion, subversion of literary canons or tenets occurs, questioning the privileges accorded to white poetics that deem one kind of knowledge inconsequential while validating another. The knowledge judged unimpor-

---

36. Adrienne Rich, *Of Woman Born: Motherhood as Experience and Institution*, 57. Rich adopts the term *matrophobia* from the poet Lynn Sukenick.

tant is the acquired knowledge of black people. Toni Morrison asserts that this knowledge is "discredited only because Black people were discredited therefore what they knew was discredited."[37]

This questioning of Western self-aggrandizement is a predominant theme in Marshall's works. Marshall not only contests this self-embellishment but also dispels the notion of absolution. In so doing, she posits "another way of knowing things," which is the focus of the fourth chapter, "'An/Other Way of Knowing Things': Ancestral Line/age, Revalidating Our Ancestral Inheritances."[38] I challenge that the revalidation of ancestral inheritances and self-validation prevent the neutralization or destruction of the Mother culture: African cultural practices and "an/other way of knowing things." This revalidation made possible by mothers, embodied and embedded in the spiritual, permits a spiritual return to the Mother-land, Africa, via the Caribbean.

The importance of the spiritual mother and spiritual conscious-ness is given full representation in Marshall's *Praisesong for the Widow*. Unparalleled, Marshall's mothers are spiritually moored, thus pro-viding the support and mainstay daughters need for self-affirmation and the acquisition of "wholeness." This spiritual return or home-coming becomes possible through the living and practicing of the mother('s) culture and the celebration of the mother and the mother's land. Notwithstanding, prior to the attainment of spiritual con-sciousness and the validation of the mother culture, the individual is engaged in constant battles with Western cultural practices and ideologies, which discredit African oral cultural practices.

This struggle between Old World and New World cultures is addressed in *Brown Girl, Brownstones*. This larger contest between cultures also functions as a guise for the struggles between the motherland, Barbados, and the mother country, the United States. To demonstrate this conflict I explore at length the plight of a sec-ondary character, Deighton Boyce, the father of the main charac-ter, Selina Boyce, who is rendered powerless because of the social castration and banishment he suffers at the hands of his fellow Barbadians. Deighton is triply exiled: from his homeland, Barbados; from his people; and from the newly "adopted" mother country,

37. Toni Morrison, "Rootedness: The Ancestor as Foundation," 342.
38. Chapter 4's title is an adopted phrase from ibid.

the United States. Adopting the mother country on its terms, the motherland is orphaned, and the Barbadian community is visibly devoid of spirituality.

Receiving spiritual guidance and nurturing from the spiritual mothers, the mother's land is claimed in the fifth and final chapter, " 'Call[ing] Your Nation': A Journey Completed."[39] I contend that in calling one's nation, the individual accepts another way of knowing things and lays claim to the mother's land. This claiming, epitomized in Avatara Johnson of *Praisesong for the Widow*, is symptomatic of an unwavering acceptance and celebration of the spiritual mothers and the homeland, a celebration of cultural unity within the diaspora among diasporic peoples. Spiritually renewed and rejuvenated, a new self is born. This rebirth, of course, is initiated by the mother, the "true" ancestress, and is accordingly staged on the mother's land. This rebirth process returns us to the beginning or, more appropriately, the conception of this study, the resisting of "zombification." Being able to "call your nation" is a marked sign of such resistance and embracing "another way of knowing things." Resisting being silenced, Condé, Kincaid, and Marshall have claimed their respective motherlands; therefore, they, like most of their protagonists, participate in the "call[ing] of [their] nation[s]."

Offering a comparative and critical analysis of the works of Maryse Condé, Jamaica Kincaid, and Paule Marshall, this study addresses the complex and complicated issues of the black woman's quest and struggle for subjecthood, self-realization, and representation. Although these women writers have varied approaches to respective themes and topics, they are undoubtedly in conversation with one another, and also with the literary world. Notwithstanding, their works challenge as well as severely critique Eurocentric values, colonialism, patriarchy, and linear narrative. Apart from this important fact, they share a common geographic home space, a Caribbean motherland. Collectively, their novels present to us a female cultural space, a mother's land, where patriarchal orders and Eurocentrism are fiercely interrogated.

39. In Paule Marshall's *Praisesong for the Widow*, the sage Lebert Joseph speaks about the importance of ancestral worshiping and of being able to "call your nation." When one can "call [her] nation," the search for self is complete.

1 Resisting Zombification

(Re)Writing/Righting the Literary Canon

Coming of age in Antigua—so touching and familiar . . . it could be happening to any of us, anywhere, any time, any place.

—New York Times Book Review

I don't think that American women have much that we can draw from. I mean the use of language is very different, and their concerns are much different. A much different sensibility. For instance, I think that American black people seem to feel almost-that being black is a predestination in some way. They have a kind of nationalism that we don't have: black nationalism. Because they are a minority, they are more concerned with their identity being extinct, whereas we don't feel that way. Everybody is black. I mean, we don't think white people are permanent. We don't feel permanent, either, but that feeling of "there will always be white people sitting on top of black people"—we don't have. . . . Black nationalism in this country is very much because there is an acceptance, in some way, of how the majority of population have thought about black people. There is very much an internalization of that. Why else have "black pride"? I mean there is no reason to be particularly proud of something you can't help. It is not an effort you made and you became black. It is just the way you are. There is nothing particularly pleasing or displeasing about it. But if you could somehow let them understand that their view of you had nothing to do with you and it remains with them, they are befuddled. But I believe that is a very West Indian trait. They have never really buckled, maybe because they are a majority.

—Jamaica Kincaid, "A Lot of Memory"

The two quotes, the first by the *New York Times Book Review*, the other by the author Jamaica Kincaid herself, illuminate as well as serve as precursors to the ambivalence and contradictions often linked to both the author and her work. Inasmuch as Kincaid's works

28

are cataloged as such, the quote by the *New York Times Book Review* suggests that the location of Kincaid's novels (*Annie John* in particular) lacks specificity and has unrestricted universal attributes.[1] This presumption not only undermines her efforts of self-assertion (explicitly stated in the second quote) as a black Caribbean woman and novelist, but also questions her position as a (postcolonial) writer. In no uncertain terms, Kincaid's becoming a writer is fashioned by her history, her colonial history, a (concrete) past with which she obsesses and to which she repeatedly returns in each of her works. This past is chronicled on the Caribbean islands, namely, postcolonial Antigua. Addressing Kincaid's work, Caribbean writer Derek Walcott asserts, "[G]enius has many surprises and one of them is geography." In response to Walcott's comments, Kincaid acknowledges that her geography, that is, her coming from Antigua, is and has been a positive influence. She confesses that the happenstance of being Antiguan, like the happenstance of being black, has molded her in becoming who she is, a black Caribbean writer. She speaks openly about her "Caribbeanness" and her reality in "I Come from a Place That's Very Unreal." The *Los Angeles Times Book Review* best summarizes Kincaid and her work in the following words: "Kincaid may reside in America but only someone with her heart in Antigua could have written with such ferocity of purpose and self-revelatory hurt."[2] Kincaid's history, her life, like the lives of her protagonists, unfolds in a fixed geographical location, the Caribbean, colonial Antigua and Dominica, respectively: the geographical locale of Annie's youth in *Annie John* is Antigua, and the geography of Xuela's entire life story in *The Autobiography of My Mother* is marked as colonial Dominica.

I quote Kincaid at length because her commentary, on one hand, gives an insight into her place, her positioning herself as a writer (although she has lived in North America for several years, Kincaid

1. Although Kincaid's works are classified as ambiguous, it is misleading and a misrepresentation of her works to suggest that the locales of her novels hold the same ambiguity as the texts. Although Kincaid's novels address universal themes, she repeatedly returns to her past that is concrete and nonambiguous. It is colonial Antigua.

2. Walcott quoted in "'I Come from a Place That's Very Unreal': An Interview with Jamaica Kincaid," 80. The *Los Angeles Times Book Review*'s revealing comment was made on the cover page of Kincaid's poignant book *A Small Place*. It further bolsters the geographic specificity of Kincaid's works.

still refers to Antigua as home, remarking that Antigua needs a writer more than it needs an American citizen), and, on the other hand, resists classification or simple categorization.[3] The statement "if you could somehow let them understand that their view of you had nothing to do with you and it remains with them, they are befuddled," although not addressed to anyone in particular, is obviously meant for the "white people" who have imposed foreign identities on "American black people." This imposition, in Kincaid's opinion, has left indelible imprints on black Americans, who as a result of colonial indoctrination have started to see themselves through and with the eyes of white America. Kincaid denounces black nationalism in America because it facilitates easy acceptance and internalization of the perception held by "the majority of population" about black people. It is rather ironic, at least in Kincaid's view, that black nationalism bears fruit on U.S. soil rather than on Caribbean soil whence the founding fathers (Garvey and Padmore, among others) hailed. She explains that the main cause of this preoccupation with black nationalism by black Americans is their minority status, and therefore they are in constant fear of becoming extinct. Kincaid's commentary on black nationalism not merely is criticism, but also offers a comparative analysis of black diasporic peoples, namely, Afro-Caribbeans and African Americans.

Because of her nonclaiming and nonacceptance of specific identities, Kincaid has come under harsh criticism for her so-called ambivalence about racial categories. Although I acknowledge a seemingly masked ambivalence, by the same token, her being black and writing about blacks, her being a woman and writing about women, in and of itself speaks of a deep kinship, a diasporic unity. Identifying strongly with her blackness, her femaleness, and her Caribbeanness, Kincaid declares: "I come from a place where most of the people are black. Every important person in my life was a black person, or a person who was mostly black, or very deeply related to what we call a black person. So I just assume that is the norm and that it

---

3. This comment was made when Kincaid, in an interview with Allan Vorda, was asked about applying for American citizenship ("'I Come from a Place,'" 98). She expressed no desire to become a citizen of the United States (though she has since become one).

is the other people who would need describing. I assume most of the people who are important to me, and not last among them is my own self, are female."[4] Kincaid celebrates not only her blackness but also her femaleness. Embracing and validating her Caribbean heritage, Kincaid writes with a black Caribbean consciousness, yet this consciousness ostensibly extends beyond the Caribbean, beyond blackness. Henry Louis Gates Jr. puts it perfectly when he states: "She never feels the necessity of claiming the existence of a black world or a female sensibility. She assumes them both. I think it's a distinct departure that she's making, and I think that more and more black American writers will assume [this world]. So that we . . . can get to the deeper themes of how black people love and cry and live and die. Which, after all, is what art is all about." Like Afro-Caribbean women, African American women are fighting a common enemy: colonialism and, by extension, cultural extinction. Not only have Kincaid, Marshall, and Condé made this "distinct departure" that Gates talks about, accordingly assuming both the black and the female worlds, but African American women writers have also assumed both a black world and a female sensibility. Toni Morrison is a perfect example of one such writer who has explored what Gates calls "the deeper themes of how black people love and cry and live and die." Kincaid admits that the act of claiming both a female sensibility (world) and a black world was not self-conscious. For her, as for other black diasporic women, this claiming is a natural unconscious act. Condé further endorses this notion when asked by interviewer Mohamed B. Taleb-Khyar about her being a woman who writes extensively about women: "I [am] just expressing my own feelings and I happen to be a woman. So I [am] speaking of me, and of people similar to me, i.e., women."[5] Hence, the women speak not only for themselves but also for all black women who share a common history, or what Marshall aptly calls a "collective history."

4. This ambivalence about racial categories is most visible in Kincaid's second novel, *Lucy*. Lucy, a black West Indian woman, appears to assimilate into a white unknown U.S. society with unusual ease. Kincaid, " 'I Come from a Place,' " 81–82.
5. Gates quoted in Kincaid, " 'I Come from a Place,' " 81; Condé, "Interview with Condé and Dove," 358.

Faced with the task of creating "a true-true self," that is, re-creating positive black self-images, Marshall, Condé, and Kincaid have had to return to the past to deconstruct the negative portrayals of black women. For example, in *I, Tituba, Black Witch of Salem,* Condé subverts the notion of a witch as someone evil and menacing to society. In her novels, Kincaid dispels the idea of femaleness and female sexuality as undesirable. Marshall observes that the history that black women have had access to is one that demonizes them and relegates them to the margins of society. She therefore calls for a revision of the historical evidence, which is documented in the fictional autobiographies. Because of the multiple literary textuality—intuition, history, and imagination—embedded in the fictional narratives, they do not conform to the customary, conventional genre of autobiography, or life writings. Though these works are fictional and pose a challenge to conventional autobiography, they possess autobiographical components and at the same time "contribute to autobiographical theory." Carole Boyce Davies appropriately observes that these writings "challenge many of the generic expectations of autobiography [forcing] a rethinking of traditional autobiographical theory. Thinking autobiography through [fictional narrative] puts into question the notion of standard autobiography as extended, linear narrative, and invites instead more complex approaches to text, discourse, author, and narrative."[6]

These complex approaches are employed on several levels. First, the fictional autobiographies created by these three women constitute a complex mixture of fiction, truth or reality or both, memory, and history. Expounding on this complex mixture, Kincaid comments:

> The process of fiction, for me, is using reality and then reinventing reality. . . . Lying is the beginning of fiction. . . . I used to be accused . . . of having a strong imagination. . . . I never forgot anything that happened. I would hear people telling something that happened, and they would leave out, in my opinion, the crucial parts. Every part was crucial. If someone left something out, then I would tell what happened and they'd look at me in amazement. So my memory was considered

6. Carole Boyce Davies, "Collaboration and the Ordering Imperative in Life Story Production," 6.

an act of treachery. . . . It was considered one of my greatest faults. . . .
I was incapable of just describing something as it really happened. I
would remember that it had happened, and I might exaggerate the
details, but other people would forget it happened. So that is essentially
what my fiction is. It really happened.[7]

Hence, the boundaries between fiction, myth, history, and reality
are blurred. Nevertheless, this blurring does not limit the narrative structure, an attestation to Kincaid's earlier comment that "every part was crucial"; rather, it is employed as a strategic device
to disclose the "real truth," black women's truth. Selwyn Cudjoe
warns that "neither form of writing [fiction nor history] should
be privileged over the other in our literary history. Each should
be judged by its ability to speak honestly and perceptively about
the experiences of [black people]." The novels suggest that both
forms of writing are crucial and integral to the black community's
sense of self-realization and identification. Kincaid aptly notes that
this style of writing is furnished to "exploit personal experiences."
Second, the notion of linearity and individualism is questioned.
The narratives follow no strict, sequential structure. Although each
fictional autobiography is personal and unique, it speaks collectively to the experiences of black women. Thus, these fictional autobiographies that serve as vehicles for the expression of female
consciousness from the black female perspective subvert the Western practice of life writing or autobiography. Offering a comparative analysis of Western autobiography and black women's writings, Sidonie Smith argues that Western autobiographies "rest upon
a shared belief in a commonsense identification of one individual with another." Instead of an individual relating his or her life
story, in these narratives we encounter a blending of voices and
discourses or "multiple lives as single text," as Davies refers to
them.[8] For example, in *Tituba* reside the voices of the ancestors
Mama Yaya and Abena. Avey is the voice of both Gran and Aunt
Cuney, and subsequently becomes the voice of the community. This

7. Kincaid, " 'I Come from a Place,' " 93.
8. Cudjoe, ed., *Caribbean Women*, 277; Sidonie Smith and Julia Watson, eds.,
De/Colonizing the Subject: The Politics of Gender in Women's Autobiography, xvii;
Davies, "Collaboration," 6.

rich mixture of multiple voices in Kincaid's view is what distinguishes black women writings from the "way grand men used to be writers."

This distinction is further articulated by Regina Blackburn, who notes that the writings of black women are "greatly shaped by their blackness and their womanhood. . . . When these women use the autobiographical mode, they reveal themselves in a unique way, one not typical of white autobiography." Although these women have made a distinct departure from "white autobiography," from conventionality, they have not completely divorced the white community from their dialogues. This departure from conventionality challenges the norm and is employed as a means of telling their stories from their perspectives. In quoting Stephen Butterfield, Blackburn argues that "the autobiographical form is one of the ways that black Americans have asserted their right to live and grow. It is a bid for freedom, a beak of hope cracking the shell of slavery and exploitation. It is also an attempt to communicate to the white world what whites have done to them." This bid for freedom exhibits not only individual attributes, but communal attributes as well, uniting those with a common history. Addressing the reciprocal relationship between the self and the community, Blackburn contends: "The self is conceived as a member of an oppressed social group, with ties and responsibilities to the other members. It is a conscious political identity, drawing sustenance from the past experience of the group, giving back the iron of its endurance fashioned into armor and weapons for the use of the next generation of fighters."[9]

The "unbreakable" link between the "self" and the community deconstructs the individualism of conventional autobiography. Apart from challenging the "generic expectations of autobiography," Davies notes that fictional autobiographies "are, as well, subversions of the definition of 'author.'" The "authorial subject" is not an individual in total and complete control of the narrative, but a collaboration of the "self" and the community. This form of narrative structure can be classified as what Davies calls "collaborative

9. Regina Blackburn, "In Search of the Black Female Self: African-American Women's Autobiographies and Ethnicity," 133–34.

storytelling," where the multiple yet distinct lives of women from various social backgrounds are recorded or documented in a single text.[10] This collaborative effort gives agency to the storyteller, the narrator (the oral), and the author (the written).

The heroines of the novels are not typical or conventional—privileged white middle-class women—another noticeable subversion. Instead, they are predominantly underprivileged, ordinary working-class black women. In applauding her "mother poets" for their tremendous courage, Marshall beautifully summarizes the social status of these heroines when she says that "these women, the 'mother poets,' never had the opportunity to be recognized, published poets. They were invisible, both as poets and women. These women were invisible on four counts: they were black, women, immigrants, and working-class. They had all of those strikes against them."[11] In Marshall's summation, these women were never applauded or recognized because they did not fit the profile of poets and as a result were deemed insignificant and peripheral. In light of these injustices, these mother poets are finally honored, and their poetic achievements are validated in the novels. The translation of their spoken words into the written diminishes their invisibility. The authorial voice, though distinct, is often conflated with the voice of the characters.

Kincaid serves as a perfect example: on one hand, she acknowledges the autobiographical content of her works, and on the other hand, she disputes her works being categorized as autobiographical, yet one cannot disregard the stark similarities between her life and her characters' lives. Like her, they migrated to the North during their teenage years. These similarities apply particularly to Kincaid's first two novels, *Annie John* and *Lucy*. Her third novel, *The Autobiography of My Mother*, is staged on the island of Dominica. Also, the mother in her works mirrors her own mother, and her first novel bears her mother's name, Annie. This is Kincaid's plot to resisting easy or simple categorization. Taking her resistance act a step further, Kincaid, engaged in the act of self-assertion, has gone

10. Davies, "Collaboration," 6.
11. Paule Marshall, "Meditations on Language and the Self: A Conversation with Paule Marshall," 286.

the length and changed her name from Elaine Potter Richardson to Jamaica Kincaid. Without a doubt, this so-called unconscious name change, on one hand, is a rejection of the name of the colonizer, and on the other hand, it is a celebration of her blackness and her Caribbeanness. She admits, "[M]y new name unconsciously had the significance I wanted it to have since that is the area of the world I'm from."[12] The name *Jamaica* bears symbolic representation to the island of Jamaica. Therefore, by renaming herself Jamaica, Kincaid claims the mother's land, as she simultaneously claims her self.

In a similar manner, resisting simple classification, Marshall and Condé incorporate specific aspects of their lives in their fiction. The lives and paths of Condé's female protagonists in her first two novels, *A Season in Rihata* and *Heremakhonon*, partially echo her own life's path. The conflict that Selina Boyce of *Brown Girl, Brownstones* experiences with her mother, Silla Boyce, is evidently emblematic of the conflict that Marshall experienced with her own mother. Hence, in the narratives, we witness not only the "blurring of the boundaries" between orality and writing, but also the conflating of the real with the imagined. The narratives give credence to the written and the spoken words, and the real as well as the imagined. Carole Boyce Davies refers to this blurring as a "critically defining feature [in black women's writings] that . . . blur[s] the boundaries between orality and writing." She defines them as "a crossover genre that challenges the oral/written separations and unites these forms as they maintain their distinct textualities."[13]

While maintaining "distinct textualities" and establishing themselves as literary genres, fictional narratives are in dialogue with other discourses, for their foundation is established on them. Their literary components are derived from

> the literary tradition of the slave narratives . . . and their integrity is derived from the historical experience of being black and female in a specific society at a specific moment and over succeeding generations. . . . Black women's autobiographies resist reduction to either political or critical pieties and resist even more firmly reduction to mindless

12. Kincaid, " 'I Come from a Place,' " 90.
13. Davies, "Collaboration," 7.

empiricism. In short, they command an attention to theory and method that respects their distinctiveness as a discourse and their relation to other discourses.[14]

As distinctive discourses, fictional autobiographies aim to get at the truth or facts. Therefore, these fictional narratives "are simply different means of arriving at, or recognizing, the same truth; the manner in which and by which the [black woman] makes and is made by [her] historical, political, and social condition."[15]

The novelists' painstaking and constant returns and references to their mothers (lands), their historical and ancestral past, are means of getting at the subjective truth in order to rewrite history and to piece together the lives of black women. This composition facilitates the re-creation of these women in their own images, images that positively reflect who they are. Kincaid admits that "the truth is important, but it's a certain kind of truth." Earlier she confesses that she does not "aim to be factual. [She] aims to be true to something, but it's not necessarily the facts."[16] Kincaid's distinction between truth, fact, and fiction illuminates the challenge that black women's fictional autobiographies present.

In writing their histories, women have had to write against the historical evidence as documented by Europeans. Marshall's quote "those negative and unflattering portrayals . . . designed to serve the fantasies and motives of the larger society . . . had little to do with us" echoes similar sentiments expressed earlier by Kincaid: "[I]f you could somehow let them understand that their view of you had nothing to do with you and it remains with them, they are befuddled." The "larger society" to which Marshall refers is the perpetrator of European aesthetics and values. Denouncing the negative portrayals of black women, history has taken on new meaning for these writers. It need not remain a subjective, biased account of black people and their lives, designed to undermine their sense of self and serving as a mouthpiece for Western values and aesthetics, but it can become

14. Elizabeth Fox-Genovese, "My Statue, My Self: Autobiographical Writings of Afro-American Women," 179.
15. Cudjoe, ed., *Caribbean Women,* 227.
16. Jamaica Kincaid, "An Interview with Jamaica Kincaid," by Kay Bonetti, 125–26.

what Marshall calls "an antidote to the lies," reflecting the way "black people love and cry and live."

This revised history that reflects black people's lives is based not only on facts as told, lived, and experienced by black women, but also on their "truths" and memory. The incorporation of memory into history is a powerful device employed by the writers to ensure the preservation of black women's life stories. Employing memory as a strategy for survival, women are not enslaved to the historical accounts of their lives as told by Europeans. Condé argues that the task of the black woman writer "is to forget the kind of superstructure which is imposed upon us by education, tradition, and going to university. We have to listen to another voice. We can write just like the whites. But we must use another method."[17] It is necessary that black women writers employ another means in their writings, because adopting the European or Euramerican method of selective exclusion only denies them agency. This other method to which Condé refers is aptly represented by Marshall's "mother poets," who utilize their memory and intuition to reconstruct their histories, thereby dismantling the "superstructure" to which Condé earlier refers, as it refutes selective exclusions. Instead, it permits the invocation and retention of past experiences, imagined and real.

Deprived of a history, black women have had to exploit their imaginative powers, which additionally speaks to the ingenuity and unconventionality of the women's writings. A perfect exploration of history with the imagination is documented in *I, Tituba, Black Witch of Salem*. Having little or no historical evidence of Tituba because of the blatant obliteration of her from the history books, Condé has had to exploit her own imagination to reconstruct Tituba's life. As privileged interlocutor, Condé confesses in her epigraph: "Tituba and I lived for a year on the closest of terms. During our endless conversations she told me things she had confided to nobody else." Possessing strong imaginations, black women are able to retell their stories in their own voices. To reiterate Condé's earlier comment, this imaginative power is rendered potent because

17. Maryse Condé, "No Silence: An Interview with Maryse Condé," 548.

black women are not tied to reality, or to actuality, espoused by the colonials.[18]

Addressing the need to re-create her historical past, Kincaid affirms that she had to resort to the autobiographical:

> My writing has been very autobiographical. For me it was really an act of saving my life, so it had to be autobiographical. I am someone who had to make sense out of my past. . . . I have to make sense of my ancestral past—where I came from, my historical past, my group historical past, my group ancestry. So I could not be a writer the way that grand men used to be writers. . . . I had to write or I would have died. I had to express myself in some way. I had to be able to do this.[19]

Thus, the autobiographical mode in fictional narratives is fundamental; it is a life-saving process that has universal attributes and diasporic connections and continuities.

Marshall conceives the struggle of Afro-Caribbean women and African American women for self-worth and recognition as a struggle of universal capacity and capability, directly linked to the struggles of the mainland Africans:

> I believe that Black women in the U.S. and the diaspora can play an important role [in the struggle]. When we who live in technologically advanced societies arrive at a consciousness of ourselves as a collective force organized to combat problems impeding Black development on an international scale, then we will be able to contribute to the future well-being of Black peoples around the world. The question poses itself as such: "How can we (as Afro-American and Afro-Caribbean women) be more effective in the world?" First, in liberating ourselves from the inferiority complex imposed by the colonial system whose vestiges are still with us. Once reconciled with ourselves, we can begin to impose our own point of view, and, in this way make ourselves

18. Condé offers a detailed description of her encounter with Tituba during which Tituba gave her sole rights to her history, which Condé sees as a necessary step in re-creating her life. In Arthur Miller's novel *The Crucible,* Tituba is footnoted as a Barbadian witch who was hanged for her deeds of practicing witchcraft.

The terms *colonial, Europeans,* and *Euramericans* are used interchangeably to refer to the powers that repress.

19. Kincaid, "A Lot of Memory," 176.

ful in the struggle for the liberation of our brothers and sisters in Africa.[20]

Like Kincaid and Condé, Marshall emphasizes the need for self-definition and takes her "campaign" a step further by including and acknowledging that Africa plays a vital and essential role to the people of African descent in the process of reinventing themselves. As a result, she calls for a "spiritual return" to Africa: "[A] spiritual return to Africa is absolutely necessary for the reintegration of that which was lost in our collective historical past. . . . [T]he role which Africa plays in determining our historical identity has been systematically de-emphasized."[21] Marshall sees the need to return, whether literally or figuratively, to her sources, as a constitutive component in rewriting and re-creating history. It fosters the piecing together of the shattered, fragmented selves of black women. Enacting a spiritual return to the past evidences a distinct departure from colonialist impositions. It is an act of liberation from what Marshall earlier refers to as "the inferiority complex imposed by the colonial system." Not only is this departure evident in the process of reemphasizing and revalidating the role that Africa plays in the liberation of the black diaspora, but it is also evident in the adoption and adaptation of the "imposed language":

> They [mother poets] had taken a language imposed upon them, and infused it with their own incisive rhythms and syntax, brought to bear upon it the few African words and sounds that had been retained. In a word, *transformed it, made it their own.* I was impressed, without being able to define it, by the seemingly effortless way they *had mastered* the form of storytelling. . . . They were carrying on a tradition as ancient as Africa, [a] centuries old oral mode by which the culture and history, the wisdom of the race had been transmitted.[22]

The mother poets have brilliantly mastered the "master narrative" through the art of storytelling. The imposition and infusion of African syntax and rhythms upon the colonial language provide the mother poets with character identification, linking them to their

---

20. Paule Marshall, "Return of a Native Daughter: An Interview with Paule Marshall and Maryse Condé," 53.
21. Ibid.
22. Paule Marshall, "Shaping the World of My Art," 103; emphasis added.

African past. This imposition bears the imprint of retribution, because it is emblematic of the intrusion blacks suffered when their (African) tongues were taken away and the colonial language was imposed upon them. The connection to the Motherland, Africa, that has been systematically severed is reestablished by this new adopted language. Rejecting the so-called standard language, Marshall invokes the past in her works: "[I]n the West Indian dialect and Black American English I employ in my work, there is a certain African dimension."[23] This invocation of "African words and sounds" and, on a larger scale, African dance rituals and practices in her works constitutes the spiritual return, which is a necessary ingredient in creating a "true" self. This adaptation of the colonial language is ironically initiated in the kitchen, the very space that should restrict women's freedom and movement. This restricted space, an exclusive female space, facilitates female bonding and, similar to the adopted language, which is rendered potent by African syntax, is converted into a place of empowerment. Conjuring "their language" in the kitchen, the talk of Marshall's "mother poets" was highly functional and was noted for its therapeutic values:

> [I]t restored the women to themselves and reaffirmed their self-worth. Through language they were able to overcome the humiliations of the work-day. . . . The exuberant talk [also] functioned as an outlet for the tremendous creative energy they possessed. They were women in whom the need for self-expression was strong, and since language was the only vehicle readily available to them they made of it an art form that—in keeping with the African tradition in which art and life are one—was an integral part of their lives.[24]

These women not only miraculously converted a language into their own, but also simultaneously practiced their ancestral culture, that of "keeping with the African tradition in which art and life are one." This re-creation of the language into their own functions as a vehicle of expression, communication, rebellion, and self-assertion.

Thus, establishing a united front, Marshall along with Condé and Kincaid have joined arms and have declared "null and void" the history that has denigrated them, falsely presenting "unflattering

23. Marshall, "Return of a Native Daughter," 53.
24. Paule Marshall, *Reena and Other Stories*, 6.

and fraudulent images of black women." The concept of history is subverted and redefined:

> History to me is an antidote to the lies, and I'm interested in discovering and in unearthing what was positive and inspiring about our experience. . . . We have the unique opportunity to create, to reinvent ourselves. So much that's been said about us—all those negative and unflattering portrayals—was designed to serve the fantasies and motives of the larger society and had little to do with us, we can declare it all null and void, all that stuff, and *fashion a self for ourselves that's more truthful and more complex.* And I think that knowing and understanding history is a part of that endeavor.[25]

Thus, the narratives of Marshall, Condé, and Kincaid are simultaneous celebrations of the self and the community. They have adopted and continued the tradition of the perpetuation of positive black self-images or portraits, espoused by Toni Morrison and others. They have also successfully fought against negative self-portrayals, illuminating the source of pride for African American and Afro-Caribbean women, and have sought to change the fate of black diasporic women by voicing their concerns.

Hence, the "fictional autobiographies" are a celebration of black (Caribbean) women, their lives and their achievements. Adequately equipped with the necessary tools—pen and language—Condé, Marshall, and Kincaid have broken the listening silence. Disputing and denouncing the historical facts that have excluded black women from the pages of history, these women novelists along with their protagonists resist being zombified; they subvert literary tenets, and rewrite (or reright) the literary canon, thereby creating a new "womanist" genre: fictional autobiography. This challenge and the subversion are evident in the coinage itself: *fictional autobiography.* Juxtaposed with *autobiography,* the term *fictional* is employed to accentuate the nonconventional use or, rather, subversion of the conventional usage of autobiography. This subversive challenge is also embodied in the titles and the narrative structures of the works. *Annie John* and *The Autobiography of My Mother,* in essence autobiography of the other, are first-person narratives. *I, Tituba, Black Witch of Salem* is a first-person narrative, and *Heremakhonon*

25. Marshall, "Meditations on Language and the Self," 287; emphasis added.

switches elusively between first and third persons. *Heremakhonon* is also noted for its inconsistent and sometimes muted monologic discourse. *Praisesong for the Widow* is a third-person narrative. *Brown Girl, Brownstones*, although seemingly an autobiographical account of the young heroine's, Selina Boyce's, life, is narrated in the third person. This distinct departure from conventional or traditional autobiography is a point of resistance, designed to set the records straight. The process of writing fictional autobiography mirrors the process of decolonization. Borrowing the title of Sidonie Smith and Julia Watson's book, these women have "de/colonized the subject," setting her free from colonial impositions. Promoting femaleness and a positive black self-image are detours from the colonial, historical account and representation of black women. The mother's land becomes the site of and for resisting zombification, promoting self-acceptance, and achieving subjectivity.

By writing "home," Kincaid, Marshall, and Condé have written the mother('s)land into history. They have not only written memory but also rewritten history, against all odds. This rewriting and righting of the self were absolutely necessary in order to avoid self-effacement and annihilation, because

> Tales of hunting will always
> glorify the hunter
> until the lioness
> is her own hiss—torian.[26]

"Hiss[ing]" themselves back into history as true "hiss-torians," Condé, Marshall, and Kincaid have created a new beginning:

> In this beginning
> [they rewrite] the history books
> put William *their* conqueror on the
> back page
> make Morgan *their* pirate
> a footnote
> Grannies to come
> will know of the Arctic Ocean
> But *will know more of the Caribbean Sea*
> *Of the Atlantic crossing*

26. Merle Collins, *Rotten Pomerack*, 63.

> *We will recall with pride our own*
> So goodbye, William
> Good
> riddance
> Kai sa c'est sa'w
> esta es nuestra casa
> In whatever language
> This is our home.[27]

This new beginning not only recalls "with pride our own" but also reclaims the self and the home space by rewriting black women's histories. The language is appropriately employed to reclaim this home space; the mother's land is the mother tongue. The once misrepresented and silenced are now adequately represented and rendered visible. The once denigrated past is embraced and celebrated and placed on the front pages of the novels. Though all-inclusive, this new beginning gives precedence to the local history and footnotes the European (colonial) history.

27. Ibid., 57; emphasis added.

2 I Am Me, I Am You

The Intricate Mother-Daughter Dyadic Relationship

My past was my mother. . . . Oh, it was a laugh, for I spent so much time saying I did not want to be like my mother that I missed the whole story: I was not like my mother—I was my mother.

—*Jamaica Kincaid*, Lucy

This quote gives an insight into the complex mother-daughter relationship as it exemplifies the existing ambivalence within this relationship. The mother-daughter relationship is classified equally by intense love and intense hatred. Noticeably, the daughter's childhood years are marked by innocence and great love and admiration for the kind, understanding mother. Inexplicably, this love is transformed into hatred and exacerbated during puberty by the mother's need to control. It is about the tumultuous adolescent years that Kincaid writes when she concludes that the relationship between the mother and the daughter mirrors the relationship between "Europe and the place that [she is] from, which is to say a relationship between the powerful and the powerless. The girl is powerless, and the mother is powerful." Although Kincaid admits that the struggle for autonomy is neither political nor public, but personal, in her works the personal is always conflated with the political. By placing the personal mother-daughter relationship within a political context, Kincaid insinuates that the personal, more often than not, is conditioned by the political. This conditioning is concretized by Rosalie Riegle Troester: "The currents that flow between Black mothers and their daughters are often tumultuous and intensified by the racism and sexism of white America. Black mothers, particularly those with strong ties to their community, sometimes build high banks around their young daughters, isolating them from the dangers of

45

the larger world until they are old and strong enough to function as autonomous women."[1]

In spite of the personal nature of the mother-daughter relationship, it is often invaded by outside forces, namely, the "racism and sexism of white America." In an attempt to protect her daughter from "such evils," the mother builds a protective wall around her. These "high banks," initially designed to protect and shield the daughter from "the dangers of the larger world," eventually function as suffocating walls or barriers that silence and subsume the daughter's subjectivity. "Isolating [daughters] from the dangers of the larger world" translates into the daughter's isolation from her mother. Though Troester's comment is pertinent and theoretically practicable, the mother exhibits impracticability when it is time to give her daughter autonomy, that is, when she is "old and strong enough to function as [an] autonomous [woman]." Seemingly unable and unwilling to grant her daughter independence, the mother functions as a deterrent to the autonomy her teenage daughter seeks. It is this unwillingness on the mother's part that Kincaid sees as a projection of the colonizer's deeds: "The mother shows her [daughter] how to be in the world, but at the back of her mind, she thinks she never will get it. She's deeply skeptical that *this child could ever grow to be a self-possessed woman* and, in the end, she reveals her skepticism; yet even within the skepticism are, of course, dismissal and scorn. So it's not unlike the relationship between the conqueror and the victim."[2] Deeply affected by colonialist teachings, the mother is unaware of the harm she is causing her daughter and their relationship, and in her effort to protect, she instead institutionalizes her daughter. Understandably, the daughter rebels against this institutionalization, another subtle form of colonization.

Yet, and in spite of this turbulence, there is no denying the mother that exists within the daughter: "I was not like my mother—I was my mother." This existence goes "beyond the verbally transmitted lore of female survival—a knowledge that is subliminal, subversive, preverbal: the knowledge flowing between two alike bodies, one

---

1. Kincaid, " 'I Come from a Place,' " 86; Troester, "Turbulence and Tenderness," 13–16.
2. Kincaid, " 'I Come from a Place,' " 87; emphasis added.

of which has spent nine months inside the other." Lucy, the titular protagonist of the novel *Lucy*, who has tried for most of her teenage life to establish a sizable distance between herself and her mother, is reminded of this "preverbal" bonding: "You can run away, but you cannot escape the fact that I am your mother, my blood runs in you, I carried you for nine months inside me."[3] The fact that the daughter spends incalculable time denying the mother in her hints at a tangible fear of becoming her mother and embodying the suffocating colonial image and presence her mother exudes. Fearful of emulating the colonial traits she detests and deplores, the daughter suffers from bouts of "matrophobia," which, according to Rich,

> is the fear not of one's mother or of motherhood but of becoming one's mother, [it] can be seen as a womanly splitting of the self, in the desire to become purged once and for all of our mothers' bondage, to become individuated and free. The mother stands for the victim in ourselves, the unfree woman, the martyr. Our personalities seem dangerously to blur and overlap with our mothers'; and, in a desperate attempt to know where mother ends and daughter begins, we perform radical surgery.[4]

A daughter's rejection of her mother is her attempt to escape the colonial yoke that binds her mother. Desperately "wanting to break free" from her mother, Lucy tries to silence her and terminate the relationship by refusing to open her letters, which is also her rejection of the colonial language and colonialism as a whole, the fundamental reason for the mother-daughter turbulence. Her decision not to open the letters is also her attempt to silence the mother-master. In spite of her refusal, Lucy repeatedly suffers from anxiety attacks whenever she is reminded of her resemblance in mannerisms and features to her mother. Repudiating the "deep underlying pull toward" her mother, Lucy vehemently denies any likenesses between her mother and herself. When told by her cousin, Maude, "you remind me of Ms. Annie, you really remind me of your mother," Lucy experiences "a dread that if [she] relaxes her guard [she] will identify with her [mother] completely." In retaliation, she counters: "I was dying and she saved my life. I shall always be grateful to her for that. She could not have known that in one careless sentence she said the only

3. Rich, *Of Woman Born*, 220; Kincaid, *Lucy*, 90.
4. Rich, *Of Woman Born*, 230.

thing that could keep me alive. I said: I am not like my mother. She and I are not alike."[5] Ironically, the mere mentioning of her mother revives Lucy. This attempt to define herself against her mother fails, for shortly thereafter Lucy complains of homesickness. Not only are daughters fearful of becoming their mothers, but mothers manifest fear as well in seeing themselves in their daughters. Perversely, it is this mutual fear, the fear of identifying and of becoming, that binds mothers and daughters. They are both colonized subjects.

In spite of the imposition of colonial doctrines on the mother-daughter relationship and its conditioning by the patriarchy, a unique female bonding is instituted outside the ramifications of colonial paternalism: a mother's land where maternal spaces and maternity are negotiated. This negotiation for female bonding is facilitated by a mother (figure), noticeably an older woman, who equips the daughter with life teachings and subsequently passes this "torch," the ability to negotiate one's identity, unto her daughter. The absence of negotiations and negotiators completely effaces mother-daughter bonding, and it is catastrophic to the individual who suffers such a deprivation. Highlighting the need for negotiations and negotiators, Troester argues, "[T]he turbulent stream may be kept from overflowing by spillways in the form of other adult women who help guide and form the young girl, thus relieving some of the pressure on the mother-daughter relationship." These adult women that Troester speaks of are either "othermothers" or grandmothers or aunts, all united by kinship with the blood or biological mother.[6] Because of their age (they are usually older women, separated by a generation or two from their "daughters"), experience, and wit, these "adult women" who possess ancestral qualities and special vision are the ones who advance and preserve the oral African (ancestral) tradition. This preservation of the culture sustains the adolescent daughters on their respective journeys to selfhood.

As a result of her ancestral status (apart from the age difference, the surrogate or othermother is not as emotionally intertwined with her surrogate daughter as the biological mother, and this minimal distancing seemingly gives her a better, wiser, and less emotion-

5. Kincaid, *Lucy*, 123; Rich, *Of Woman Born*, 235; Kincaid, *Lucy*, 123.
6. Troester, "Turbulence and Tenderness," 13.

driven perspective on the mother-daughter relationship), the surrogate mother bridges the rift created by the tumultuous mother-daughter relationship. Often, this relationship forges and forces a mother-daughter separation that usually occurs during the daughter's pubescent years. Such a separation greets us in the first few pages of Kincaid's *Annie John*. Significantly, the first chapter is titled "Figures in the Distance," speaking of unidentifiable origins and separation. The mother and daughter, evidently, represent these "figures in the distance." Commenting on this first chapter, Laura Niesen de Abruña notes, "[T]he first chapter, in a novel ostensibly about coming of age, ironically concerns death. This is Kincaid's deliberate strategy since the novel is not about a beginning but about the end of the narrator's intimacy with her mother and her island."[7]

The end of this intimacy between mother and daughter is chronicled by the numerous deaths and funerals that pervade the novel and about which Little Annie obsesses.[8] *Annie John* opens with relentless descriptions of various deaths: both the young and the old die. Annie equally obsesses over the deaths of the young and the old, but she seems to have a fascination and fixation with the deaths of young children, particularly young girls. She describes in graphic details the deaths of two girls, one younger than herself, named Nalda, and another, her own age. Evidently, Annie's obsession with the death of young girls is indicative of her own fear of death, and separation and abandonment. This obsession almost becomes a reality, for she suffers a near-death experience at the end of the novel. Closely linked to death is the notion of abandonment, which is often staged by parents who desert their young, powerless children. Because of such desertion, Annie views the adult world as the world of the powerful, a cruel and unfathomable place. Annie's disillusionment with the adult world will surface again when she experiences direct personal severance from her own mother, who inexplicably withdraws from her upon her entrance into womanhood. She views this brutal severance as a loveless act, a mother's betrayal of her own child. Although

7. Laura Niesen de Abruña, "Family Connections: Mother and Mother Country in the Fiction of Jean Rhys and Jamaica Kincaid," 279.
8. Annie bears the name of her mother and is often referred to as "Little Annie" by her parents.

it is the parent who abandons the child, it is the child who bears the shame of being abandoned. Commenting on the death of another little girl, Annie admits, "[S]he seemed a shameful thing, a girl whose mother had died and left her alone in the world."[9]

Annie's own father, Alexander, bears the shame of abandonment, for at a tender age he is also forsaken by his parents, who "after kissing him goodbye [left] him with his grandmother, and boarded a boat and sailed to South America" (23). This abandonment of children by parents translates into a power relationship. Alexander's parents exert power by deserting their helpless and powerless—and young—son. Annie vocalizes her own fear, her own powerlessness, in an essay that becomes a recurring haunting dream in which her mother, similar to Alexander's parents, abandons her at sea. In leaving their children, the parents become inaccessible like the sea identified by its drowning depths.

Before the actual mother-daughter separation, Annie experiences a tangible fear of abandonment as she witnesses her mother engrossed with the deaths of others, exclusively female. She becomes the village undertaker. Annie's mother's association with death gives her a transcendental power over others, including her daughter (both the young and the old die in Mrs. John's hands or else collapse at her feet while in conversation with her). Ironically, it is the mother who introduces Annie to her first encounter with death by having her daughter witness a ritualized death bath of a young girl. As the mother plays an active role in the ceremonies (she bathes and prepares the dead for burials), Annie stands aside and looks on, uninvolved, out of touch with the ritual, indicative of the daughter's powerlessness and her lack of control over the imminent loss of her mother and their relationship.

The final moment of imposed separation between Annie and her mother culminates in the scene "The Circling Hand," classified as deathlike, white and bony and out of its elements. This deathlike hand signals the symbolic death of the loving, nurturing relationship Annie once shared with her mother. It is no mere coincidence that the chapter "The Circling Hand" precedes the chapter "Gwen,"

9. Jamaica Kincaid, *Annie John*, 8. Future citations will be given parenthetically in the text.

significant of the final separation between mother and daughter and the beginning of a relationship between Annie and her new-found friend, Gwen. These hands once remembered lovingly, for they caressed Annie and tended to her every need—"We [mother and daughter] would sit in this bath in a darkened room with a strange-smelling candle burning away. As we sat in this bath, my mother would bathe different parts of my body; then she would do the same to herself" (14)—are now equated with betrayal and death. The caresses once meant exclusively for Annie are now directed at other girls, significantly dead, a clear invasion of the privacy Annie once shared with her mother. This female invasion of privacy is later replaced by a male invasion of privacy, the final disruption of possible negotiations for the continuance of the loving mother-daughter relationship. Walking in on her parents' lovemaking, all Annie saw was her mother's circling hands:

> It didn't interest me what they were doing—only that my mother's hand was on the small of my father's back and that it was making a circular motion. But her hand! It was white and bony, as if it had long been dead and had been left out in the elements. It seemed not to be her hand, and yet it could only be her hand, so well did I know it. It went around and around in the same circular motion, and I looked at it as if I would never see anything else in my life again. If I were to forget anything else in the world, I could not forget her hand as it looked then. (30–31)

The hand that once bathed little dead girls is now linked to sex: it provides sexual gratification. Similar to death, sex is abhorrent to Annie. Although she confesses that the actual sex act did not bother her as much as the circling hand, the sex act is of great significance. The circling hand is inextricably linked to the sex act, which heralds the final moment of intimacy between mother and daughter. By partaking in this sex act with Alexander, Annie sees her mother as a betrayer of her love and trust, for Alexander had succeeded in doing exactly what Annie had hoped to do before walking in on her parents' lovemaking that fateful day: "reconquer [her] mother—a chance for her to smile . . . again" (30). Suffering from bouts of disappointment, Annie views not only her mother as the enemy but her father as well, who in her young eyes has both invaded the mother-daughter privacy and imposed his will on their relationship. Noticeably, it is after the sex act, which culminates into

Annie's emergence into womanhood, that Annie's mother initiated a break from her daughter.

Accustomed to unrivaled intimacy in her earlier years and growing up under her mother's protective wings, Annie suffers a wrenching and inexplicable separation from her mother in her pubescent years, a period in a young girl's life that is punctuated by conflict and tension and therefore difficult to negotiate. Her mother abruptly terminates their ritual of dressing alike:

> "You are getting too old for that [dressing alike]. It's time you had your own clothes. You just cannot go around the rest of your life looking like a little me." . . . Because of this young lady business, instead of days spent in perfect harmony with my mother, I trailing in her footsteps, she showering down on me her kisses and affection and attention, I was now sent off to learn one thing and another. I was sent to someone who knew all about manners. (26–27)

This severance from her mother has a devastating effect on Annie, and her relationship with her mother is now one born out of conflict and tension. Similar to her daughter, who has undergone transformation from a young girl to a "young lady," Mrs. John, once a loving and caring mother, has been transformed into a distant, hateful other, embodying the colonizer. Like the colonizer, who colonizes the female body by regarding it as an object of shame and filth (it becomes desirable only when sexual connotations are attached to it), Mrs. John's rejection of her daughter's body is inadvertently a rejection of the black female body. Whereas Annie's body was a site of harmony during childhood, upon entering womanhood her body becomes a site of conflict. Such a rejection forces Annie to view female sexuality as a woman's worst enemy because of the stigma likened to it, and as a result she condescendingly refers to her menstruation as this "young lady business" (26). Her mother's reference to her maturing into adulthood evidences a visible detachment. Unlike childhood, a period of innocence, which is prized and valued, adolescence is a period of guilt and shame. Thus, along with Annie's burgeoning sexuality comes an onslaught of new and unprecedented problems. A young lady now, dressing like her mother might attract unwanted and unsolicited attention and advances, making her a desirable object. Annie confirms her mother's prediction, embodying "the slut she [was] so bent on becoming," for she is seen by her mother engaged in conversation with a childhood male friend, Mineu.[10] Annie has committed the ultimate sin: she engages in the abominable act of talking to boys. Subsumed by colonialist beliefs, Mrs. John's vision is colored, perhaps by a generation of similar experiences, and therefore she buys into the myth that a woman's burgeoning sexuality allures the opposite sex, thereby providing a "powerful rationale for sexual assaults."[11] Apparently, this "rationale for sexual assaults" is present in the conversation Annie has with the boys (Mineu and three friends). Significantly, her mother observes her "speaking *to young men*," and not *with* them. They are respectable "young men," while Annie, who has become a "slut," is not deserving of respect. Talking has taken on new meaning; it is now synonymous with sluttishness. Annie's sexuality is regarded as a curse and is treated exactly like one by her mother, who unjustly punishes her by alienating her from her world. Sexuality is taught to be feared and repressed by girls and is celebrated by boys (Mrs. John readily warns her daughter of becoming a slut, yet she never questions her husband's allegedly lewd and lascivious sexual behavior: he has fathered many children, some of whom he does not know). Unquestionably, Mineu's maturing into a sexual being is an asset, in contrast to Annie, whose sexuality has transformed her into a slut. Annie is no longer her mother's little girl but becomes a budding sexual being. The friendship and love that mother and daughter once shared are now inexplicably lost, and in its place stand misunderstanding and intense hatred. This inexplicable loss of friendship can be best explained as a sign of resistance on the mother's part to her daughter's inevitable entrance into the realm of womanhood. A woman now, Annie has disheveled her childhood Eden.

Because female sexuality is deemed taboo, a young girl is denied "proper" initiation into womanhood. A clear indication of this denial is chronicled in the novel *Lucy*. The protagonist, Lucy, scared to death by the changes in her body, "immediately cries out for [her] mother to come and help [her]"; upon witnessing her daughter's predicament,

10. Jamaica Kincaid, *At the Bottom of the River*, 3.
11. Patricia Hill Collins, *Black Feminist Thoughts: Knowledge, Consciousness, and the Politics of Empowerment*, 77.

the mother cautions that "finding blood in [her] underpants might be something one day [she] would get down on [her] knees and pray for." Lucy later remarks: "[W]ithout telling me exactly how I might miss a menstrual cycle, my mother had shown me which herbs to pick and boil, and what time of day to drink the potion they produced, to bring on a reluctant period." Instead of enlightening her daughter with the cause of missing her menstrual cycle, Lucy's mother, Mrs. Potter, instead presents her with the cure. However, the cure is presented in disguise, eliciting the following comments from Lucy: "She had presented the whole idea to me as a way to strengthen the womb, but underneath we both knew that a weak womb was not the cause of a missed period. She knew that I knew, but we presented to each other a face of innocence and politeness and even went so far as to curtsy to each other at the end."[12]

Mother and daughter are unable to speak openly of female sexuality; instead, it is cloaked in innuendo and conspiracy. In a similar fashion, never given an explanation for the shattering of her childhood innocence and the severance of the relationship between herself and mother, Annie is left on her own to decipher what it means to grow into a young woman. From her mother's unexpected reaction, she knew that this "young lady business" was offensive, something that causes hurt and pain, the ultimate cause of the mother-daughter estrangement. Marking her entrance into puberty, Annie seemingly "trades in" her innocence and purity. Upon entering this "imperfect" space, Annie is sent off to learn perfection: good manners and how to become a "perfect" lady. Harmony with the biological mother is replaced by learning colonial habits, a subtle worshiping of the colonial mother.

For Annie, being a "perfect" lady signals self-effacement, for it mirrors colonial habits and ways. Whereupon, in her young eyes, her mother is transformed into the enemy, she is a perpetrator of colonial habits, first, for denouncing female sexuality and renouncing her own femaleness and, second, for adopting and thereafter attempting to inculcate and indoctrinate her daughter into colonialist values and teachings. This perpetration of colonial customs is accorded full agency in Kincaid's collection of short stories, *At the Bottom*

12. Kincaid, *Lucy*, 69, 70.

of the River, in a chapter appropriately titled "Girl." This lyrical, poemlike essay functions as a manual for the girl or, rather, for all Caribbean girls, for whom it is written. The voice of the story is singular, yet it seems to speak for all Caribbean mothers admonishing their daughters of female sexuality and its severe consequences in a patriarchal, colonial society. It offers a fixed code of conduct for young women to live by, namely, how to become "good" women and "good" wives, and rules for their surviving in a male-dominated society. If not adhered to, the young girl risks becoming a "slut." By imposing these rules upon her daughter, Mrs. John advocates patriarchal law and order. As such, she sheds her femaleness and if not literally then figuratively enters the asexual zone. She no longer identifies through her sexuality or femaleness with her daughter; instead, she appears to adopt a masculine, colonial role, as she colonizes her daughter's body. Female sexuality becomes an enemy, while the "real enemy," colonialism, is masked and is therefore overlooked.

Denouncing female sexuality in general, and renouncing her own sexuality, Mrs. John plays what Trinh Minh-ha calls the "double game." On one hand, she "asserts [her] right, as woman, an exemplary one; on the other hand, [she] quietly maintains [her] privileges by helping the master to perpetuate his cycle of oppression." It is apparent that Minh-ha did not envision the "double game" being played by mother and daughter, for she acknowledges that it is played by women against other women (specifically First World women against Third World women), the powerful against the powerless, "I-who-have-made-it [against] You-who-cannot-make-it." Notwithstanding, her coinage is applicable to the relationship Annie has with her mother. Imposing colonial values upon her daughter, Mrs. John is perpetuating the cycle of oppression initiated by the colonial master. Not only is she subsumed by colonialist beliefs, but her identity is also conflated with the colonizer; she thereby fits the profile of the distant "other." Interestingly, her daughter earlier visualized her head, like that of the queen's, on a sixpence (18–19). This vision is twofold: it simultaneously speaks of intense yearning and wrenching estrangement. On one hand, Mrs. John is still Little Annie's mother, embodied by the queen figure, and on the other hand, she is the distanced "other." This "otherness" culminates in the "end of specialness," but not for the reasons, "competition and rivalry," that Minh-ha underscores.[13]

The overriding reason for Mrs. John's ironclad behavior is fear, fear of the consequences of her daughter's burgeoning sexuality. By succumbing to her fear and yielding to societal pressures and sending her reluctant daughter to become a "perfect lady," she appears to relinquish her rights as mother and woman. Ironically, as she relinquishes her womanly qualities and rights, Mrs. John is training or, more appropriately, colonizing her daughter in accordance with societal standards on how to become a "good" wife and mother.

Attaining womanhood, there is no noticeable distinction between Annie and other women, notably Alexander's alleged "outside" women. Similar to the alleged "outside" women with whom Mrs. John refuses to speak, she refuses to exchange words or communicate verbally with Annie. Herein begins the mutually accepted silence to which mother and daughter secretly adhere concerning matters related to sexuality and the body. Although not an instigator, Annie has a complicit alliance to this code of silence. When informed by her mother in a "matter of fact manner" that she was on the verge of becoming a young lady, Annie admits that she was glad of the brief mentioning of such matters: "She didn't say exactly just what it was that made me on the verge of becoming a young lady, and I was so glad of that, because I didn't want to know" (26). Thus, Annie has become an accomplice in the "secret" code of silence, and as a result verbal communication and dialogues are replaced with gestures and monologues, and "the frightening black thing," representative of the hate and animosity between mother and daughter: "My mother turned to face me. We looked at each other, and I could see the frightening black thing leave her to meet the frightening black thing that had left me. They met in the middle and embraced. . . . To me she said, You are late. . . . She was using that tone of voice: it was as if I were not only a stranger but a stranger that she did not wish to know" (101). This war of silence is later replaced with a battle of words. Drowning in a well full of the word *slut*, Annie manages to survive the current, as she accordingly "talks back," attacking her mother equally with words: "[L]ike father like son,

13. Trinh T. Minh-ha, *Woman, Native, Other*, 86–87.

like mother like daughter" (102). In Annie's response the subversion of the proverbial male saying is starkly visible and lends to her transforming the "colonial" language into her own. At the same time, her revealing comment hints at the sameness between mother and daughter. It also insinuates the fear that Mrs. John experiences, which is that her daughter is becoming her, a rebellious teenager who left her parents behind and migrated to Antigua because of a family misunderstanding.

Talking back to her mother creates a larger void between mother and daughter, and power is seemingly transferred from Annie the mother to Annie the daughter. Bell hooks celebrates the act of talking back in an entire book that bears the appropriate title *Talking Back*. In her words, talking back is a "rite of initiation. It is that act of speech, that is no mere gesture of empty words, that is the expression of our movement from object to subject—the liberated voice." Talking back is indeed an empowering source, but in the case of Annie with her mother, it does not fully liberate her from the powerful grasp of her mother. As a result, this transferal of power is fleeting, and Annie's joyous moment is short-lived as her mother not only talks back but also turns her back on her. Back turned, Annie the mother is strong and powerful, and it is young Annie who trades places with her mother. In spite of her youth, Annie now appears old, broken, and helpless: "*It was I who was tired and old and broken*, and as I looked at my mother, *full of vigor, young and whole*, I wanted to go over and put my arms around her and beg forgiveness for the thing I had just said. . . . But I couldn't move" (103; emphasis added). By "turning her back" on Annie, the mother silences her. Consequently, Annie suffers defeat. She becomes powerless in spite of her talking back. Though the act of talking back is "the expression of [Annie's] movement from object to subject," it does not give her the redemptive power and liberation she seeks from her mother.[14]

Notwithstanding, talking back culminates with self-recognition. It is only after talking back to her mother that Annie for the first time looks at herself naked in the mirror and sees her black face and self, and is significantly repulsed by what she sees. This repulsion of her being speaks to her lack of identity and acceptance of self:

14. Bell hooks, *Talking Back: Thinking Feminist, Thinking Black*, 9.

I stood naked in front of a mirror and looked at myself from head to toe. I was so long and bony that I more than filled up the mirror, and my small ribs pressed out against my skin. I tried to push my *unruly hair* down against my head so that it would *lie flat*, but as soon as I let it go it bounced up again. I could see the small *tuft of hair* under my arms. And then I got a good look at my nose. It had suddenly *spread across my face almost blotting out my cheeks, taking up my whole face*, so that if I didn't know I was me standing there I would have wondered about that strange girl—and to think that only so recently my nose had been a small thing, the size of a rosebud. (27; emphasis added)

Instead of seeing the reflection of her mother, which she repeatedly saw before this rift, Annie sees herself, symbolic of the end of the mirroring stage between mother and daughter. She becomes aware of her color difference or, rather, her blackness. This blackness, once invisible, becomes doubly visible as she matures and grows apart from her mother. Annie's mother's rejection of the adult, mature body forces Annie into self-loathing, evidence that she is not a fully liberated subject and therefore has not attained the final stage of becoming of which hooks makes mention.

Rejected by her mother, Annie in turn rejects her self, her body, further shattering her childhood serenity and her sense of self. This self-rejection contributes to her self-destruction as she perpetuates her mother's crime by adopting and accepting the negative view of blackness and womanhood. Annie denigrates her African features— her dark skin, broad nose, full lips, and kinky hair—as she colonizes her appearance. In stark contrast to this blackness (ugliness) stands her mother's whiteness (beauty):

When my eyes rested on my father, I didn't think very much of the way he looked. But when my eyes rested on my mother, I found her *beautiful. Her head looked as if it should be on a sixpence.* What a *beautiful long neck*, and *long plaited hair*, which she pinned up around the *crown of her head* because when her *hair hung down* it made her so hot. Her *nose was the shape of a flower on the brink of opening.* Her mouth, moving up and down as she ate and talked at the same time, was such a *beautiful mouth* I could have looked at it forever. . . . Her *lips were wide and almost thin*, and when she said certain words I could see small parts of big *white teeth—so big, and pearly*, like some nice buttons on one of my dresses. (18–19; emphasis added)

Constant references are made to her mother's beauty: straight, long hair, chiseled nose, and white hands. This reference of beauty speaks of the (negative) effect of colonization, where the colonized are brainwashed into accepting a European standard of beauty. While Mrs. John is conflated with the colonizer, Annie's black skin links her with the colonized. Mrs. John's white hands, long neck, and thin lips are synonymous with the colonizer, the mother country, England, while Alexander and Annie with their dark skin embody the colonized, the powerless. Kincaid brazenly makes this distinction between the colonizer and the colonized in *A Small Place* when she vocalizes the obvious: the black people seen on exclusive holiday resorts are slaves or servants to the white tourists or colonists.

Mrs. John's powerful presence serves only to remind Annie of her weakness and her dependency. Annie's powerlessness is noticeable not only by her mother talking back and turning her back on her, but also by her cooking Annie's dinner and attending to her other needs: "When I looked down it was as if the ground had opened up between us, making a deep and wide split. *On one side of this split stood my mother, bent over my dinner cooking in a pot; and on the other side stood I, in my arms carrying my schoolbooks* and inside carrying the thimble that weighed worlds" (103; emphasis added). In spite of the estrangement, Annie is dependent upon her mother for her livelihood. This dependency and powerlessness are underscored as her mother stands cooking Annie's dinner. The "deep and wide split" symbolizes alienation and disaffection between mother and daughter and also illuminates Annie's dependency. Standing on her "side of the split," the kitchen, Mrs. John is a master of her domain. She cooks, concocts, and conjures her culinary art in her kitchen. On the other side of the split, which figuratively functions as the classroom, stands Annie. While Annie is subjected to colonial teachings in the classroom, Mrs. John, arguably, is unaffected by colonial dominion because she creates her own recipes.

In contrast to her mother, Annie has yet to master her domain. She is still aspiring to become, which is marked by her *carrying* her schoolbooks and a thimble, speaking to and of competing discourses. It also hints at a negotiation between the domestic (maternal) world and the literary world. Annie bears the burden of fetching her schoolbooks, a burden she is compelled to bear if she is to master the literary domain. Carrying a thimble, Annie is also aspiring to master the domestic domain. The thimble is also suggestive of Annie's need for protection, her lack of mastery, hence the need for a protective coat or cover, represented by the thimble. This thimble is symbolically linked to the domestic world and the mother whose protection Annie still needs.

Although competing discourses, literary training and domestic training, are both symbols of freedom, the juxtaposition of the literary (written) and the domestic (oral) speaks to the need for negotiation between them. Mrs. John epitomizes this negotiation, for although her domain is the kitchen, she instills in her daughter the importance of literary training. (Not only does Kincaid call for a blending and acceptance of the two worlds, the literary and the domestic, but Marshall and Condé also hint at the necessity of this balance.) The literary world is one of freedom, freedom achieved through books. The reading or interpreting of books facilitates the acquisition of (colonial) language, and thereafter its reinterpretation, permitting freedom of expression. The adoption and adaptation of the colonial discourse functions as a powerful tool and is used as a weapon.

Using language as a weapon is no novelty to Kincaid. In her book *A Small Place*, although she concludes that the language of the colonizer only glorifies his acts, she uses the same language to curse him by exposing his foul deeds. Similarly, Annie's schoolbooks represent her endeavor to master the colonial language. Though Mrs. John's domain is distinctly the kitchen, she does not decry the literary world. Actually, she is a contributor to it, for she negotiates with this world for her daughter's livelihood. She provides and to a great extent empowers Annie with the oral teachings, which Annie later transcribes. A clear example of this transferal of power or, more appropriately, bestowal of authorship occurs in a classroom scene where Annie scribbles under a portrait of *Columbus in Chains* words spoken by her mother about her father and Annie's grandfather Pa Chess: "The Great Man Can No Longer Just Get Up And Go." Annie enjoys a moment of victory as she further enslaves the enslaved Columbus—crowned discoverer of the New World—with words and language. Significantly, the language she uses is Old English, the oldest form of the colonial language. Annie masters the language of the colonizer only to enslave him. Columbus now shares a common fate with the colonized, for his movement is restricted as he sits at the bottom of a ship fettered in chains.

Although seemingly possessing some sense of circumscription, the kitchen, arguably, is also a powerful metaphor for freedom. Denied direct access to the literary world (she never attended school because investing in the education of women was not feasible), Mrs. John acquires her power in this circumscribed space. It seems as though Kincaid's earlier quote "If I actually ran the world, I'd do it from the kitchen" speaks directly to and for Mrs. John, who runs "the world" from her kitchen. Repeating Marshall's observation, the kitchen can equip one with life's teachings and has therapeutic values as it functions as an "outlet for tremendous creative energy." It is rather interesting that Annie once again finds herself caught between two domains.[15] In this instance, she is caught between the literary and the domestic, symbolized by her simultaneous carrying of her books and the thimble, two distantly varied teachings that at once repel and fascinate her. On one hand, Annie is obsessed with books, resulting in her often stealing them from her school library out of mere fascination. Significantly, it is her mother who introduced her to her first books. Unable to access books directly, Mrs. John ensures that her daughter has unrestricted access to them. On the other hand, Annie openly rejects the colonialist teachings printed in the books. She concludes that the reason for the rejection is that the printed literature did not truthfully and adequately depict the lives of her people, the colonized people. As such, she expresses her hatred for and rejoices at the celebrated founder of the New World, Columbus, "fettered in chains attached at the bottom of a ship" (77). Annie views her moments of rejoicing as justly deserved, for this ship within which Columbus is contained is reminiscent of the slave ships her ancestors forcibly boarded centuries ago.

15. Marshall, *Reena and Other Stories,* 6. Here I am referring to the love-hate relationship within which Annie is trapped with her mother and the ambivalence that characterizes their relationship. Annie repeatedly finds herself "between places"—love-hate, literary-domestic—that are significant to both her development and her sense of self, and as such, she has to negotiate by arriving at a medium.

In another classroom scenario, Annie discerns the colonizers' attempt to camouflage their deeds and the ills inflicted on the colonized: "With our teachers and our books, it was hard for us to tell which side we really now belonged—with the masters or the slaves— for it was all history, it was all in the past, and everybody behaved differently now; all of us celebrated Queen Victoria's birthday, even though she had been dead a long time. But, we the descendants of the slaves, knew quite well what had really happened" (76). Without a doubt, the colonizer's agenda is to beguile the colonized, denying her a sense of self and her story, and to impose his (hi)story on her. Though the colonizer's attempt is to befuddle the individual, Annie asserts that the "descendants of the slaves" were well aware of the past, which the colonizer deemed history, an uncelebrated one. Annie dismantles the colonizer's attempt to zombify the colonized as she reinterprets his (hi)story. Obsessing over these rebellious thoughts in the classroom, characterized by its colonial atmosphere, is an act of resistance against colonialist teachings.

Like the books, the domestic world both captivates and eludes her. The magic of the kitchen, represented by her mother, possesses her. Annie is fascinated by her mother's ability to concoct various dishes. She describes with painful detail her mother's preparation of various foods and delicacies. Food is used initially as a metaphor for intimacy. Annie is rewarded with her favorite dishes whenever she does things that please her mother. When she is cast out of her mother's intimate world, food becomes a means of deceit and betrayal. Annie is tricked by her mother into eating the hated breadfruit (83–84).

This theme of deceit and betrayal is given full attention in Sandra Gilbert and Susan Gubar's *Madwoman in the Attic*. Reconstructing the fable "Snow White and the Seven Dwarfs," Gilbert and Gubar focus on the mother-daughter relationship between the Wicked Queen Stepmother and her stepdaughter, Snow White. This relationship is marred by deceit, trickery, and betrayal. Annie's rejection by her mother seems to be linked directly to the rejection suffered by Snow White at the hands of a wicked stepmother. She confesses: "I tried to imagine that I was like a girl in one of the books I had read—a girl who had suffered much at the hands of a *cruel step-parent*, or a girl who had suddenly found herself *without any parent* at all. When reading about such a girl I would heap more suffering on her if I felt the author hadn't gone far enough" (86; emphasis added). Annie seemingly suggests that having a cruel stepparent equals having no parent at all. This link between Annie and Snow White is further endorsed by Annie's allusion to her suffering a fate similar to that of Snow White. She angrily remarks: "I would have chosen going off to live in a cavern and *keeping house* for *seven unruly men* rather than to go on living with my life as it stood" (130; emphasis added). Similar to Snow White, who becomes an obedient servant to the seven dwarfs, Annie implies that she is willing to become a "housekeeping angel" as long as she escapes the "Wicked Stepmother," her mother. Rejecting her daughter, Mrs. John relinquishes her motherly role and instead becomes a transformed and alien parent, embodying a stepparent.

The alienation that Annie experiences equals being parentless. Similar to the Queen Stepmother, who tricks her stepdaughter into eating a poisonous apple, Mrs. John tricks Annie into eating the hated breadfruit. This act of treachery is one of many. Gubar and Gilbert pose the question: "Why do parents begin to seem like step-parents when their daughters reach puberty?" They contend that "when the child gets old enough to become conscious of her parents as sexual beings they really do begin to seem like fiercer, perhaps even younger versions of their 'original' selves. They [seem] more threatening because the child's own sexual awakening disturbs them almost as much as their sexuality, now truly comprehended, bothers the child."[16] Contrarily, Annie and her mother's relationship is not one of sexual rivalry, but one that is aggravated by the social constructions of black womanhood. Though Annie's mother becomes fierce upon her daughter's entrance into womanhood, this ferocity is not as a result of being personally threatened, for Mrs. John is not so much threatened by her daughter's burgeoning sexuality as she is deeply concerned by societal conventions of femaleness and the apparent threats that exist if these conventions are not honored. Although parental sexuality bothers teenage children, evidenced by Annie's reaction upon witnessing her parents' lovemaking, the

16. Sandra Gilbert and Susan Gubar, *Madwoman in the Attic: The Woman Writer and the Nineteenth-Century Literary Imagination*, 69.

overriding concern is what it means to be black and female in a male-oriented and male-dominated colonized society. As a result of female demonization, Mrs. John has to train Annie in accordance with societal, patriarchal conventions, lest she be seen in an unfavorable light. This training seemingly and unavoidably entails her adopting the profile of the colonizer. Regardless, the central theme in both stories, Annie's and Snow White's, is the end of female bonding and the beginning of betrayals and deceit.

This act of deceit, the episode where Annie is tricked by her mother into eating the hated breadfruit, is one of many. Attempting to make Annie confess about her marble playing, Mrs. John tells her a childhood tale of unknowingly carrying a snake hidden between a bunch of figs: "The weight of the green figs caused her to walk slowly. She . . . was very glad to get rid of [them]. She no sooner had taken the load from her head when out of it crawled a very long black snake" (69). This story mirrors the history taught in the classroom, which has an agenda to beguile, efface, and obfuscate identity, because it is told with the intention of tricking Annie into relinquishing her marbles. The snake imagery is symbolic, because Mrs. John uses snakelike tactics to get Annie to confess. Full of pity for her mother, Annie almost falls for the bait but regains her composure and manages to escape her mother's venom.

Deceit and betrayal become the order of the day. Despite her efforts to retaliate against the deceptions and betrayals, Little Annie is no match for the powerful mother; she is repeatedly portrayed as the betrayed. Understandably, she accuses her mother of betrayal, of neglecting her and directing her undivided attention to the patriarchy, in the form of colonial values. The fear of her loss is so tangible that she is haunted by it in dreams. In a premonitory dream, Annie foresees her fractured future with her mother: "I kept having a dream about my mother sitting on a rock. Over and over I would have the dream—only in it my mother never came back, and sometimes my father would join her. When he joined her, they would both sit tracing patterns on the rock and it must have been amusing, for they would always make each other laugh" (44). Having no control over the imminent loss, Annie records her dream in an autobiographical essay, which she relates to her class. This transcription is another attempt to negotiate for her mother's lost love. In telling her story, she "placed the old days' version before [her] classmates, because [she] couldn't bear to show [her] mother in a bad light before people who hardly knew her. But the real truth was that [she] couldn't bear to have anyone see how deep in disfavor [she] was with [her] mother" (45). In her storytelling, similar to her mother's, Annie uses deception and betrayal by omitting the truth surrounding her mother and their relationship. This omission evidences Annie's yearning for her lost mother. Lying is employed as a means of saving her and her mother's relationship, or what is left of it. Ironically, the very act of lying and deceit that unites these two women simultaneously creates a larger void between them.

Annie employs the very colonialist teachings and language that her mother seemingly reveres in her autobiographical essay, attempting to reestablish that mother-daughter connection and rekindle the mother's lost love. In contrast to her mother, who uses the teachings to keep her "in line," Annie is unable to penetrate her mother's world and is forced to seek motherly affection elsewhere, specifically by attaching herself to other girls, namely, Gwen and the Red Girl. These attachments do not diminish the difficulty of negotiating with the onset of maturity, nor do they efface the great love she has for her mother. Annie's friendship with Gwen is short-lived when she becomes aware that Gwen embodies the very colonial sentiments she detests. Apart from being a "perfect" lady, Gwen apparently subscribes to societal standards of becoming a "good" wife: she suggests that Annie marry her brother, Rowan. Annie instantly ends the friendship.

At the same time, Annie's deliberate choice of the Red Girl is an act of rebellion against her mother and against colonial standards and values. The Red Girl's way of life stands in stark contrast to Mrs. John's and colonialist teachings. She is the embodiment of anticolonialist sentiments. She subverts the notion of the "good" woman, representing wildness and freedom as she carelessly engages in unconventional, so-called masculine sports: tree climbing and marble playing. She never bathes or washes, and wears torn and tattered clothing. In a deliberate attempt to reject everything that reminds her of her mother, and the conventions of colonialism, Annie develops an affinity for the Red Girl. Notwithstanding, Annie's underlying desire for motherly love soon becomes apparent because this relationship mirrors the relationship she once had with her mother. She re-creates a real-life experience her mother had at sea, substituting the Red Girl for her mother: "I dreamed that the boat on which she had been traveling suddenly splintered in the middle of the sea, causing all the passengers to drown except for her, whom I rescued in a small boat. I took her to an island, where we lived together forever" (70–71). The splintering of the boat and its drifting off at sea is reminiscent of Annie's own mother's experience of sailing on a boat from Antigua to Dominica, which, after being ravaged by tempestuous waves, fractured in the middle. Miraculously, Mrs. John was the only one, along with her trunk, who survived the trip and escaped the sea's brutality (noticeably, Annie and the Red Girl's relationship does not survive because the Red Girl departs for Anguilla). Annie's dream of rescuing the Red Girl from peril is a subconscious attempt to rescue her and her mother's relationship. This story is as much a retelling of the mother's tale as it is an implication of a deep yearning for her. This longing is later put into words: "At the moment, I missed my mother more than I had ever imagined possible and wanted only to live somewhere *quiet and beautiful with her alone*" (106; emphasis added).

Similar to the colonial mother, England, which ambiguously establishes itself as both victor and vanquished, the biological mother, Mrs. John, embodies both devouring and nurturing images.[17] Attracted by the nurturing image, the daughter seeks herself in the mother, only to be later "seduced" and zombified. Mirroring the colonial mother, the biological mother takes possession of her daughter's body, mind, and soul. Zombification of daughters is crucial because it signals death of the self and the spirit. Zombified, daughters are deprived and dispossessed of their spirits and selves.

A perfect example of this self-dispossession is seen in Marshall's *Brown Girl, Brownstones*. After the heroine's, Selina's, father's death and the eviction of her surrogate mother, Suggie Skeete, the mother's desire to control intensifies: "She [Silla] touched the tears that had

17. Earlier in the discussion where *Columbus in Chains* is addressed, Annie mentions being devoured and subsumed through trickery by the colonialist teachings. These teachings that purport to intellectually nurture the individual actually surreptitiously deprive the subject of her identity.

dried white on her [Selina] dark skin. . . . Despite the tenderness and wonder and admiration of her touch, there was a frightening possessiveness. Each caress declared that she was touching something which was finally hers alone."[18] Selina is conscious of her mother's intentions and concludes that her mother wants her "to have no one." This spirit possession is also at the core of the relationship that Annie develops with the Red Girl, and continues until the Red Girl's migration to Anguilla.

Ironically, the Red Girl's departure culminates with Annie's entrance into womanhood. This passage is seemingly a forced one because it coincides with Annie's loss and deprivation of mother figures. Deprived of mothers, Annie is forced to "come into her own." Soon after the Red Girl's departure she starts menstruating, linking the color of the Red Girl with the color of blood. Like the "objectionable" Red Girl, Annie's first impression of womanhood is offensive. Trading places with the Red Girl, Annie also becomes objectionable: "I had turned into a strange animal" (25). Her strangeness, triggered by the onset of maturity, creates a larger unbridgeable gulf between herself and her mother. Unable to bridge this rift, Annie suffers a mental breakdown.

At this point the mother-daughter separation is most tangible, for Mrs. John is unable to revive or initiate her daughter. Annie's grandmother Ma Chess assigns herself this task. The inability of biological mothers properly to initiate their daughters is a recurring theme in the writings of (Caribbean) women. In Marshall's *Brown Girl*, we witness that Silla is able to reclaim her role as mother to her daughter Selina only after Selina's rite of passage into womanhood. Symbolically, this entrance is spearheaded by Silla's friend Florrie, who "with a casual fleeting gesture, brushed one of [Selina's] small breasts." This raises the question: why is the biological mother incapable of successfully initiating her daughter into womanhood? Arguably, this inability of the mother is linked to generational changes and the effect of colonization on the different generations. Velma Pollard's comment that "a whole generation has to pass before blood links take on passion" is pertinent. She notes that grandparents experience a "closeness that parents can't really feel [because] parents

18. Paule Marshall, *Brown Girl, Brownstones*, 185.

with their concerns that are practical, that allow us to be all the things that make grandparents proud, can't afford [passion]."[19] Pollard addresses the shared relationship between grandchildren and grandparents, and not specifically the relationship between mother, daughter, and grandmother, nor does she address specifically the sexuality issue. However, her theory provides a partial answer to this complex mother-daughter relationship. Without a doubt, first-generational women, represented by Ma Chess, feel more secure and confident in discussing personal matters that they themselves were never told or did not pass on to their own daughters. This self-confidence and security, as evidenced, are acquired only when the mother has finished raising her own children and has learned to better cope with growing (childhood) pains. Then she becomes functional as a grandmother and mothers her grandchildren.

Motherhood is seemingly bondage, a form of colonization, for the biological mother, who, unlike the grandmothers and mothers of previous generations, is directly affected and conditioned by existing colonizing principles. Battling for her own identity and struggling to sustain a mother-daughter relationship mediated by colonization, the biological mother is unable to extend the passion of which surrogate mothers and grandmothers are capable. While the mother-daughter relationship is often defined and mediated by colonization, the relationship that the grandmother has with her granddaughter is more spiritual than material. Deprived of this spiritual knowledge that their own mothers were ostensibly unable to give them in their teenage years, a gap is created between biological mothers and their daughters, and the cycle of silence and oppression is perpetuated. Having themselves gone through the hurt of not being told forthrightly and of not being properly initiated, biological mothers unconsciously distance themselves from their daughters because they are unable to "bridge that gap" created by the previous generation. Themselves "uninitiated," mothers do not have the language to communicate with the also "uninitiated" child. This noncommunicative atmosphere creates further misunderstanding, alienation, and estrangement between mother and daughter. Hence, an "other-mother," spiritually endowed, mediates this fractured relationship

19. Ibid., 77; Velma Pollard, *Considering Woman*, 47.

and bridges the misunderstanding and pain between mother and daughter.

Apart from being spiritually embodied, othermothers "live different lives and exemplify values widely divergent from the biological mother. [They] provide a safety valve and sounding board and release the teenage girl from the confines of a single role model. They can be gentle and affectionate where the blood mother must be stern and demanding. . . . Sometimes they give gifts mothers find hard to give, such as sexual initiation." A perfect example of a gentle and affectionate othermother is depicted in *Lucy,* where Lucy's surrogate mother, Mariah, is often described as kind and understanding. Of this affection Lucy confesses: "Mariah was like a mother to me, a *good* mother. . . . Always she expressed concern for my well-being."[20] Mariah and Lucy also discuss their sexuality and sexual encounters with great ease.

Similarly, Ma Chess is gentle and understanding to Annie. Spiritually secured, she nurtures and initiates her granddaughter into womanhood. In contrast to the mother-daughter relationship, the relationship between Ma Chess and Annie is not threatened by Annie's entrance into womanhood, nor is it deeply affected or mediated by colonization. Deeply rooted in African oral practices and cultures, Ma Chess rescues her granddaughter from peril. Indeed, she leads a different life, exemplifying divergent values from those of her daughter, who conveniently practices both Old World and New World cultures. Mrs. John's lack of mastery of African cultural and oral practices becomes evident during the illness Annie suffers: she is unable either to revive her daughter from the illness or to diagnose its cause. This inexplicable illness is the ultimate signal of Annie's identity crisis:

> Nothing seemed wrong. I did not have a fever. No wild storms raged through my stomach. My appetite was as poor as it had always been. My mother tugging at my eyelids this way and that, could not see any signs of biliousness. All the same, I was in no condition to keep up in my usual way, so I had to take to my bed. For over a year no rain fell. There was nothing unusual about that: drought was such a big part of our life. . . . Then suddenly the rain started to come down in torrent. (108)

20. Troester, "Turbulence and Tenderness," 13; Kincaid, *Lucy,* 110.

Paradoxically, in a drought-ridden land, Annie's illness is punctuated by torrential rains that lingered the entire three and a half months of her breakdown. Rather than a welcoming presence, the rain is suffocating: "[T]he sound the rain made as it landed on the roof pressed me down in my bed, bolted me down, and I couldn't even so much as lift my head if my life depended on it" (109). The rain that pressed Annie down in her bed is symbolic of her containment within the womb. It is also symbolic of her mother's resistance to her entrance into womanhood and her desire for her to remain childlike, retaining her childhood innocence. Rain or water is also a powerful symbol of rejection and separation. In the dream in which her mother leaves her behind, it is the sea of water that separates Annie from her mother. Her father, Alexander, also suffers alienation and desertion by water, for his parents sailed away on a boat to South America, leaving him behind. Noticeably, Ma Chess avoids the sea and has little or nothing to do with water. She mysteriously appears on the island of Antigua, although no steamer was due. She "never [took] a bath in just plain water and soap. She took a bath, once a month or so, in water in 'which things animal and vegetable had been boiled for a long time'" (123–24).

Ma Chess's presence facilitates new life for her granddaughter, Annie. Just as mysteriously as Annie's illness had appeared, it left. Similarly, the rain left with the illness. The departure of the rain signals the commencement of Annie's rebirth and her coming into being. Ma Chess literally re-creates those childhood moments of pleasure that Annie once shared with her mother, reenacting the intimacy that mother and daughter once enjoyed. She sleeps in the same bed with Annie. She provides Annie with the very intimacy she seeks and yearns for: "*When I would feel that I was locked up in the warm falling soot and could not find my way out, Ma Chess would come into my bed with me and stay until I was myself*—whatever that had come to be by then—again. I would lie on my side, curled up like a little comma, and Ma Chess would lie next to me, curled up like a bigger comma, into which I fit" (125–26; emphasis added). Surviving the initiation rite and having received Ma Chess's blessings, Annie is well on her way to achieving selfhood. In contrast to her mother, who wants Annie to maintain her childlike purity and innocence, Ma Chess brings Annie out of her childlike stage: "When I would feel that I was locked up in the warm falling soot and could not find my way out, Ma Chess would come into my bed with me and stay until I was myself" (125). Annie's struggle to find her way out of the "womb" reflects her desire to be born, to signify. The "comma," fetuslike, is indicative of Annie's fetal-like position. Ma Chess, the bigger comma, gives birth to the little comma. Thus, Annie, on the verge of death, is brought back from the dead by her grandmother. Unlike Annie's mother, who lays the dead to rest, Ma Chess revives them.

Annie emerges from her breakdown with a clearer sense of self. In her construction of selfhood she objectifies and annihilates those who hindered her growth and self-development. During her illness, Annie gives some family photographs "a good bath." These pictures (one of herself in her white school uniform, one in which she was her aunt Mary's bridesmaid, one of her father wearing his white cricket uniform, and another in which she was dressed in white, having just received her Communion in church) "loomed up big" in front of Annie's miniature frame. Resisting being subdued, she washes them "thoroughly with soap and water" (here again water is a source of separation). Later, looking at the washed pictures, Annie observes: "In the picture of my mother and father, I had erased them from the waist down. In the picture of me wearing my confirmation dress, I had erased all of myself except for the shoes" (120). The erasure of her parents from the waist down implies castration and impotence. This deed seemingly is Annie's attempt to prevent further "abominable" sexual acts. Overall, the erasure of her family members deprives them of their identities while she asserts hers. By erasing her aunt Mary and her new husband, Monsieur Pacquet, in the wedding picture, Annie deprives them of a new beginning and a new life, represented by marriage. In erasing herself from the wedding picture, Annie is no longer a lady-in-waiting, a bridesmaid who attends to the bride's needs and wants. White, a symbol of purity and chastity, does not reflect reality; instead, it is a misrepresentation of their lives, and Annie makes this point by wearing her "decorative cutout on the sides" shoes. As expected, her mother objects to the pair of shoes, remarking that it is unfitting for the occasion. In response to her mother's objection, Annie wishes her dead. The wearing of these shoes silences her mother. In the washed-out family photograph, only Annie's shoes remain, signaling her imminent departure and, she hopes, a new beginning.

Annie's "coming into being" coincides with her imminent departure: "[M]y name is Annie John. These were the first words that came into my mind as I woke up the morning of the last day I spent in Antigua, and they stayed there, lined up one behind the other, marching up and down, for I don't know how long" (130). As she is about to leave her mother and her mother's land, Antigua, for the mother country, England, Annie for the first time affirms her name "Annie John." Significantly, shortly after enunciating her name, she adds, "[M]y mother's name is Annie also" (132). Her enunciating her name is simultaneously an affirmation of her "self" and an attempt to make peace, or her acknowledging that she is a part of her mother, that she is her mother's child. Annie enacts a journey similar to one her mother enacted years ago when she left her mother and mother's land, Dominica, for Antigua. Unlike her mother, Annie expresses her reluctance to go to England: "I did not want to go to England, I did not want to be a nurse" (130). Annie's comment is indicative of uncertainty and arguably is foreboding of her unpredictable future. Inasmuch as Annie confesses that she hates England and has no desire to go there, there nonetheless exists a subconscious, subliminal need to journey. This desire, even if not actualized, always exists in the imagination and in the numerous allusions to the colonizer. This imaginative pastime is a direct result of the educational system, the colonial indoctrination instilled in the mind of not only Annie but also other colonized peoples. A clear example of this colonial indoctrination is in a passage of *Annie John* in which the students are asked to recite their autobiographical essays. Every child, with the exception of Annie, reminisces about life outside the Caribbean. Giving commentaries on the different autobiographical narratives, Annie observes: "One girl told of a much revered and loved aunt who now lived in England and of how much she looked forward to one day moving to England to live with her aunt and one girl told of her brother studying medicine in Canada and the life she imagined he lived there" (40). As trained Anglophiles, the children aspire for the mother country. It is rather ironic that Annie, whose narrative speaks of love for her mother and her mother's land, Antigua, is the one who suggestively leaves for the mother country, England, by the end of the novel. It is also paradoxical that once imbued with anticolonial sentiments, Annie eventually chooses the (m)other country.

Nevertheless, Annie's journey to the mother country is another phase in her negotiation and her quest for identity. Her simultaneous speaking of love for her mother and her mother's land, followed by her departure to the mother country, speaks to the ongoing, though complex, negotiation in which she is embroiled. Perversely, this negotiation entails rejection, and Annie needs to create distance among herself, her mother, and her mother's land "to (be)come." In her search for a new identity, Annie attempts to reject her former self and life:

> I was feeling how much I never wanted to see a boy climb a *coconut tree* again, how much I never wanted to see the *sun shine day in, day out* again, how much I never wanted to see my mother bent over a pot cooking me some thing that she felt would do me good when I ate it, how much I never wanted to feel her long, bony fingers against my cheek again, how much I never wanted to hear her voice in my ear again, how much I longed to be in a place where nobody knew a thing about me and liked me for just that reason, how much the *whole world into which I was born had become an unbearable burden and I wished I could reduce it to some small thing that I could hold underwater until it died.* (127–28; emphasis added)

Annie's rejection of the sunshine (a rejection of her mother and her mother's land) is a clear call for a colder climate. England, perhaps? While yearning for a colder climate, reference is made to the tropics, where the "sun shines day in, day out." The tree-climbing scene that defined Annie's world and was once a symbol of pride and joy, and a distinct Caribbean identity has been reduced to an "unbearable burden." Her wanting to submerge this world underwater is indicative of her desire to distance herself from it.

The distance Annie manages to establish among herself and her mother and the Caribbean is merely physical. Although she seemingly rejects the domesticated world of her mother—"I never wanted to see my mother bent over a pot cooking" (131)—her departure is marked by things domestic. She notes, "[T]he things I never wanted to see or hear or do again now made up at least three weeks worth of grocery list" (134–35). She recalls her seventeen years of life: the things her father made her, the things her mother did for her, the life they shared together. The reliving of these earlier years spent in harmony with her parents speaks to the unbreakable connection, the inability to erase memory:

> When I look at things in a certain way, I suppose I should say that the two of them made me with their own hands. For most of my life, when the three of us went anywhere together I stood between the two of them or sat between the two of them. I had made up my mind that, come what may, the road for me now went only in one direction: away from home, away from my mother, away from my father, away from the everlasting blue sky, away from the everlasting hot sun. (134–35)

Annie, although convincing herself that her recollection of her childhood memories is a final, defiant act, gives agency to her past, her mother. It is an act of recalling, re-membering; reconnecting with her past, a past that she has come to understand is nonexistent without her mother. Her walking through the entire town to the jetty where she will board the steamer for England is no mere coincidence. She is re-creating lost memories, refamiliarizing herself with her mother and her mother's land. This is the final, determining memory she takes with her to the mother country.

On the verge of departing for England, Annie confesses: "My name was the last thing I saw the night before, just as I was falling asleep; it was written in big, black letters all over my trunk, sometimes, followed by my address in Antigua, sometimes followed by my address as it would be in England" (130). The trunk she takes is a treasured memorabilia of the womenfolk of her family (after one of many arguments with her mother, Annie had requested that her father make her her own trunk; notwithstanding, there is no indication that this request was honored). It once belonged to her grandmother Ma Chess, was later used by her mother when she departed for Antigua, and is now used by Annie, who is leaving for the mother country. In this trunk, their different, yet similar, lives are stored. This trunk holds a legacy; a history that try as she may Annie cannot escape. The trunk significantly survived the water, the sea journey from Dominica to Antigua, symbolic of the unbreakable bond between these generations of women: grandmother, mother, and daughter. Hence, to attain subjectivity, Annie has to negotiate between her past, her present, and her future. This incipient negotiation is already in progress; rather than rejecting forthrightly her mother's land and the mother country to which she is about to depart, Annie seemingly attempts to reconcile the two mother figures: her name "*was* written in big, black letters all over [her] trunk, sometimes, followed by [her] address in Antigua, sometimes followed by [her] address *as it would be* in England" (130; emphasis added). Thus, her past will be a constitutive part of her future.

At the heart of *The Autobiography of My Mother* is a lost daughter, a colonized female subject mourning the loss and death of a parent, a people, a culture, and a language all at once. In recounting her mother's history, the protagonist, Xuela Claudette Richardson, relates a history of generations: the history of her mother's people, the Caribs, and her mother's land, the Caribbean island of Dominica, and the devastation that these indigenous people and the land suffered as a result of colonial intervention on the island.[21] Thus, Xuela's mother embodies an entire history: a people and their colonization. She is a metonym for the mother's land. These haunting absences pervade the entire novel, specifically, the haunting absence of a mother and mother figures. This severe lack haunts Xuela as she obsesses about the provocative thought of who she is. Born without love, comfort, or the protection of a mother, Xuela is unable to find herself within this void. Cataloged by colonized geographies and bodies, the novel chronicles the detrimental absences that hinder Xuela's self-actualization.

Similar to the life of challenge that Xuela experiences, the title of the novel is challenging, for it purportedly relates the life story or, rather, death of a woman and a mother. The personal, "autobiographical" title of the novel stands in stark contrast with its strong political undertones. The loss of the mother is emblematic of the loss and devastation of the island and the island's inhabitants to colonization. As a result of this loss and emptiness, Xuela expresses a strong desire to identify and to belong, which presents a challenge, probably insurmountable, because it is around a void, around absence, loss, and death, that she has to create herself and establish her

21. The earliest known inhabitants of the West Indies were two Amerindian tribes, the Arawaks, who migrated from South America, and the Caribs, who later drove them away. At the time of Columbus's arrival, the Caribs inhabited Dominica. Xuela's mother is one of the few remaining descendants of the Caribs.

presence. This challenge is made more complicated because Xuela has to grapple not only with the death of her mother and the loss of her mother's land, but also with the loss and absence of a history. Many theorists who write on the mother-daughter theme illuminate the importance of a mother in a daughter's life, contending that the absence or presence of a mother is crucial in a daughter's identity formation. Alison Donnell contends that "[a daughter's] ties to the motherland are most intensely realized through her bond to the mother. . . . [I]t is the relationship with the mother which forms the primary focus for the protagonist's intense and ambivalent emotions."[22] The relationship that Xuela has with her dead mother cannot be considered a "normal" relationship; nonetheless, similar to a "conventional" mother-daughter relationship, this so-called relationship is not devoid of emotions or ambiguities. Unlike the "conventional" mother-daughter relationship, it is not the presence of a mother (figure) that arouses or awakens Xuela's intense emotions; rather, it is the absence, the loss of her mother, that deprives her of love and loving altogether. This deprivation embitters Xuela while it intensifies her indifference to life itself. The untimely death of her mother, which prohibits her self-growth, is accountable for her intense indifference.

Similar to *Annie John*, which opens with the theme of death, from the onset of *The Autobiography of My Mother* we are confronted with the death of Xuela's mother, who dies shortly after giving birth to her. The novel opens with these haunting and prophetic words: "My mother died at the moment I was born, and so for my whole life there was nothing standing between myself and eternity; at my back was always a bleak, black wind. . . . At my beginning was this woman whose face I had never seen, but at my end was nothing, no one between me and the black room of the world."[23] Xuela's referral to the world as a "black room" is symbolic, suggesting darkness or gloom and containment. The "bleak, black wind" at her back emblematizes her mother, who like the wind is invisible. Hence, Xuela's world is one of darkness and gloom, resulting from a lack

---

22. Alison Donnell, "When Daughters Defy: Jamaica Kincaid's Fiction," 21.
23. Jamaica Kincaid, *The Autobiography of My Mother*, 3. Future citations will be given parenthetically in the text.

of love and the loss of her mother. Left in the care of her father, she is first attended to by his laundress, Ma Eunice, after which she lives with her father, her stepmother, and their two children. She later becomes involved in a series of affairs and subsequently marries an English doctor, after presumably poisoning his wife. Xuela's nomadic existence is symptomatic of her lack of self and her lack of identity. On a desperate quest for selfhood, she is obsessed with finding her origins: "For I was lonely and wished to see people in whose faces I could recognize something of myself. Because who was I? My mother was dead" (16). Although on a quest for self, Xuela's brooding simultaneously seems to hint at the impossibility of this quest. Born in an atmosphere devoid of maternal love and nurturance, this void becomes her wall of protection, for it is within this wall that Xuela narrates and attempts to piece together her life story. It becomes her space of narration. Yet, this wall of protection momentarily functions as a prison, locking Xuela within its confines and prohibiting her from seeing or reaching beyond her quest.

As a result of the loss of her mother, Xuela is transformed into a vulnerable and hard person who, deprived of love, is unable to love herself. Solitary life has made Xuela insensitive. Though she is incapable of externalizing joy or happiness, she easily externalizes hatred. This inability to love is reflected in her indifference to people and places alike. She walks in and out of people's lives, yet remains untouched or unaffected by them. She completely rejects everyone, and all of her relationships are devoid of love and compassion. She is most at home in a loveless atmosphere, as she readily acknowledges: "Love would have defeated me. Love would always defeat me. In an atmosphere of no love I could live well; in this atmosphere of no love I could make a life for myself" (29). Defeated by love, Xuela appears to be defeated by life itself. Inasmuch as she tries to construct her life around the lack and absence that she has been surrounded by all her life, is it possible for Xuela to "make a life for [her]self" in this loveless climate? Her hatred for people and places alike undoubtedly results from her lack of memory and history. There is not sufficient historical evidence that documents the life and the deaths of her mother and the Carib people, who suffered extinction by the colonials. Having no knowledge of her mother's past, the memory she possesses is fragmented and insignificant:

> I realized that there were so many things I did not know, not including
> the very big things I did not know—my mother. I did not know my
> father; I did not know where he was from or whom or what he liked;
> I did not know the land whose surface I had just come through on an
> animal's back; I did not know who I was or why I was standing there in
> that room. . . . A great sea of what I did not know opened up before me,
> and its powerful treacherous currents pulsed over my head repeatedly
> until I was sure I was dead. (28)

Xuela is drowned in the sea of absences: the death of a mother, the absence of a father, the absence of a mother's land, and in turn the lack of self. Though Xuela engages the numerous absences to record her presence, these wells of absences and losses appear to suffocate her very being. Her entire life, beginning to end, is marked by absence and suffocating presence, which has dispossessed her. Can Xuela repossess herself without a past? Self-repossession is possible only when one has a strong sense of self. Deprived of seeing her mother's face, Xuela has no mirror in which to see her self-reflection. She is denied both the mirroring bond that allows a daughter to identify with her mother and the maternal discourse, which are pivotal in a daughter's identity formation. They provide a daughter with a sense of self and are essential tools for self-construction. In her revealing essay, Ronnie Scharfman contends that "mirroring and mothering" are inextricably linked, and often merge, making it impossible to delineate where mother ends and daughter begins, and to demarcate the mother's story from the daughter's. Xuela's mother's life ended even before hers began. Hence, the mirroring-mothering link is severed from the inception. It is crucial that Xuela's mother's face remains hidden throughout the novel, while the only visible signs are her heels. The absence of a face suggests a lack of identity, while the heel is suggestive of departure, or rejection and abandonment. Addressing the mother-daughter relationship in Jean Rhys's *Wide Sargasso Sea*, Scharfman maintains that the mother-daughter relationship is unwholesome because "we are confronted with a colonial culture incapable of reproducing itself." However, in this case, "this impasse is mirrored [not simply] in the inadequacies of the mother-daughter bond," but also in the colossal lack, the absence around which revolves not only the novel, but Xuela's life as well.[24] Although Scharfman sees the mother's inability to bond with her daughter as largely a function of the mother's inadequacy, in this instance, it goes beyond the personal relationship between mother and daughter. Instead, it is the imposition of a foreign culture, a colonial culture that prevents bonding and identification. Therefore, the inability to bond on the mother's and daughter's parts is not of their own making, but is mediated and prohibited by outside force: colonial intervention and indoctrination.

Denied both her mother and mothering, Xuela is simultaneously denied the mirroring bond, resulting in her inability to perceive her mother's reflection in a loving gaze. The only reflection that Xuela sees is the reflection or the gaze of the colonial mother (country) or colonialism, which as evidenced does not give her the "true" self-reflection or identity or "wholeness" she seeks. Xuela's earlier wish to see "people in whose faces [she] could recognize something of [her]self" remains unfulfilled (16). Instead of recognition, she is faced with further alienation. The only reflection she encounters is that of a fragmentary self.

This fragmentation questions the notion of wholeness. Does a colonized self ever achieve wholeness? The writing of the novel itself seems to question as well as dispute the notion of wholeness. Similar to the title of the novel, *The Autobiography of My Mother*, which is logically impracticable, Kincaid's adoption of this title is probably her attempt to establish the impossibility or impracticability of a colonized subject achieving "wholeness." Fragmentation seems to be inherently linked to the colonized subject. Not only is Xuela fragmented, but so is her dead mother. She has no face, no defining features, suggestive of her lack of identity and her lack of self. She is defined by her heels and the hem of her dress. Although Xuela desperately attempts to create an image of her mother, her mother remains invisible and elusive throughout the entire narrative. Xuela is also defined by this invisibility. Her intense yearning for her dead mother and her identification with this absent-present figure characterize not only her childhood but also her entire adult life. This

24. Ronnie Scharfman, "Mirroring and Mothering in Simone Schwarz-Bart's *Pluie et vent sur Télumée Miracle* and Jean Rhys' *Wide Sargasso Sea*," 88.

invisibility that becomes her defining principle is also a critical factor in her alienation.

The manner in which Xuela remains disconnected to places and people eludes our grasp and our understanding in much the way in which her search for self-affirmation eludes her. This seems to suggest that the quest for "wholeness" is just as elusive as the notion of wholeness, the notion of an "authentic" (Caribbean) self. At first we know neither Xuela's name nor the place where her life story unfolds. Even after she reveals her name, her identity still eludes us. This elusiveness comes about because she believes that names are not a true depiction of the self. She in fact questions the naming of people, as, in her opinion, it does not reveal the "true" self:

> And your own name, whatever it might be, eventually was not the gateway to who you really were, and you could not ever say to yourself, "My name is Xuela Claudette Desvarieux." This was my mother's name, but I cannot say it was her real name, for in a life like hers, as in mine, what is a real name? My own name is her name, Xuela Claudette, and in the place of the Desvarieux is Richardson, which is my father's name. . . . The name of any one person is at once her history recapitulated and abbreviated. (79)

Xuela questions this recapitulation of history. In her opinion it is insufficient because it does not adequately chronicle peoples' lives. This abbreviated history is a plot to obfuscate the individual's identity and history and, thereafter, obliterate it altogether. The obliteration of a people and their history prompts Xuela to pose the critical question: what is a "real" name to a colonized person? Although her comment that "your own name . . . was not the gateway to who you really were" is valid, nonetheless, her and her mother's names do speak of their history, though a colonized one. Her name is her mother's name, whose name is in turn the colonizer's name, or the name of the father, the biological and the colonial. Hence, her name is an adopted one. Similarly, she becomes an adopted daughter after her mother's death, though she despises the notion of adoption. Xuela rejects any and all forms of surrogacy. She rejects her adopted, colonized name, her adopted land, and her adopted mothers. Adoption or surrogacy bears resemblance to colonization. It imposes a foreign identity on its subject, molding this subject to its own liking while denying it any sense of self.

A perfect example of this resemblance between adoption and colonization is depicted in *Lucy*. At war with her mother, Lucy, full of enthusiasm, leaves her mother and her mother's land, Antigua, for her adopted mothers, the United States and Mariah, with whom she will work as an au pair. Her search for a safe haven and a surrogate mother is shattered because she finds neither the nurturing mother nor the solace she envisioned. Instead, she is confronted by "cold hearts and foreign tongues."[25] A new identity is imposed upon Lucy the very day of her arrival. She is placed in a room labeled the "maid's room," a clear indication of her status. She is certainly not one of their (Mariah's, her family's, and friends') equals, contrary to what they espoused and what we are led to believe. This labeling of the room as the maid's room not only identifies the room but also labels Lucy, objectifies her, and, indeed, contains her in a palpable way:

> The room in which I lay was a small room just off the kitchen—the maid's room. I was used to a small room, but this was a different sort of small room. The ceiling was very high and the walls went all the way to the ceiling, enclosing the room like a box—a box in which cargo traveling a long way should be shipped. But I was not cargo. I was only an unhappy young woman living in a maid's room, and I was not even the maid. I was the young girl who watches over the children and goes to school. . . . How nice everyone was to me, though, saying that I should regard them as my family and make myself at home.[26]

Just as clearly as the room is labeled, Lucy is labeled. Dinah, one of Mariah's many rich friends, affirms this with her condescending question: "So you are from the islands?" This somewhat derogative comment denies Lucy a distinctive, individualistic identity. Lucy intuitively concludes that to a person such as Dinah, she or someone else in her position is and will always be "the girl—as in the girl who takes care of the children."[27] This island girl is in reality neither the maid nor cargo, yet in a sense she is both. Her fear of being valued as a kind of exotic "other" or possession is realized, if not as a maid,

25. This is a borrowed phrase from Helen Tiffin's article "Cold Hearts and (Foreign) Tongues: Recitation and the Reclamation of the Female Body in the Works of Erna Brodber and Jamaica Kincaid." The phrase is a combined title of two of the five chapters of *Lucy*: "The Tongue" and "Cold Heart."

26. Kincaid, *Lucy*, 7.

27. Ibid., 56, 58.

then as an alien "other" from the islands, an "object" in either case. Having left her mother and island behind, Lucy soon realizes that her new surrogate (colonial) mothers do not fill the void left from the severed relationship with her biological mother. These colonial mothers, Mariah and the United States, cannot substitute for the biological mother.

Xuela endorses this notion by her denouncement of surrogacy and downright rejection of adoptive lands and mothers. Xuela's total rejection of surrogate mothers can be viewed as a confirmation that surrogacy is not a substitute for the biological (real) mother. It is a misidentification of the "real" self. It does not furnish "wholeness" but heeds further fragmentation. Xuela is living testimony of this further fracturing and severance of the self.

Denied a developmental bond with her biological mother, Xuela is unable to bond with or love her surrogate mothers or her adoptive mother's land, Dominica. For her, the loss of her mother signals the simultaneous loss of her mother's land. Because the mother is a metonym for the mother's land, her death signals the death and devastation of the mother's land. Hence, Xuela's indifference extends to her place of origin, Dominica. Distanced from it, Dominica becomes the other's land—strange and alien. She confesses that "in a place like this, brutality is the only real inheritance and cruelty is sometimes the only thing freely given" (5). Transformed and defaced by colonialism, Dominica is defined by its cruelty and brutality. It is a paradise lost. It is not a place for positive self-definition and self-affirmation, but is figured as a prison, a place that suffocates and inhibits subjecthood.

Ann Morris and Margaret Dunn affirm that when a "daughter has been denied a developmental bond with her own mother, then the mothers' land itself may provide a surrogate."[28] Evidently, Morris and Dunn did not foresee or envision the rejection of the mother's land by a daughter who has lost her mother to death (understandably so, because they apply this theory to Kincaid's earlier novel *Annie John*), and as such, their theory does not apply to Xuela. For a meaningful relationship with the mother's land to develop,

---

28. Ann R. Morris and Margaret M. Dunn, " 'The Bloodstream of Our Inheritance': Female Identity and the Caribbean Mothers'-Land," 219.

a mother's presence and love are necessary. The mother does not necessarily have to be biological, but she must possess maternal and nurturing qualities to advance her daughter's coming into being. Having no real mother or surrogate, the mother's land, Dominica, is no surrogate to Xuela.

Dominica is employed as a metaphor for all the Caribbean islands, ravaged and raped by colonialism. This experience has left the inhabitants indifferent and incapable of giving or extending "true" love. Not only are daughters affected by this devastation, but mothers are also incapable of expressing or giving love. Of this catastrophic lack, Xuela observes: "Ma Eunice was not unkind: she treated me just the way she treated her own children—but this is not to say she was kind to her own children. . . . I did not like her, and I missed the face I had never seen. . . . I never grew to love this woman my father left me with, this woman who was not unkind to me but who could not be kind because she did not know how—and perhaps I could not love her because I, too, did not know how" (5–6). Mothers themselves are victims of the colonial regime. Ma Eunice, a mother of six, is not spared the trauma of colonization; she is just as indifferent as everyone else. Her apathy extends even to her own children. Because the mother's love is the initial love, when deprived of it a child is seemingly deprived of loving altogether. In a place where everything is defined by lack or absence, it is no surprise that the people ultimately mirror this place.

By mirroring the colonials, the inhabitants of the island are both forced and forged into a mothering relationship with the mother country, which purportedly claims motherhood. Instead of a nurturing and caring mother, the colonial mother is a suffocating other, making life unbearable for the island's inhabitants. They become prisoners in their own home space, which is suffocating and prison-like in nature. However, the island's brutality is not of its "own making," but is a result of colonial intervention. Observing the distance created among the island's inhabitants as a result of colonialism, Xuela comments:

> That "these people" were ourselves, that this insistence on mistrust of others—that people who looked so very much like each other, who shared a common history of suffering and humiliation and enslavement, should be taught to mistrust each other even as children, is no longer a

mystery to me. The people we should naturally have mistrusted were beyond our influence completely; what we needed to defeat them, to rid ourselves of them, was something far more powerful than mistrust. To mistrust each other was just one of the many feelings we had for each other, all of them the opposite of love, all of them standing in the place of love. It was as if we were in competition with each other for a secret prize, and we were afraid that someone else would get it; any expression of love, then, would not be sincere, for love might give someone else the advantage. (48)

Rudely awakened by the island's devastation, Xuela had come to "realize that [her] presence on the island—[her] ancestral history— was the result of a foul deed."[29] Deeply affected by colonization, the island now mirrors the colonial mother. It sets the inhabitants against each other, retarding the individual's growth and annihilating any sense of self. Xuela is a true embodiment of this retardation. Having lived her entire life on the island, cataloged by its ceaseless *droughts*—drought of love, drought of kindness and compassion— Xuela mirrors this drought-ridden land and is unable to reproduce literally or figuratively. This inability is in turn cataloged by her rejection of motherhood. This downright rejection of the mothering role stems from the cruel fact that Xuela herself is orphaned. This "shameful" experience, that of being motherless, voiced in *Annie John,* is lived by Xuela. In addition to being orphaned, she is also haunted by cruel stepmothers. Unparented, Xuela cannot parent anyone, let alone herself. Xuela hails from a generation of women plagued and haunted by motherlessness:

> The attachment, spiritual and physical, that a mother is said to have for her child, that confusion of who is who, flesh and flesh, that inseparableness which is said to exist between mother and child—all this *was absent between my mother and her own mother.* How to explain this abandonment, what child can understand it? That attachment, physical and spiritual, that confusion of who is who, flesh and flesh, which was *absent between my mother and her mother was also absent between my mother and myself,* for she died at the moment I was born, and though I can sensibly say to myself such a thing cannot be helped—for who can help dying—again how can a child understand such a thing, so profound an abandonment? I have refused to bear any children. (199; emphasis added)

29. Kincaid, *Lucy,* 135.

Brutally expelled from her mother's womb, Xuela is deprived of the spiritual and physical bond a daughter experiences with her mother. As a result, she does not experience "the knowledge [that flows] between two alike bodies."[30] Her conscious refusal to bear children is an act of fear. Xuela is afraid to perpetuate the cycle of abandonment and the cycle of motherlessness and lack of love that have plagued the women in her family. Her womb mirrors the island womb, Dominica. It is a wasteland.

Abandoned at birth, Xuela adopts a defensive position, refusing love, and instead attempts to exact revenge for her mother's death by not only rejecting love but also avoiding it. She vows never to allow the "full weight of desire to make a pawn of [her]" (65). The defense mechanism she employs is to prevent the perpetuation of this cycle of abandonment, which from all indications ultimately spirals into wells of oppression and alienation. However, this defensive position, though it offers temporary refuge and protection, leaves her in a permanent state of insecurity, which inhibits and lends falsity to all her relationships. This defensive stance also fosters the devaluation of the self. Xuela's stance is not to love in order to avoid abandonment and rejection. Doomed to a life that is characterized by indefiniteness and uncertainties, Xuela is secure in her refusal to bear children:

> I had just recently refused to become one, and I knew then that this refusal would be complete. I would never become a mother, but that would not be the same as never bearing children. I would bear children, but I would never be a mother to them. . . . *I would condemn them to live in an empty space frozen in the same posture in which they had been born.* I would throw them from a great height; every bone in their body would be broken and the *bones would never be properly set, healing in the way they were broken, healing never at all.* . . . It is in this way that I did not become a mother. (97–98; emphasis added)

Xuela's refusal to bear children hints at the "death sentence" to which they will be destined, because "death is the only reality, for it is the only certainty, inevitable to all things" (228). Her confession is emblematic of her own life. Xuela rightly observes that bearing children does not qualify a woman as a mother. Her own mother bore her, but never mothered her. Similarly, both Ma Eunice and

---

30. Rich, *Of Woman Born*, 220.

her stepmother bore children but never mothered them. Denied mothering, these children, including Xuela, are never emancipated from infancy; instead, they remain children, fetal-like, locked within the womblike space represented by the island. The death of Xuela's mother during childbirth condemns her to a frozen childhood. Although she is physically a grown woman, mentally and spiritually she is still infantlike, an embryo, "frozen in the same posture in which [she] had been born." She has suffered a fractured psyche, symbolized by the broken bones resulting from this fall, meaning her mother's death, and has not yet healed, and probably never will, as the novel's end indicates. Xuela equates her abandonment with broken bones that never heal. Her inability to love and be loved leaves her in dire need of healing and nurturing. The privileged position of being both mother and daughter—"we are, none of us, either mothers or daughters; to our amazement, we are both"—that Rich discusses escapes Xuela, who never experiences the power of love and bonding with other women. Denied and deprived, Xuela remains uncommitted: "Women, mothers or not who feel committed to other women, are increasingly giving each other a quality of caring filled with the diffuse kinds of identification that exist between actual mother and daughters."[31] Unfortunately, deprived of and denied the love of both mothers and othermothers, Xuela has no commitment to other women and as such does not identify with anyone other than the image of her dead mother. This fractured image cannot provide Xuela the definition she craves. Not having an "actual" mother, Xuela is not an "actual" daughter.

Actuality does not define Xuela, nor does it define the inhabitants of Dominica. Although the inhabitants are taught to mistrust each other, they place their trust in material possessions, as exemplified in Ma Eunice's worshiping of a china plate that depicts the English countryside. The breaking of this plate by Xuela sent Ma Eunice into a period of intense mourning. Ma Eunice's first emotional reaction to anything, let alone an object, enthralled Xuela: "[T]he sadness she expressed over this loss fascinated me; it was so thick with grief, so overwhelming, so deep, as if the death of a loved one had occurred" (8). Xuela could not understand what Ma Eunice found so intriguing

31. Ibid., 253.

about this plate with a picture painted on its surface, which in Xuela's words was "nothing but a field full of grass and flowers on a sunny day, but it had an atmosphere of secret abundance, happiness, and tranquility; underneath it was written in gold letters the one word HEAVEN" (9). This picture of the English countryside idealized is a colonizing, deceptive image. Ma Eunice and Xuela are momentarily colonized by the image of this picture that promises "a life without worry or care or want" (9). While presenting the mother country, England, as heavenly, the Dominican inhabitants live and experience a hell-like existence. This image and "atmosphere of secret abundance, happiness and tranquility" is far from the reality that the Dominican inhabitants live. In actual fact, this picture exposes the abusive colonial history where the existence of the vanquished is erased. Idealizing the mother country, the inhabitants' own history is erased. Ma Eunice's worshiping of the mother country via the plate indicates that the victors had scored yet another victory over the vanquished. It is rather ironic that Ma Eunice relinquishes her motherly role and seeks her identity in (an)other mother, England. Xuela later realizes that the depiction of England as heavenly was a device to beguile the inhabitants, establish further mistrust, and create further distance between them. The achievement of this heavenly existence was as distant as the false hope they, the inhabitants, lived, that of achieving "wholeness" and the ability to love. Xuela sarcastically remarks that Ma Eunice "had died; perhaps she went to heaven and it fulfilled the promise on that plate" (9). On one hand, Xuela's speculations hint at the remoteness of the colonized ever achieving wholeness, and on the other hand, it illuminates the relationship between captor and captive, the powerful (colonizer) and the powerless (colonized). Ma Eunice, the colonized, died as she lived: powerless.

The relationship that Xuela has with her father is also redolent of the relationship between the victor and the vanquished. After her mother's death, Xuela is handed over to the care of her surrogate mother, Ma Eunice, by her father. Like the bundle of clothing, Xuela was dropped off at Ma Eunice's to be taken care of. Like the clothing, Xuela is treated like soiled goods by her father. Although the soiled clothing is eventually cleaned and "wrapped up like a gift in two pieces of clean nankeen cloth and place on a table, the only table in the house . . . Xuela remains discarded goods" (6). The nankeen cloth, a durable fabric, is contrasted with Xuela's frail, fragmented self. Even the clothing has a "place on a table, the only table in the house." In contrast, Xuela is orphaned and homeless. It is of utmost significance that homelessness and alienation are often linked to the mother, to the female. Similarly, it is the mother's land, Dominica, that suffers devastation and destruction.

Inasmuch as both men and women suffer from traumatic experiences at the hands of the colonials, the men seemingly because of their status as men are exempted from some social injustices. Xuela's father exerts some level of power because of his possession of material wealth and his status in the community as a policeman. Similar to the colonials, he polices the inhabitants, subjecting them to a life of terror. He is identified and defined by his wealth and his possessions. It is rather interesting that in a place where identities are elusive men have access to them. Lacking self-definition, Xuela defines her male friend Roland, a stevedore:

> His name is Roland. His mouth was like an island in the sea that was his face; . . . I could see only his mouth. . . . His mouth really did look like an island, lying in a twig-brown sea, stretching out from east to west, wider near the center, with tiny, sharp creases, its color a shade lighter than that of the twig-brown sea in which it lay. . . . He was not a hero, he did not even have a country; he was from an island, a small island that was between a sea and an ocean, and a small island is not a country. And he did not have a history; he was a small event in somebody else's history, *but he was a man.* (163–64, 167; emphasis added)

Even though Roland is not heroic, he has a name, an identity, "he was a man," unlike the woman. This point is alluded to earlier when Xuela classifies the woman as *any one person:* "the name of any one person is at once *her* history recapitulated and abbreviated" (79; emphasis added). The choice of the pronoun *her* is no mere coincidence. Xuela insinuates that his (hi)story does not represent the black woman. Roland's history is not recapitulated. He embodies the island, the island that gives him his birthright, the same island within which Xuela is contained. Interestingly, his name, Roland, spells *land.* Roland represents the freedom and self-definition that Xuela seeks.

In spite of the assumed carefree life that he enjoys, Roland is a member of the oppressed, the colonized, as is made clear from the onset of Xuela's description of him. She notes that Roland was "Philip's [her English husband's] opposite" (163). Roland's difference is evident in his race, class, and history. Whereas Roland "was a small event in somebody else's [Philip's] history" (167), Philip, a name that alludes to the colonizer's name, represents his history.[32] Similar to the small islands that are made indistinguishable because they are swallowed up by "the sea and the ocean, and by countries" (167), Roland's history is obfuscated by the colonizer's history. The islands' smallness-cum-insignificance does not qualify them as countries. Therefore, they remain islands with histories just as islandlike and just as insignificant. Regardless, the colonials have left behind a group of dispossessed peoples who, similar to Xuela and Roland, are seeking answers to their past with the hope of constructing a "whole" new future and self. Dispossessed of their homeland, the islands' inhabitants are left homeless. They become the adopted daughters and sons of the colonial mother (country), and the island functioning as surrogate becomes the adopted mother's land.

Colonization in the islands has deprived Xuela of not only a mother and a mother's land but also her mother's tongue. Surprisingly, the first words that Xuela uttered were "in English not French patois or English patois, but plain English—a language [she] had never heard anyone speak" (7). Xuela's rejection of surrogacy and of all things reminiscent of the colonizer and colonization, and her now speaking in the colonizer's language, is rather ironic, but nonetheless speaks of a negotiable space. Xuela admits: "[That] the first words I said were in the language of a people I would never like or love is not now a mystery to me; everything in my life good or bad, to which I am inextricably bound is a source of pain" (7). Speaking in the colonizer's tongue Xuela expresses her anguish. Inextricably bound to the colonizer, the colonized female subject has to negotiate for her identity. In order to voice or articulate her palpable hatred for colonialism, Xuela must revert to the language of the colonizers. Kincaid speaks of this irony in her book *A Small Place:*

---

32. I contend that the name *Philip* alludes to the colonizer Prince Philip, duke of Edinburgh. In the broad sense, it is an allusion to the mother country's colonization of the Caribbean islands.

> Isn't it odd that the only language I have in which to speak of this crime [colonialism] is the language of the criminal who committed the crime? And what can that really mean? For the language of the criminal can contain only the goodness of the criminal's deed. The language of the criminal can explain and express the deed only from the criminal's point of view. It cannot contain the horror of the deed, the injustice of the deed, the agony, the humiliation inflicted on me.[33]

Inasmuch as the language of the colonizer is limiting, the colonized subject has but two choices: either be silent, allowing his or her subjectivity to be subsumed, or utilize the language of the "criminal." Xuela chooses the latter, exposing the brutality and injustices of the colonizers. Like Caliban, with whom she shares a history of oppression, Xuela uses the language of the criminal to curse him.

Xuela's undying and unwavering love for her dead mother is another expression of her defiance. Her mourning for her dead mother is an act of remembrance. She keeps her bloodline alive by reliving and re-creating the memories, the lives, and the brutality suffered by her mother and a people. In so doing, she exposes the brutality and the foul deeds of the colonials and, at the same time, rejects their version of history. Xuela's only form of identification with her mother is through death, and by embracing her mother in death she identifies with her. While her mother is physically dead, she lives a deathlike existence in a colonized mother's land. Perversely, death lends some kind of intimacy. It is what unites the inhabitants. It is what unites Xuela with her stepbrother, Alfred (here again, noticeably, the man is defined or named, while the stepsister remains nameless), and stepsister: "My brother died. In death he became my brother. When he was alive I did not know him at all. . . . She became my sister when shortly after she was expelled from school she found herself with child and I helped her rid herself of this condition" (110, 114).

Death, in spite of its alien characteristic, evidently brings closeness and familiarity, for it is only after Alfred's death that Xuela acknowledges him as her brother and refers to him by name. Similarly, she acknowledges her stepsister only when she is found in a vulnerable position, pregnant and close to death after an abortion that she,

33. Kincaid, *A Small Place*, 31–32.

Xuela, performed. Xuela further confesses, "I came to love my father, but only when he was dead, at that moment when he still looked like himself but a self that could no longer cause harm, only a still self; dead" (214). Like hatred, death intrigues Xuela, giving her some perverted sense of strength. Death also lends a feeling of superiority:

> Seeing him [her father] dead, I felt superior in the fact that I was alive and he was dead, and even though I knew and believed that death was my fate also, I felt superior to him, as if such a humiliation, death, would never happen to me. I was a child then, but you are a child until the people who brought you into this world are dead; you remain a child until you understand and believe that the people who brought you into this world are dead. (213)

Xuela does not have the same feeling of superiority over her dead mother as she has over her dead father. This speaks to and of the "magic" that the mother has over her daughter, even in death. Paradoxically, it is within this "death-trap" that Xuela fosters a relationship with her dead mother. She experiences intimacy through death, establishing a mother-daughter bonding, though rather unconventional, outside patriarchal dominion. Nonetheless, this bonding does not foster growth, but leaves Xuela in a stagnant, childlike position because of her strong desire for maternal love. She discloses that "you remain a child until you understand and believe that the people who brought you into this world are dead." Fittingly, Xuela is still a child, and her childlike existence is evidenced by her confession that her mother's death "was not a death at all" (211). Never entirely revealing herself, Xuela's mother exerts power over all those who cannot see her, especially Xuela. Her presence is omnipotent. Page after page of the novel offer exhausting details of her death. Everything and everyone are contrasted against her. Everything is defined through and by her. Her palpable absence speaks for her powerful presence. Night after night the mother invades the daughter's dreams, appearing to reveal herself to her daughter, yet she never does. Notwithstanding, death has not spared the mother life's cruelty. She is just as indifferent as those alive. The lullaby she sings to her daughter is not sentimental, is not geared to console Xuela and help her through life's trials and tribulations; instead, it gives her a false sense of serenity. It is wordless, yet holds some kind of magic over her.

Thus, death both imprisons and liberates Xuela. It keeps her alive and going in her quest for self. Her mother's death provokes Xuela's quest for knowledge of her. She is identified and defined by death. Her birth coincides with her mother's death. She becomes her mother's daughter by and in death. She is named after her mother's death. Xuela's mother is also named after her own mother's disappearance or death. The death of Xuela's Carib mother is employed as a subtext for the death of the Caribs, the Amerindians, who also suffered extinction at the hands of the colonials. They are stripped of their home, land, and subjectivity. Extinct, they are written out of history:

> Who are the Carib people? Or, more accurately, Who were the Carib people? For they were no more, they were extinct, a few hundred of them still living, my mother had been one of them, they were the last survivors. They were like living fossils, they belonged in a museum, on a shelf, enclosed in a glass case. That these people, my mother's people, were balanced precariously on the ledge of eternity, waiting to be swallowed up in the great yawn of nothingness, was without doubt, but the most bitter part was that it was through no fault of their own that they had lost, and lost in the most extreme way; *they had lost not just the right to be themselves, they had lost themselves.* This was my mother. (198; emphasis added)

Sharing the same history with her mother, Xuela has seemingly both lost the right to be herself as well as lost herself. This loss is symptomatic of that suffered by the inhabitants of the Caribbean island of Dominica: the loss of their identities, a mother's land, and the mother's tongue. Dispossessed, they are unable to identify with a "true" motherland and a culture that are inseparable from that of the colonizer's. This inseparableness blurs and more often obfuscates individual identities. This conflation of identities seemingly questions and challenges the notion of a Caribbean identity. Significantly, a few pages after questioning the identity or, rather, extinction of the Carib peoples, Xuela questions her own existence:

> Who was I? *My mother died at the moment I was born. You are not yet anything at the moment you are born.* This fact of my mother dying at the moment I was born became a central motif of my life. I cannot remember when I first knew this fact of my life, I cannot remember when I did not know this fact of my life; perhaps it was at the moment I could recognize

my own hand, and then again there was never a moment that I can remember when I didn't know myself completely. . . . *I refused to belong to a race, I refused to accept a nation.* I wanted only, and still do want, to observe the people who do so. *The crime of these identities,* which I know now more than ever, I do not have the courage to bear. Am I nothing, then? I do not believe so, but if nothing is a condemnation, then I would love to be condemned. (226; emphasis added)

It is of great significance that like the Caribs, Xuela refers to herself in the past tense—"Who *was* I?"—which is indicative of the loss or death of the "original" self. The X that begins her name evidently speaks of her extinction. She is an ex-self. Similar to the Caribs, Xuela's "extinction" is intensified by the imposition of a foreign colonial culture on the island. Her unnerving confession speaks to her deathlike existence: "My mother died at the moment I was born. You are not yet anything at the moment you are born." It also spells disaster for the child, the daughter, abandoned in the world without a mother, a mother's tongue, or a mother's land. The damage caused by this abandonment has severe consequences, causing the victim untold suffering; it has left Xuela scarred for life. She is unable to claim or "accept a nation," and refuses to "belong to a race," let alone lay claim to the island. Claiming the mother equals claiming the island. She is the vital link, the connecting cord that sustains the mother-daughter relationship and in turn links daughters to the mother's land. Unable to fully claim her (dead) mother, unable to claim the "invisible current" that runs from mother to daughter, Xuela cannot claim her mother's land. She, therefore, remains fractured and incomplete:

No life is complete, no life is really whole, without this invisible current, which is in many ways a definition of love. No one observed and beheld me, I observed and beheld myself; the invisible current went out and it came back to me. I came to love myself in defiance, out of despair, because there was nothing else. Such a love will do. . . . It will do, it will do, but only because there is nothing else to take its place; it is not to be recommended. (56–57)

Xuela candidly admits that self-love is no substitute for a mother's love, and it therefore should not be encouraged. It is a poor substitute or surrogate for the mother's love. Entrapped within a destructive narcissism, Xuela's quest for identity is futile.

Denied all paradigms of female bonding—motherhood, daughter-hood, and, last but not least, childhood—Xuela is arguably doomed for eternity. Daughterhood and motherhood, argues Adrienne Rich, are two key concepts in identity formation and definition as women. Xuela does not have the anchor of a real mother, nor does she forge any connection with surrogates. Unable to identify with her mother and her mother's land, Xuela is unable to truly find herself. Due to her mother's untimely death, Xuela never experiences any formative relationship with her. She is disarmed of the strength, "the invisible current," that fosters this mother-daughter connection. She never receives the empowerment passed on from one woman to another; she never receives the "kind of strength which can only be one woman's gift to another, the bloodstream of our inheritance" and therefore is left "wandering in the wilderness."[34] This strong line of love never existed for Xuela, as the "bloodstream of [her] inheritance" was disrupted from birth. At the narrative's end, she confesses: "This is an account of the person who was never allowed to be and an account of the person I did not allow myself to become" (228). Thus, Xuela never "becomes," and is still "wandering in the wilderness." She admits that "[she] had been living at the end of the world her whole life" (213). Even after the narrative's end, Xuela appears to be still living at the end of the world. Embittered by her mother's death, she withdraws from her mother's land. The death of a mother, followed by withdrawal from the mother's land and the island community, spells disaster—annihilation of the self. Xuela has disarmed herself; she has no womb to which to return, or to seek refuge, not the island womb or the mother's womb.

Xuela's narrative is her attempt to fill the void left by her mother's death. In a moment of self-reflection, she muses: "This account of my life has been an account of my mother's life as much as it has been an account of mine, and even so, again it is an account of the life of the children I did not have, as it is their account of me. In me is the voice I never heard, the face I never saw, the being I came from. In me are the voices that should have come out of me" (227–28). Mother and daughter are inextricably bound in spite of death. In Xuela's autobiographical account, the present, the past, and the

34. Rich, *Of Woman Born*, 246.

future, though dismal, merge. Her narration of her life story speaks either directly or indirectly to all mothers and daughters, born and unborn. Her story speaks volumes to generations of women who have been denied identities, who have been denied the mother-daughter bond, and who have been silenced. The devastating results of these denials are personified in Xuela. "In [her] are the voices" of daughters trapped in a childlike state: "In me are the voices that should have come out of me." Her narrative appears to be a plea for a meaningful mother-daughter connection. Thereby, she speaks for every woman, every mother, biological and "other," and every mother-daughter relationship mediated by colonization. In spite of her deprivation, Xuela refuses to be defeated, refuses to be resigned, even though she questions: "Am I nothing, then?" In the same breath she rebuts: "I do not believe so" (226). But there is no mistaking that her life "was changed forever" (93).

Kincaid's symbolic return to her mother's land, Dominica, and her representation of a Caribbean people are her attempts at reclaiming a Caribbean sensibility. It can be interpreted as her search also for a "lost" Caribbean identity. Her constant returns and references to the mother illuminate the profound way in which a mother is linked to the mother's land and the mother culture. The mother embodies that culture. She embodies the island and the island's history.

3 Imagined Homelands

Engendering a Mythic Return "Home"

Back to Africa Miss Matty?
Yuh noh know wha yuh dah-sey?
Yuh haffe come from some weh fus,
Before yuh go back deh?

Me know sey dat yuh great great great
Gramma was African,
But Matty, doan yuh great great great
Grampa was Englishman?

Den yuh great grandmada fada
By yuh fada side was Jew?
An yuh grampa by yuh mada side
Was Frenchie parley-vous!

Den is weh yuh gwine Miss Matty?
Oh, you view de countenance,
An between yuh an de Africans
Is great resemblance!

Ascorden to day, all dem blue-y'eye
Wite American,
Who-fa great granpa was Englishman
Mus go back a Englan!

Wat a debil of a bump-an-bore,
Rig-jig an palam-pam!
Ef the whole worl' start fe go back
Weh dem great granpa come from!

Ef a hard time yuh dah-run from
Teck yuh chance, but Matty, do
Sure o' weh you come from so yuh got
Someweh fe come-back to!

Go a foreign, seek yuh fortune,
But noh tell nobody sey
Yuh dah-go fe seek yuh homelan
For a right deh so yuh deh!

—*Louise Bennett, "Back to Africa"*

I quote Jamaican poet Louise Bennett's "Back to Africa" at length because it is integral to the discussion of, or apparent obsession with, "going back" to Africa. Bennett's poem appears to be a direct response to the "Back to Africa" movement spearheaded by Marcus Garvey in the early 1920s.[1] Garvey's call for all blacks to return "home" understandably never materialized because of its prematurity and impracticability. Illuminating the multicultural, multiethnic, hybrid composition of the Caribbean, Bennett speaks to this impracticality in her phenomenal poem. She harshly questions the notion of a "return" and a search for a homeland that is often imaginary: "Back to Africa Miss Matty? / Yuh noh know wha yuh dah-sey?" Bennett concludes that the "real" homeland is the place of birth, "a right deh so yuh deh!" and cautions that it is necessary to know the homeland as a means of achieving self-identification and self-definition: "Sure o' weh you come from so yuh got / Someweh fe come-back to!"

Condé continues the tradition of critiquing and arguing against the Back to Africa movement a decade after Bennett.[2] Her first novel, *Heremakhonon*, is arguably her attempt to illuminate the impracticability of this call for a return home. This return is disastrous and ends in disillusionment and disappointment. This disenchantment has affected not only the protagonist, Veronica Mercier, but Condé as well, for there is a marked shift away from this obsession with going

1. Garvey's ideologies helped actualize Pan-Africanism. His philosophical ideologies would also eventually grow into the Rastafarian movement. The Négritude movement governed by Aimé Césaire found its roots in Garvey's "Back to Africa" movement and later in the Harlem Renaissance.

2. Condé's novel *Heremakhonon* (1976) was published exactly ten years after Louise Bennett's *Jamaica Labrish*. Although *Heremakhonon* does not directly focus on the "Back to Africa" movement, the novel's protagonist, Veronica Mercier, physically and unsuccessfully enacts this return, confirming Condé's doubt about such a return, which is fully addressed in "Pan-Africanism, Feminism, and Culture."

back to Africa in *I, Tituba, Black Witch of Salem*. This palpable shift results from the disillusionment that Condé herself has experienced while in the Motherland, Africa. Condé blames the Pan-Africanist movement and Négritude for instilling in the minds of Caribbean peoples that all blacks are the same and that Africa is "home," a place where the West Indian can seek refuge and achieve "wholeness." She admits her generation expected too much from Africa:

> It was naive, simplistic and overly idealistic to assume that African countries, just liberated from the yoke of colonization, and facing so many problems and subject to so many pressures from the imperialist powers, could provide the model we were looking for. We expected to be welcomed by the Africans with open arms and seen as long-lost brothers and sisters. We expected them to help us in our struggles while theirs were still raging. But this was not possible.[3]

Vévè Clark offers an enlightening explanation for the disillusionment experienced by those in search of an ideal homeland in her groundbreaking research on diaspora literature. She notes that "ironically, it is through disillusionment that the reader's diaspora literacy develops into post-colonial consciousness." She defines diaspora literacy as the "ability to comprehend the [multicultural, multilingual] literatures of [the diaspora]: Africa, Afro-America, and the Caribbean, from an informed indigenous perspective."[4] Similar to her protagonist, Veronica Mercier, Condé has experienced diaspora literacy, that is, the transition from incomprehensibility to acceptance, understanding, and comprehension. As a result, both Veronica and Condé have had to reevaluate and reexamine their notions of home, and their concepts of self. In spite of its multiple definitions and interpretations, home is figured as a geographic, concretized location in the novels.

Heremakhonon chronicles the life's path of Veronica Mercier, an Antillean who journeys from her homeland, Guadeloupe, to the mother country, France, and then to the Motherland, Africa, to "find herself." The entire narrative is structured around journeys—arrivals and departures. This substantiates Grace Nichols's claims that the

3. Condé, "Pan-Africanism, Feminism, and Culture," 59.
4. Vévè A. Clark, "Developing Diaspora Literacy and Marasa Consciousness," 42, 49.

sense of journeying always exists in Caribbean people's imagination, whether the return is real, metaphoric, or imaginary.[5] Veronica's constant journeys initiated by a loss or lack of sense and self are visible signs of displacement. The novel opens with Veronica's departure to an unnamed African country and ends with another departure, her "return back" to France. These continual journeys or wanderings illuminate Veronica's uprootedness and her ambiguous relation to her homeland, Guadeloupe, and her Motherland, Africa. Having left her mother's land, Guadeloupe, Veronica has severed all ties, disrupting negotiations with her mother, who serves as a direct connection to and a metaphor for the homeland. From the onset of the novel she hints at this disruptive relationship: "Why am I here? They were right to sneer. Not my mother, she never sneers. She sighs. . . . That's it misunderstanding all the way. Tons of them, right up to the first goodbye. *They,* standing behind the *glass doors* at the airport. *Me,* climbing the gang way with wobbly legs and misty eyes."[6] Veronica's "otherness" is elucidated by her use of the pronoun *they* versus *me*. *They* is suggestive of togetherness, of community and collectivity. In contrast, *me* accentuates severance and alienation from the collective, and the community. "Climbing the gang way with wobbly legs and misty eyes" illuminates Veronica's uncertainty and her lack of selfhood and vision.

The glass doors that separate Veronica from her mother are reminiscent of the queen's looking glass that Sandra Gilbert and Susan Gubar make habitual reference to in *Madwoman in the Attic.* This is the glass that creates distance and difference among women and ultimately sets them apart. Deserting her mother('s)land, Guadeloupe, for the Motherland, Africa, Veronica rejects both the mirroring and the nurturing gazes of the mothers and therefore is faced with further desertion and alienation. This alienation precedes her actual arrival in and welcome (*Heremakhonon* means "Welcome House") to Africa. Detailing various events about the flight, she observes: "Seven hours in a DC-10. *On my left, an African* desperately trying to make small

5. Grace Nichols herself makes this observation in her commentary on the film version of her book of poetry, *I Is a Long Memoried Woman.*

6. Condé, *Heremakhonon,* 3–4; emphasis added. Future citations will be given parenthetically in the text.

talk. *Behind me, a French* couple as average as they come. Why am I doing this?" (3; emphasis added). The quoted passage alludes to Veronica's "in betweenness," her "nowhereness." The African on her left and the French couple behind her serve as metaphors for the Motherland, Africa, and the mother country, France. Neither the representatives of the mother country, the French couple, nor the African representative have an effect on Veronica. The French couple, in her eyes, is insignificant, "average," and she distances herself from the African, who is "desperately trying to make small talk." Veronica precariously sits between two continents, belonging nowhere, to neither, and alienated from both. While her musing "Why am I doing this?" questions her intentions, that of going to Africa to find herself, it simultaneously predicts her uncertain future, one plagued with alienation, exile, ambiguities, and indecisiveness. This ambiguous position that the protagonist takes to both her motherland and her mother country is directly linked to the (non)relation she has with her homeland. Louise Bennett cautions

> Yuh haffe come from some weh fus,
> Before yuh go back deh . . .
> [And] sure o' weh yuh come from so yuh got
> Someweh fe come-back to![7]

Deliberately severing all ties and rejecting any form of negotiations with her mother and her mother's land, Veronica has no "real" home or mother's land to which to return. Brathwaite appropriately concludes that it is "not the society which sends the West Indian seeking exile, but [her] own basic rootlessness and lack of direction." Her aimless wanderings and uprootedness account for her indifference and ambiguity to her Caribbean homeland and culture, resulting in her inability to establish any meaningful relationships with people or places. In quoting Frantz Fanon, Françoise Lionnet notes that Veronica falls victim to Fanon's concept of the "double alienation of the intellectual who cannot embrace his or her own geopolitical and historical situation and gets caught in a hopeless dualism." Veronica does not equivocally claim her mother's land or the Motherland, resulting in her being precariously trapped between

---

7. Bennett, *Jamaica Labrish*, 214.

the two worlds. This entrapment further illuminates the hopelessness of her cause, her search for subjecthood. This hopelessness, in turn, leads to aimless and futile wandering. In a conversation with Maryse Condé, Françoise Pfaff questions: "[M]any of your characters seem to be doomed to wandering and wishing to be where they are not. Is this constant search for a Promised Land the distinguishing feature of human beings? Since this Promised Land does not exist, should we see this search as life's ultimate chimera?"[8] Condé affirms Pfaff's observations. Although this constant search for home is indeed a "distinguishing feature of human beings," it is often, if not always, initiated by a lack of self and rootedness. Illuminating the consequences of "aimless" wandering, the novel suggests that if a woman is rooted in her culture, she will foster a true sense of self, thereby eradicating any false internalization of the self. Linked to confinement, rootedness is often seen as suffocating and also as doom. Notwithstanding, rootedness also suggests selfpossession and is often necessary for developing a sense of the self. Yet, it should not prohibit wandering, which leads to creativity only when one has a deep sense of rootedness and of self. An individual can be situated in several different cultures, which holds true for Caribbean peoples whose entire history is founded on difference and multiplicity. Bennett addresses the danger of Caribbean peoples claiming one identity and refuting another:

> meh know sey dat yuh great great great
> Gramma was African,
> But Matty, doan yuh great great great
> Grampa was Englishman?[9]

This preference of one identity over another is a rejection of the "true" self.

Rather than journeying back to the Caribbean to find herself, to find her roots, Veronica instead chooses exile both in the Motherland, Africa, and in the mother country, France. In the final stanza of her poem, Bennett hints at the foolhardiness of such a venture:

8. Edward Kamau Brathwaite, *Roots*, 38; Lionnet, *Autobiographical Voices*, 176; Françoise Pfaff, *Conversations with Maryse Condé*, 131.
9. Bennett, *Jamaica Labrish*, 214.

Go a foreign, seek yuh fortune,
but noh tell nobody sey
Yuh dah-go fe seek yuh homelan
For a right deh so yuh deh![10]

In other words, it is an admissible claim to go abroad to seek one's fortune, but migrating in search of one's roots is pointless because Guadeloupe, substituted for Bennett's Jamaica, is home. Questioning her own motives for seeking a homeland in Africa, Veronica accedes that Guadeloupe is home and knows that her "true" self could be found only on the island, in that womblike space, in spite of its turmoil:

> If I want to come to terms with myself, i.e. with them, i.e. *with us,* I ought to *return home.* To my *island specks* tossed to the four corners of the Atlantic by Betsy, Flora and *other females.* Back to the obscene caricatures of my childhood. . . . [Back] to my *mother's womb which I never should have left.* . . . It's not surprising then that Ibrahima Sory denies me the love which, *according to my theory,* could save me. He's got *better things* to do. . . . It's not the first time, but perhaps never as clearly, *I realize my place is not here.* At least *what I came to do is absurd.* Yet I know I won't move. Held back by a hope I know is thwarted from the start. (71, 86, 100; emphasis added)

After pointlessly trying to find herself in the other (country), Africa, and a man, in the form of Ibrahima Sory, whom she refers to endearingly as her "nigger with ancestors," Veronica finally admits that her theory is distorted, that she needs to return to the island, the mother's womb, to the warmth and support of other females. Although openly acknowledging her thwarted hope, Veronica has yet to answer her ancestral calling, meaning she has yet to expedite her return back to her mother's land.

In Africa, Veronica remains rootless and is unable to establish any significant relationship with the inhabitants because of her decision to remain neutral in the midst of her friends' struggle. From the onset of the novel Veronica's quest for selfhood in the Motherland, Africa, is futile because of her rootlessness in her Caribbean culture. Lacking a sense of belonging, one is forced to take flight into dreams and illusions—hence her flight to France and subsequently to Africa.

10. Ibid.

George Lamming perfectly summarizes Veronica's plight when he argues: "We are made to feel a sense of exile by our inadequacy and our irrelevance of function in a society whose past we can't alter, and whose future is beyond us." Haunted by her past, embodied by her parents, Veronica attempts to kill it symbolically by self-exile. Refuting her Caribbean past, she desires to capture or return to her African past, or what remains of the past. Unfortunately, for the colonial woman there can be no true return. Nevertheless, frozen in both space and time, Veronica continues to believe that there is an easy, painless way: "I came to seek a land inhabited by Blacks, not Negroes, even spiritual ones. In other words, I'm looking for what remains of the past. I'm not interested in the present" (56). Veronica foolishly thinks that she can access the remnants of the past while dismissing the present. Uprooting and coming to terms with one's past become a prerequisite. Bettina Soestwohner observes that one has to deal with the past other than in passing, because it is a constructive factor of the present. The past is constantly renegotiated through the present. There should exist a dialogic exchange between the past and the present. Killing the past, contends Edward Said, "help[s] the mind to intensify its own sense of itself by dramatizing the distance and difference between what is close to it and what is far away. This is no less true of the feelings we often have that we would have been more 'at home' [elsewhere]."[11] Said's theory holds true for Veronica. Distancing herself from her mother('s)land, she creates an idealized image of the Motherland, Africa, a lost paradise that she hopes to recapture. Apart from functioning as a mythic home space, Mother Africa is equated with the phallus. For her, Africa is a phallocentric world where the phallus is the law of the land. She fools herself into believing that the love of and for a man can sustain her love of and for the mother('s)land.

Veronica's world, to borrow Kincaid's words, starts at the crotch. She speaks incessantly about sex, and in Arthur Flannigan's words, "it is her sexuality and her sexual activity that define her very

---

11. Lamming quoted in Brathwaite, *Roots*, 38; Bettina Soestwohner, "Uprooting Antillean Identity: Maryse Condé's *La Colonie de nouveau monde*," 694; Edward Said, *Orientalism*, 55.

essence."[12] Her relationship with Ibrahima Sory is a sexual one; beyond that there is nothing between them. Well aware of this void between them, she muses: "[W]oman [she] is a field and man [Sory] her ploughman. Plough me, ploughman" (66). Sory is obsessed with Veronica's alienness and her exoticism, and moreover her willingness to be seduced, in spite of her intellectual capabilities (she is a teacher of philosophy). Commenting on his fascination, she confesses: "I'm a foreigner. But mainly because I'm more interesting sexually than my head or my heart or both. Come on let's make love. And jump to it" (78). She readily acquiesces to the role of the exotic, alien "other": "If I had a bit of respect for myself, I'd leave. But there's a secret unhealthy voluptuousness in being treated like an object" (89).

While Sory is fascinated with Veronica's exoticism, she is fascinated with Sory's not being branded: "This man who is about to take me does not know that I am a virgin of sorts. Of course the wrapper won't be stained with blood and the griotte won't hold it up proudly to reassure the tribe. It will be another blood. Heavier and thicker. Before letting it flow, black and fast, I now realize why he fascinates me. He hasn't been *branded*" (37). Unlike Sory, Veronica is branded and always has been, and she actively contributes to her being branded. While Sory is exempted because of his status as original African and as man, Veronica is branded for sleeping with both black and white men, and she is also branded by or as the Middle Passage. She recalls: "With Jean-Marie [her mulatto lover], I was called Marilisse. With Jean-Michel [her white lover], too—*especially* Jean-Michel" (71; emphasis added). Her admission that she was condemned a whore especially with Jean-Michel, her white lover, is significant. Frantz Fanon addresses the relationship between a white man and a black woman in his book *Black Skin, White Masks*. Specifically, he addresses the disrespect a woman of color calls upon herself by being with a white man. Veronica's life(style) bears resounding similarities to Mayotte Capécia's, an Antillean also, who is subjected to harsh and unadulterated criticism by Fanon for her

12. Kincaid, "Interview with Jamaica Kincaid," by Perry, 509; Arthur Flannigan, "Reading below the Belt: Sex and Sexuality in Françoise Ega and Maryse Condé," 306.

choices of men, specifically white men. Like Mayotte Capécia, before her voyage to Africa Veronica sought acceptance in a white elitist society. Although her present relationship is with an African, Sory, it mirrors her previous relationships. Though not white, the minister of defense and interior, Sory, is an embodiment of the colonials, both in his livelihood and in his mannerisms; he exploits the less fortunate, a likely source of his affluence. And he is of great stature and social standing, assets that are well guarded. As a result of this relationship with Sory, Veronica is deemed a whore by her students for sleeping with her "nigger with ancestors," who later re-echoes her students: "I wonder how one can love a white man. After all they did to us. . . . For me, only whores should deal with white men" (152). Sory's comment is arguably directly linked to Mayotte Capécia's observation of the disrespect a black woman endures in the white man's eyes, even when the relationship is based on love.[13] Noticeably, Sory poses the question in an accusatory tone: how can a black woman love a white man? seemingly suggestive of the derision Veronica has brought upon herself. Having slept with a European, Veronica, as a black woman, is in complicity with the sisterhood of the whore and prostitute. Subtly referring to Veronica as a whore, Sory tries to despoil the part of her that escapes him:

> "You have an identity problem?"
> The tone is somewhat mocking . . .
> "There was a young black American girl here who had the same sort of problem, I believe. She ended up having her hair plaited like *our women* and having herself renamed Salamata."
> What an amusing story! How it amuses him. I can imagine this poor Shirley alienated by white America and trying to cure herself. Amidst their laughter. Perhaps you made love to her? Perhaps you're the specialist for neurotics from the Diaspora? We are after all the Diaspora! He laughs louder.
> "Oh no! My weak point is pretty women. And in the name of Allah she was very ugly!"
> Yes, just a question of sex.

13. Frantz Fanon, *Black Skin, White Masks*, 42. Fanon severely criticizes Mayotte Capécia and her autobiographical narrative, *Je suis Martiniquaise*, and refers to her as delusional because of her choice of white men and her expressing desire to marry one. He dedicates an entire chapter, "The Woman of Color and the White Man," to this criticism in his book, *Black Skin, White Masks*.

[Later] It's not worth a damn to him. He speaks to me like a sick or else a very stupid child. (52–53)

Veronica is simultaneously an object of desire, a pretty face, and an object of disgust, a black West Indian woman who sleeps with both white and black men. She, like her American (diasporic) counterpart, is reduced to body parts, a pretty or ugly face, a barren womb, and a body. Sory's reference to the American girl with an identity problem is double voiced. The identity problem, obviously, is one that plagues diasporic, not continental, Africans, thus his emphasis on "our women." Making such a distinction between the diaspora and the mainland, he seems to hint at the notion that Africa is for Africans. He also hints at the absurdity of the diaspora in coming to the Motherland in order to find oneself, contending that it is much deeper than changing one's name and appearance. Aside from entrusting the identity problem to the diaspora, Sory insinuates that the problem is gendered, exclusively female, a notion that appears to support the idea that "femaleness was in and of itself a deformity."[14] As the specialist for neurotics from the diaspora, Sory diagnoses this illness that plagues the diaspora: identity crisis.

Branded by Sory, Veronica is belittled as a "sick" or "deformed" child. He does not see her as a subject (woman): "[D]on't you ever speak to the women in your bed?" (51). Reinforcing a sizable distance between himself and her, he even refers to her in the informal "tu" instead of the formal "vous." Despite the fact that they have known each other for a period of time, Veronica remains an outsider: "In my opinion it's not the first time you make love, but the second, that is the most delicate. You are no longer strangers, eager to get to know each other. . . . It has always been recognized from time immemorial that pillows are a place for confidences. True, some have nothing to confide. . . . So he doesn't want to know who I am, where I come from, and what I've come to do so far from home?" (51). Thus, as a woman, a black West Indian woman, an outsider, Veronica is barred from Sory's aristocracy, his society. Disrespected by Sory, she is nothing to him other than his loveless possession. For him, she exists only in body, and she submits to his every sexual need. He is

14. Quoted in Gilbert and Gubar, *Madwoman in the Attic*, on Aristotle's notion, 53.

not interested in defining her or knowing her beyond their sexual encounters.

Penned in the Welcome House (Heremakhonon), in a luxurious room, Veronica reduced to nothingness becomes Sory's possession. As a prisoner in Sory's Welcome House, Veronica is denied access to the Motherland. Denying others access to the Motherland, can Sory truly represent Mother Africa? Lemuel Johnson's commentary on *Heremakhonon* attempts to provide an answer to this question. "Veronica's desire in *Heremakhonon*," he observes, "is to remember and to be re-membered. It is, for sure, 'un destin' made all the more 'difficile à dechiffrer' because the attention is so focused on la chose genitale. Caribbean Veronica's investment in an ancestral phallocentricity, as the means of getting through to the 'other side,' only results in a myth-making and myth-mocking copulation." He later adds that Veronica "once more, must shake her arse if she is to save her soul," suggesting that sex proves her only savior. As Flannigan notes, it "alone has the regenerative and transformative effects that she seeks."[15] Equating Mother Africa with the phallus is Veronica's need for a Father('s)land rather than a mother's land. Not actively participating or taking control of the narrative discourse, Veronica condemns and sentences herself to a symbolic death, voicelessness.

Thus, Veronica is rendered inarticulate because she has allowed Sory to subsume her subjectivity. She asks nothing, demands nothing, except acceptance in his world. She plots her own death or silence, acceding to the self-entrapment that some women bring upon themselves, as noted by Gayatri Spivak. She asserts that "the relationship between woman and silence can be plotted by women themselves." Veronica entraps herself in the narrative by her inability or unwillingness to be involved in dialogue with her interlocutors. Instead she is engaged in internal monologues. These monologic discourses render her powerless and insignificant, for they are not "oriented toward an addressee." "The word," according to Bakhtin, "is a two-sided act. It is determined equally by whose word it is and for whom it is meant. As word, it is precisely the product of the reciprocal relationship between addresser and addressee. . . . A

---

15. Lemuel Johnson, "A-beng: (Re)Calling the Body in(to) Question," 134; Flannigan, "Reading below the Belt," 309.

word is a bridge thrown between myself and another. . . . [I]t is territory shared by both addresser and addressee." Veronica's internal monologues are never worded or articulated, and as such she is never able to bridge the differences among Sory and herself and the other Africans. Frantz Fanon expounds further upon Bakhtin's idea when he maintains that to speak is to assume a culture and that the act of speaking is a two-way dialogic engagement. He adds that the mastery of speaking and language affords remarkable power. Directing her thoughts within, Veronica relinquishes her bargaining power, and her speech is misdirected and displaced. H. Adlai Murdoch argues that "the discursive representation through internal monologue amounts to a conscious strategy of displacement, the fragmentation of subjectivity figures the absence of a valid place of enunciation."[16] By refusing to dialogue, Veronica does not exist for Sory, and as a result she suffers cultural extinction. There is no verbal reciprocity between the addresser, Veronica, and the addressee, Sory. The reciprocity is of a sexual nature. Although the addressee of the protagonist's discourse is discernible, her discourse carries no agency, and as a result she seems to be in conversation with herself. Murdoch further observes that monologic discourse inscribes the subject into a sort of discursive neutrality that both desires and denies recognition of and by the other.[17] This ambivalence is the core of the relationship Veronica has with Sory. While she seemingly wants Sory to define or comprehend her, she simultaneously denies him entrance into her world by her refusal to speak to him directly. She yearns to tell (her)story to Sory, yet she is repeatedly unable to do so and instead falls into a silent stupor. When for the first time Sory asks her why she came to Africa, she responds by telling him, "I was fed up. I was living in Paris. With a white man" (52). (Her) story turns out to be (his) story. She repeatedly recounts her story through the lens of the other/male: Sory, Jean-Marie, Jean-Michel, her father, the Mandingo marabout, other countries: France and Africa.

16. Gayatri Spivak, "Can the Subaltern Speak?" 82; Bakhtin quoted in V. Vološinov, *Marxism and the Philosophy of Language,* 214; Fanon, *Black Skin, White Masks,* 18; Adlai H. Murdoch, "Divided Desire: Biculturality and the Representation of Identity in *En attendant le bonheur,*" 580.
17. Murdoch, "Divided Desire," 583.

This liminal position of being neither here nor there, in-between cultures, evidences a fragmented, lost self. Her liminality results from her indifference to the culture and languages of the African peoples and the Africans themselves. Susan Andrade claims that Veronica's "inability to engage with the Africans among whom she now lives [is illuminated by her] reading African issues exclusively and narcissistically through her Caribbean lenses of absence and loss."[18] Refusing to enter in and partake of either culture, African or Caribbean, Veronica remains an exile in both the Motherland and the homeland. This refusal precipitates and accounts for her loss and failure in her quest for selfhood.

In *Speech Genres,* Bakhtin says that a certain entry as a living being into a foreign culture offers one the possibility of seeing the world through the eyes of the other, which constitutes a necessary part of the process of understanding the other through his or her culture. As an outsider (Bakhtin's concept of outsideness does not preclude rootedness; rather, it is founded on rootedness), Veronica occupies a privileged position of understanding the other and living the other('s) culture, but her rootlessness in her Caribbean culture prefigures her indifference to African culture, resulting in alienation from both cultures and peoples, leaving her doubly exiled. In the realm of culture, to quote Bakhtin,

> outsideness is a most powerful factor in understanding. It is only in the eyes of another culture that foreign culture reveals itself fully and profoundly.... [T]hey engage in a kind of dialogue.... [W]e seek answers to our questions and the foreign culture responds to us by revealing to us its new aspects.... Such a dialogic encounter of two cultures does not result in merging or mixing. Each retains its own unity and open totality, but they are mutually enriched.[19]

Bakhtin's emphasis on "dialogic encounters" between cultures and peoples underscores the necessity and urgency for dialogue and contact with the other. He sees this "encounter" as meaningful and mutually enriching. Notwithstanding, Veronica cannot find a

18. Susan Z. Andrade, "The Nigger of the Narcissist: History, Sexuality, and Intertextuality in Maryse Condé's *Heremakhonon,*" 218.
19. Bakhtin, *Speech Genres,* 7. Bakhtin addresses in detail the notion of "outsideness" and cultural identity in his work.

common ground on which to relate to the Africans. This indifference is spawned by her dismissal of her island's culture and her refusal to enter into the African culture. Françoise Lionnet contends that "Heremakhonon indicts 'neurotics from the Diaspora'—who come to Africa in a selfish search for fulfillment, remaining safely uninvolved in the revolutionary struggles of the local population." Veronica admits and later deplores this selfish act as she questions her motives: "Do they really believe that Africa has nothing else to do but give and give? . . . But is it up to me to criticize? When I too have my hand outstretched. I'm a first rate beggar. A parasite. A louse" (104). Blinded by her selfishness and narcissism, Veronica still hopes to find herself in the country and the natives that she openly rejects. Her refusal to interact with the Africans is a denial of dialogue between the diaspora and the continent, between diasporic Africans and continental Africans, which in turn is an indirect denial and rejection of the self. She and Sory function as metaphors for the two peoples, Africans and Caribbeans, for the nondialogue between them. Just as she engages solely in monologues, Veronica views society as a monolithic entity. She does not envision the two societies, the Caribbean and the African, dialogically. Hence, she rejects her Caribbean past and desperately clings to an elusive African past. Divorcing her personal problems from the real political problems of the African people constitutes Veronica's crucial mistake and eventual downfall. Frozen in the past, she rejects the present. Clark views her inability to communicate as a breakdown "between diaspora literacy and delusion." She further adds that "Veronica's literacy is deceptive, having failed to evolve beyond the 1950s, and is further compromised by her indulgence in sentimental images of the noble revolution and the African homeland embraced by New World blacks."[20] Delusional, Veronica is unable to give herself verbal shape and remains alienated and exiled from (an)other point of view, and ultimately the community's point of view.

Retreating into the past, Veronica remains a foreigner, easily identifiable among the Africans by her looks and undoubtedly by her disassociation from them. She resides on the exclusive island com-

20. Lionnet, *Autobiographical Voices,* 181; Clark, "Diaspora Literacy and Marasa Consciousness," 49.

pound of Heremakhonon away from the inhabitants. This welcomed isolation speaks to the fact that although she hopes to find herself in Africa, her intention is not to become "one of them": "I didn't come to get mixed up in their quarrels and take sides. I came to find a cure. Ibrahima Sory, I know, will be the marabout gree-gree. We'll exchange our childhoods and our past. Through him I shall at last be proud to be what I am" (42). Although Veronica convinces herself that she will not take sides, she does exactly that, seriously "compromis[ing] the non-partisan she has adopted."[21] By refusing to question Sory, Veronica "fears that she will lose her objectivity were she to believe Saliou's crusade rather than the pro-government rhetoric of Ibrahima."[22] Her "objectivity" is seemingly worth more than the lives of her African friends. Little does Veronica know that the identity she seeks is dependent upon the struggles from which she distances and dissociates herself. Distancing herself from the people's struggles equals severance from the community. Her avoidance of the local people and their real political problems perpetuates the crime of the black bourgeoisie that, according to her, serves as a mouthpiece for the glorification of the race and its terrified conviction of its inferiority (52). Mirroring the black bourgeoisie who "sugarcoat" reality, Veronica resorts to such avoidance as a means of escape—unfortunately, an invalid one. Sory does not represent the ordinary citizens, and his royalty serves only as a justification of his oppressive power. In a purportedly nonaligned country, Veronica aligns herself with the elite masses, cloaked as assassins.

Minimized to nothingness, Africa is seen through the lens of an assassin, Ibrahima Sory. The traditional maternal role of Mother Africa is compromised in the novel through a masculine figure or figures. Aside from this relegation of duty, according to Andrade, Veronica "experiences Africa not only through her lover, Ibrahima Sory but in relation to other males—her favorite student, Birame III and her friend and potential lover, Saliou and her close friend, Pierre-Gilles." This identifying with the phallocentric society gives

---

21. Clark, "Diaspora Literacy and Marasa Consciousness," 47.
22. This is an earlier version and variation of Vévè A. Clark's discussion of diaspora literacy and literature, "Developing Diaspora Literacy: Allusion in Maryse Condé's *Heremakhonon*."

the patriarchy, appropriately represented by the men, agency and voices, while it further stifles the already silenced females in the novel. Veronica endorses the patriarchy by refusing to bond with the Mother(land). Offering a meaningful diagnosis for Veronica's inability to bond with the women in the novel, Jonathan Ngate remarks that Veronica's problem, her alienation, is compounded because "she is unable to bridge the gap between herself and the two African women, Sory's sisters, Oumou Hawa and Ramatoulaye."[23] While Veronica reveres the African men, she relegates the African women to the margins of society. While she admires and attempts to identify with the men's unbridled freedom—Sory is not branded, Jean-Marie is (identified) defined by his free spirits, and for her father, the Mandingo marabout, aside from having his name printed on the title pages of literary magazines and his signatures on speeches and similar ceremonies, "freedom [is] an iron weight encircling his feet and [theirs]" (8)—the women, like herself, are marked. The iron weight around their (her, mother's, and sisters') feet suggests imprisonment and confinement, whereas it is a source of empowerment for the Mandingo marabout.

Endorsing the men's unbridled freedom with her unwavering admiration, Veronica is not impressed in the least by the women. She places them into two categories: those who are defined by the domestic and lack substantial wealth and those of affluence who readily adopt and promote colonialism and its principles. This endorsement of colonialism compromises the maternal, the motherlands, Africa and Guadeloupe. First, Oumou Hawa, Sory's sister, is insignificant compared to her brother, the "nigger with ancestors." She is introduced to us after the Fanonian theory that the white woman is the black man's obsession. This introduction is timely, suggestive that the black woman is not only the black man's obsession but also his possession: "This is my wife, Oumou Hawa" (5), as introduced by Saliou. Her identity is dependent upon and conflated with her husband's. Commenting on the introduction, Veronica observes: "The black gazelle extolled by the poet. Pregnant, not that it mars her beauty. Nothing could. The table is set for two. They're right, a

---

23. Andrade, "Nigger of the Narcissist," 222; Jonathan Ngate, "Maryse Condé and Africa: The Making of a Recalcitrant Daughter?" 11.

woman's place is in the kitchen" (5). As Saliou acclaims his black gazelle, he claims her. The small black gazelle stands in contrast to the composer of poetry. The gazelle is prided for her beauty as the poet is revered for his artistry and his poetic and political insights.[24]

In spite of her beauty, Oumou Hawa is marked by her pregnancy. Her movement is restricted to closed spaces: the kitchen where she spends most of her time and days, apparently the bedroom, a fact to which her numerous pregnancies testify, and the hospital where she spends incalculable time giving birth. Her appearance in the novel is marked by the thud of her pestle, by her carrying or fetching food and babies alike on her back, and by the frequent "hold[ing] out [of] her breast to her bab[ies]" (92). Oumou Hawa's weakness is that she refuses to negotiate or bargain for her subjectivity, and she apparently surrenders to her plight, succumbing to the prescribed role assigned women by the society.

Oumou Hawa's sufferings, like her life, are alien to Veronica. Even in their sufferings, the women do not identify with Veronica, who appropriately observes that "this apparent submission [Oumou's], this apparent detachment hides a world I shall never comprehend" (95). It is also a world that Veronica refuses to become a part of: "Don't they know I don't care a damn for their town? I'm not an ordinary tourist. I don't care a damn for the women lined up at the well with their babies on their backs" (9), yet she hopes to satisfy her narcissistic desires: "[Oumou] could be my guide nevertheless. Be the chief linguist who interprets the words of the oracle" (95). Ironically, despite Oumou Hawa's prescribed domain, Veronica accords her the status of soothsayer, whose presumed task is to interpret the "words of the oracle." This speaks to Oumou's hidden potential that remains incomprehensible to Veronica.

When the women are not distinguished by their domesticity, they are acclaimed for their strong propensity for colonial things. Ramatoulaye, Sory's older sister, aggrandized for her strong colonial taste, is "decked out like a tournament horse, proud and sulky" (22). A perpetrator of colonialism, Ramatoulaye "niggerfies herself for pleasure":

24. Saliou is a political advocate.

Is the exuberant nigger, spontaneous like a child, another of Europe's inventions? No. They're not niggers. But we are! We, the so-called Diaspora! They're not niggers but Africans. For many unfortunately, *the process of negroization seems to have already begun.* . . . Ramatoulaye has just come back from the reception at the Ghanian embassy where the ambassador's wife was holding her weekly party. With a sigh of relief, Ramatoulaye removes her heavy wig which makes her look like one of the Supremes. Her hair emerges, rose-plaited. Now here is someone who niggerfies herself for pleasure! (122; emphasis added)

Significantly, this French African (unnamed) country that should be historically colonized by France has adopted the United States as its colonial mother. Ramatoulaye models the Supremes, indicative of the strong colonial influence of the United States, despite France's territorial dominance and occupation of this country. Veronica's conviction is that niggers are one of Europe's many inventions, recognizing that Europe, specifically England, played the first role in inhabiting Africa and colonizing Africans. She makes distinctions between Africans and niggers: "No. They're not niggers. But we are! We, the so-called Diaspora! They're not niggers but Africans." Her theory suggests that the diaspora, despoiled by colonization and slavery, creates niggers, meaning diasporic Africans.

Veronica's identification with colonialism, on one hand, is a downright rejection of the mother line and, on the other hand, her desire to identify with power or what she terms *freedom.* Veronica's mistake, as described by Joycelynn Loncke, lies in the fact that she seeks liberation not through herself or the mother's land or line but through men, in the "feverish hope that by attaching herself to one who is 'free' that freedom would somehow transfer itself to her. Her tragedy arises out of the fact that she has not recognised that the shackles which bind her exist within herself." Relinquishing her identity and freedom is an act of self-betrayal, which comes about because of a lack of maternal and sororal bonding and comfort. Addressing the absence of sisterly bonding, Ngate notes that "no sororal comfort from the African women can be counted upon when she finds herself betrayed because of her investment in a phallocratic aristocracy." This act of identifying with the "phallocratic aristocracy" strips her of her (female) subjectivity, and she becomes the same thing that she accuses her mother of being: "the moon round the paternal planet"

(24). In her words, she despises her mother because of her weakness, her inability to stand up to the father. Nonetheless, Veronica's passivity rivals her mother's. Her weakness, like that of her mother, who succumbs to the Mandingo marabout's every wish, is purportedly loving Sory too much and obsessing about her ideal creation of her "nigger with ancestors." This blind obsession disables her and prevents her from seeing beyond his aristocracy and beyond his tyrannical acts. Love is beyond Veronica for the same reasons Fanon concludes that "love is beyond the reach of the Mayotte Capécias of all nations." He contends that "the beloved should not allow me to turn my infantile fantasies into reality: On the contrary, he should be able to go beyond them."[25]

Veronica expects her infantile fantasy, which is to have Sory give her the self-definition she seeks, to be transformed into reality and to realize her dream and her creation of her "nigger with ancestors." Sory denies her all her dreams and expectations, and he repeatedly tells her: "I won't do anything to save you" (88). Unable to see beyond her obsession, Veronica succumbs to Sory's bewitching colonial powers. Beguiled, she is reduced to nothingness, a nonbeing, by Sory, worse than her mother, whom she accuses of being an echo of her father. Denied verbal expression by Sory, Veronica is denied the opportunity of even becoming an echo of Sory. The underlying truth behind her hatred for her mother arises out of her need to identify with the mother she despises. Viewing her mother as a perpetrator of colonialism, Veronica sees her as the enemy, but she, Veronica, strikingly mirrors this enemy by perpetuating the same crime, the worshiping of the patriarchy. While mother and daughter see the enemy in each other, they continue to worship patriarchy and colonialism, blind to the fact that this is the source of the estrangement between them.

The love-hate relationship Veronica has with her mother fashions the ambiguous love-hate relationship she has with her mother's land. Decidedly refusing to negotiate with her mother, Veronica identifies with her father and patriarchy; she is papa's baby because

25. Joycelynn Loncke, "The Image of the Woman in Caribbean Literature with Special Response to *Pan Beat* and *Heremakhonon*," 273; Ngate, "Maryse Condé and Africa," 11; Fanon, *Black Skin, White Masks*, 44.

she opts to identify with her powerful father rather than through the line of her mother. Veronica's refusal to be identified with the marked women, in spite of her "captive body," is her denial of a common bond among her, her mother, and the other women. Arthur Flannigan observes that all "that is associated with the male, is esteemed; and all that is woman or associated with the female is disesteemed and even scorned." He further observes that Veronica holds all the women that populate her past and present more or less in contempt. She even blames the great-grandmother for what he terms the contamination of the family's bloodline by the sperm of a *béké*.[26] And her mother, Marthe, accused repeatedly of being unaffectionate and insignificant, along with the other women of the novel, is also subjected to Veronica's wrath. They are all held in rather low esteem. Veronica's comment that the women, including her mother, never impressed her is a desecration of mother(hood) and sister(hood) and a validation of father(hood). She openly denounces the motherlands, the Caribbean and Africa.

Veronica's lack of significant relationships with any women induces her failure and downfall. She convinces herself that as a "virgin of sorts," that is, having Ibrahima Sory, her "true" born-and-bred African, she can be saved by the brother(hood). This investment proves a bad one. "My ancestors, my ancestors via Ibrahima Sory are playing a dirty trick on me. A very dirty trick. . . . Yes, my ancestors are playing a dirty trick on me. They are laying a trap. They are making me choose between the past and the present. Take sides in this country's drama. As if they too are fed up with my objectivity. . . . A very dirty trick" (160–61). Contrary to Veronica's belief, she sets her own trap and stages her own drama. She voluntarily rejects both her past and her present with the hopes of constructing an imaginary future. Her relationship with her "nigger with ancestors" turns out to be a farce. Sory's "niggerish" qualities go unnoticed by Veronica. Despite being a product of the Motherland, Africa, Sory is tainted by colonialism, hence overturning Veronica's earlier conviction that niggers are products exclusively from the diaspora.

---

26. I coined the phrase "papa's baby" by inverting Hortense Spillers's "Mama's Baby, Papa's Maybe: An American Grammar Book"; Flannigan, "Reading below the Belt," 307.

Spared from the trauma of the Middle Passage, Africa, according to her, is and should be inhabited by purebred Africans, but little does she know Africa is "already painted with a Western varnish" (111). Referring to Sory as her "nigger with ancestors," a term that is supposed to single him out from others and lend credence to his privileged status, incongruously suggests that like the diaspora he is despoiled by colonization or, rather, "negroization," to borrow her words. She notes that, unfortunately for many, "the process of negroization seems to have already begun" (122), and Sory is no stranger to this process, despite her nonacknowledgment of this fact. Naively, she confesses: "Quite frankly, I don't care a damn for the past and present crimes of this aristocratic [Sory's] family. They are the ones I came to see. Genuine aristocrats. Not monkeys" (24). The genuine aristocrats are nothing but mere monkeys who mimic the colonials. They "fight and kill each other in the name of Africa" (94). And so Sory's deeds, "niggerish" in nature, mirror the aristocracy.

Offering an apt interpretation for Veronica's apparent blindness, Françoise Lionnet maintains that because Sory "corresponds to an authentic mythical idea of the nigger with ancestors," he functions as a "symbolic screen that prevents Veronica from decoding the nature of his brand of tyranny." Veronica's vision of Sory as "the symbol of her dreams of an Africa as it was before colonialism and the slave trade" is distorted and fallacious. She becomes a figure of ridicule, says Andrade, seeking "an authentic African history while fleeing her own."[27] While Sory and the aristocrats, his sister Ramatoulaye included, "niggerize" themselves, Veronica came to the Motherland with the intention of "Africanizing." To her dismay, the Motherland, Africa, like the mother's land, Guadeloupe, is populated with niggers. Thus, she is left with the task to create (her) story, because to echo her, (his) story "never bothered about niggers because they weren't worth the fuss" (11).

The first step to the creation of (her) story lies in the feasible investment in the matrilineage. First and foremost, Veronica needs to stage a return to her immediate past, her mother's land, Guadeloupe, a return that constitutes a physical return to the insular, womblike

27. Lionnet, *Autobiographical Voices,* 171; Loncke, "Image of the Woman," 275; Andrade, "Nigger of the Narcissist," 220.

space and a symbolic return to her mother's womb. She has to make amends with the mother and thereafter the mother's land before she can have a meaningful relationship with the Motherland. She needs to return to her homeland and establish her roots before her routes take on any significance. It is also imperative that she initiates a negotiation with both her mother and her mother's land. Her rebirth, her symbolic return to the womb, can be effected only by the love and nurturance, compulsory ingredients, of a mother or a mother figure, a fact of which Veronica is well aware, for she constantly broods: "[H]ow can I return to my womb? How can I be born again?" (85).

She seeks love in the wrong places, in the arms and, ultimately, the beds of men, an act that leaves her "literally and figuratively screwed," as Ngate aptly describes it. Confessing that she should never have left her mother's womb, she subsequently accepts and acknowledges the futility of her quest: "I didn't find my ancestors. Three and a half centuries have separated me from them. They didn't recognize me anymore than I recognized them. All I found was a *man with ancestors* who's guarding them jealously for himself and wouldn't dream of sharing them with me. If we could swap child-hoods" (136). In actuality, Sory cannot guard the ancestors because his aristocracy does not permit the ancestral presence, and like Veron-ica, he is also in need of the ancestors. Sory is indeed a nigger, for he is imbued by colonialism. With Sory spiritually disembodied, Veronica too is denied spiritual access and entrance into the Motherland. She admits her error in journeying to Africa, as she admits her misecon-ception of the "nigger with ancestors": "I almost take him [Ibrahima Sory] for a ghost. Does Ibrahima Sory exist? Or is he a figment of my imagination? Of my frustration?" (50). She no longer refers to him as her "nigger with ancestors"; instead, he becomes a man. Both Africa and Ibrahima Sory exist in Veronica's imagination. They are both Veronica's creation. To paraphrase Wangari wa Nyatetu-Waigwa, Veronica has clearly understood the misguided nature of her quest; Africa has never been, and never can be, her native land. I would add that Sory as the embodiment of Africa, a "metonymical displacement," to borrow Françoise Lionnet's words, can never assist her in her quest for selfhood. He can never give her a sense of self, nor can he initiate her return (back) to her ancestors. Her association with him heeds only further alienation, and he figures as the "locus of her most profound alienation." Nyatetu-Waigwa concludes that Veronica's ancestors are to be sought elsewhere, ostensibly in the mother's land, Guadeloupe. The necessity to return to Guadeloupe becomes apparent as the protagonist admits that she ought to return home, to her "island specks," if she wants to come to terms with herself (71). Condé herself acknowledges that such a return is necessary: "An Antillean quest for identity can be resolved without having to go to Africa; or, if you like, a trip to Africa simply proves that Africa is not indispensable to an Antillean identity." Veronica's voyage to Africa substantiates Condé's claim. It costs Veronica a trip to Africa to find out the difficulty or, rather, impossibility of finding self-definition in or through Africa. Veronica, like her Africa, is "frozen in an imaginary dimension, where time stands still and myths contribute to the paralysis of future generations."[28]

Addressing why it is impossible for the Antillean to find self-definition through Africa, Nyatetu-Waigwa cites two reasons. First, "Africa becomes an obstacle because the protagonist cannot identify with the milieu. Far from finding the place 'where time stands still' . . . Veronica discovers in Africa that the 'transformations that cultures undergo through time and transplantations' render a return impossible." This actual return to the past is and will always be impossible because connections have been severed since the Middle Passage, rendering the return impossible, not only for the slaves but for their descendants as well. However, a spiritual return can be enacted, but the participant has to be at home with herself. Refusing to identify with the milieu, Veronica stages her own self-alienation. Second, "for the Africans to acknowledge the protagonist as one of them, she would have to accept adaptation (that is, deny her true identity and allow herself to be defined by others and re-created in their likeness)."[29]

Adaptation does not require the relinquishing of the (entire) self or being. In the first place, it is such an act, that is, a denial of her

---

28. Ngate, "Maryse Condé and Africa," 12; Wangari wa Nyatetu-Waigwa, "From Liminality to a Home of Her Own? The Quest Motif in Maryse Condé's Fiction"; Lionnet, *Autobiographical Voices,* 171; Maryse Condé, "L'Afrique, un continent difficile: Entretien avec Maryse Condé," 22; Lionnet, *Autobiographical Voices,* 170–71.

29. Nyatetu-Waigwa, "Liminality," 556.

(Caribbean) self and depending entirely on the other to define her, that caused and later heightened Veronica's alienation. Veronica's identity is determined equally by herself and the community of which she is a part. Although she is re-created and is given verbal shape by the community, it is a reciprocal relationship between the self and the community. But this reciprocity is possible only if and when one has a sound and spirited sense of self. Veronica needs to transcend her liminal status, which first and foremost calls for identification with and acceptance of her neglected past. It is incumbent that she unequivocally claims her birthright, a Caribbean identity, and initiates the process of adaptation. She needs to return to her island home, and she needs to make "peace with her island."[30]

Her constant references to the mother's womb and Guadeloupe, the island womb, hint at a return to and reconciliation with both the mother and the mother's land. Her denouncement of the patriarchy for the first time, referring to Sory as a "figment of [her] imagination [and] frustration" (50), speaks to this imminent negotiation and reconciliation. A return is necessary to put Veronica in touch with herself. Out of touch, Veronica's (re-)creation of Africa and Sory remains mythical. This symbolic (non)creation is linked to her literal nonprocreation. Perpetually liminal, she is in no position to make or fashion herself or anyone for that matter. The inability to create or make herself is inextricably linked to her inability to procreate; hence the sterility of her womb. Unable to fashion herself, Veronica can give birth neither literally nor figuratively. Rejecting the mother line, she has no tradition, no legacy. She negates her "true" self and goes in search of a nonexistent self and other. As a result, Africa, which mirrors her womb—"a great black hole [and] the dark continent" (56)—accordingly turns out to be sterile like her womb. Her reference to the African night as "opaque as the womb" (30) is indicative of the impenetrability of her womb. It is rather ironic that Veronica's barrenness stands in stark contrast to the fecundity of the African

30. This is a borrowed phrase from the title "Je me suis reconcilié avec mon île (I have made peace with my island): An Interview with Maryse Condé," in which Condé speaks about her own negotiation with the mother's land chronicled by her physical return.

women, alluding that for the Caribbean woman (who has no sense of self), Africa remains alien and sterile.

By the conclusion of the novel, Veronica is apparently on a journey to self-awareness. She looks herself in the face (eyes) for the first time as she vows that if given the chance, she would bond with the African natives:

> If men, women and youngsters had come out of their huts, I would certainly have marched with them. Their determination would have given me strength. And here I am. Face to face with myself. Trapped. For ever. All this time *he's talking. What's he saying?* . . . Yet another flight! One day I'll have to *break the silence*. I'll have to explain. What? This mistake, this tragic mistake I couldn't help making, being what I am. My ancestors led me on. What more can I say? I looked for myself in the wrong place. In the arms of an assassin. (176; emphasis added)

"Face to face" with herself forces her to confront herself, and to look within. This confrontation gives her a sense of self, and it provides her the medium for self-assessment and self-recognition. It presents her the opportunity of meeting and welcoming herself in a harmonious way. Ironically, her self-entrapment is a form of liberation from the suffocating gaze or grasp of the "other," a liberation that provides her the opportunity to see herself for the first time with her own eyes and not through the eyes of the "other."[31] This self-recognition yields to her verbal shaping. Possessing the ability to see (herself), Veronica is galvanized to act. Speaking of breaking her silence, she in turn silences Sory. She no longer hears or listens to him. His words are undecipherable.

Veronica finally realizes the importance of the matrilineage and the need to sustain the bloodline. Her acknowledgment of its importance is promising. Jonathan Ngate poignantly states that "the understanding that she is not African and does not need to look for her self via her ancestors on the continent is, in the end, a liberating truth." She needs to effect this separation from Sory and Mother Africa in order to assume and valorize her own identity. The breaking of her silence will free her from the walls of her self-

---

31. Self-entrapment, similar to the island, although it connotes enclosure, is a protected space where one seeks refuge. It forces a confrontation with the self. Though figured as a restrictive space, it is a positive, empowering one.

inflicted imprisonment. This monumental event will be enacted on the mother's land, the island of Guadeloupe. The novel ends on a promising note: Veronica's departure en route to her mother's land, Guadeloupe, via the mother country, France. Because the connection between "Africa and the Caribbean has from its very beginnings existed through Europe," Veronica's going back to France, according to Nyatetu-Waigwa, "is a logical and necessary step in her implied return to Guadeloupe."[32]

As Veronica leaves the Motherland, Africa, for the mother's land, Guadeloupe, to negotiate and reclaim her selfhood, Condé initiates a similar negotiation in *I, Tituba, Black Witch of Salem*. Africa is no longer a designated homesite, but the Caribbean is reclaimed as the "true" native land. In *I, Tituba, Black Witch of Salem*, there is a marked shift away from alienation and exile toward rootedness and spiritual consciousness. Although the homeland, Barbados, of Tituba, the eponymous heroine, is characterized by havoc and poverty, it is rich with spirituality and communal kinship. Tituba's rootedness in spirituality and in her community sustains her on the island. This evolution from uprootedness to rootedness marks maturity in Condé's fiction. Condé recounts the story of the witches of Salem, giving agency and voice to Tituba, a Barbadian slave. Tituba falls in love with John Indian and follows him into slavery in Massachusetts, where she is accused and tried for witchcraft. Bought by a Jewish merchant, Tituba is returned to freedom, after which she returns to Barbados, where she spends her final days.

Severance from her native island, Barbados, and severance from those who loved her was catastrophic for Tituba. Commenting on this devastating severance, Nyatetu-Waigwa observes that "separation from her native Barbados automatically entails severance from her life-source, the Barbadian community, and thereby, isolation and nostalgia."[33] Tituba's separation from the island space itself is not as devastating as her severance from her mothers, her "othermother," Mama Yaya, and her biological mother, Abena.

32. Ngate, "Maryse Condé and Africa," 11; Nyatetu-Waigwa, "Liminality," 556–57.
33. Nyatetu-Waigwa, "Liminality," 557.

In spite of this separation, Tituba is protected because of the nurturing and mothering she received from her mothers, Mama Yaya and Abena. Unlike Veronica, Tituba unequivocally claims a Caribbean identity, and is strongly grounded in ancestral heritage. In constant dialogue with her ancestors, she is sustained by her strong beliefs in her ancestral heritage. This communication is maintained even after her ancestors have passed on. Thus, Tituba is doubly empowered: maintaining close contact with, and being a part of, this earthly world as well as a great part of that other (ancestral) world. Tituba is not liminal but deeply rooted in both worlds. This rootedness, along with the great intimacy she shares with the ancestors, Mama Yaya and Abena, provide Tituba the necessary protection and function as her life-giving forces and sources. Tituba's temporary departure from her native land entails a separation from her life-giving forces, which creates an apparent unbridgeable distance between her and her ancestors. When informed by Tituba of her desire to leave the island, Mama Yaya responds, "[S]oon, I won't be able to be of any help. I'll be so far away. It'll take so long to cross the water. And it'll be so difficult."[34] Her leaving the island shores equals being "dragged off to the other side of the water" (15). The ocean waters function as an inhibiting force that limits contact with the ancestors. Crossing the borders from Barbados to Massachusetts, Tituba relinquishes her communal status and therefore is no longer part of the spiritual community. She relinquishes not only her communal status but also her freedom in order to be with her lover and future husband, John Indian.

Although Tituba is no longer a part of the spiritual community, she does not give up her spirituality and her practicing of witchcraft. Even in the midst of sexual gratification, Tituba remains spiritually grounded, which, nonetheless, does not inhibit sexual gratification. Before full acceptance of her ancestral leanings, her relationship with John Indian mirrors Veronica and Sory's, in that it is of a mere sexual nature: "What was there about John Indian to make me sick with love for him? Not very tall, average height, five feet seven, not very big, not ugly, not handsome either. I must confess it was downright

---

34. Maryse Condé, *I, Tituba, Black Witch of Salem*, 29–30. Future citations will be given parenthetically in the text.

hypocritical of me to ask myself such a question, since I knew too well where his main asset lay and I dared not look below the jute cord that held up his short, tight-fitting *konoko* trousers to the huge bump of his penis" (19). John Indian pointedly alludes to the inevitable sexual nature of their relationship upon meeting Tituba for the first time: "[H]ave you looked at yourself recently? You don't know how to talk and your hair is a tangle. You could be lovely if you wanted to" (13). His suggestive comment not only invites her but also challenges her to "makeup herself," that is, make her body more desirable. As with all sexual relationships, Tituba's beauty and body become the focal points of contention. Having never before given her body second thoughts, Tituba for the first time after John Indian's comment sees herself as a sexual being and decides to explore and harmonize her body:

> Up until now I had never thought about my body. Was I beautiful? Was I ugly? I had no idea. What had he said? You know, you could be lovely. . . . I took off my clothes, lay down, and let my hand stray over my body. It seemed to me that these curves and protuberances were harmonious. As I neared my pudenda, it seemed that it was no longer me but John Indian who was caressing me. Out of my body gushed a pungent tidal wave that flooded my thighs. (15)

Thoughtlessly "placing her body in John Indian's hands," Tituba momentarily becomes a slave to him.[35] She becomes the object of his desire. Mama Yaya's prophecy that "men do not love. They possess. They subjugate" (14) comes to fruition. John Indian becomes the possessor of Tituba's body, resulting in her being added to the list of the many hens "that this cock has coupled" (15). Even before Tituba had an inkling of John Indian's betrayal of her, Mama Yaya saw through the "shallow nigger, full of hot air and bravado" (15).

Consumed by sex and sexual activity, Tituba allows herself to be taken back into slavery. Though she admits that she was taking a risk by returning "to the white man's world," she is unable to fathom her actions, "her uncontrollable desire for a mortal man" (19). Categoriz-

---

35. Tituba, a free woman, literally becomes a slave as she follows John Indian to Massachusetts, where she lives with him and toils in his master-mistress Susan Endicott's household and later in Reverend Parris's, who bought them from Susan Endicott.

ing her acts as madness and betrayal, Tituba nonetheless eventually gives in to her madness and betrayal and follows John Indian to the other side. Her betrayal is twofold: first, she relinquishes her freedom fought and won by her ancestors and returns to the white colonial world as a slave, and second, her leaving for Massachusetts with John Indian is equivalent to her offering her body to him. This offering is a betrayal of her mother, whose own body functions as a conflicted site of oppression because she was brutally raped, resulting in Tituba's birth: "You know very well that I don't want to return to the white man's world. . . . My mother had been raped by a white man. She had been hanged because of a white man. I had seen his tongue quiver out of his mouth, his penis turgid and violet. My adoptive father had committed suicide because of a white man. Despite all that, I was considering living among white men again, in their midst, under their domination" (19). This return to the white world is the ultimate betrayal of the mother. Tituba is under not only the white man's dominion but the black man's as well. This double dominion or domination is closely linked to her birthright, for she is the product of a rape: the daughter of a white European, the rapist, and an African, her mother, Abena.

In a revealing statement, Jeanne Snitgen observes that "Tituba symbolizes the West Indian who can look to neither continent for an affirming mirror. Rejected by her African mother because she is born of a violation by a white European, Tituba embodies the problem of Caribbean subjectivity."[36] Abena's temporary rejection of her daughter is understandable and can be seen as a rejection of the colonizer, who imposes on and violates the colonized against her will. Mirroring her mother, Tituba becomes a valuable commodity as her body is commercialized. Abena's rape and, later, Tituba's lend testimony to their sameness—femaleness, "otherness," and blackness—and to the fact that the (black) body is a site of both desire and oppression.

Pregnant, Abena is bought into slavery by Darnell Davis, who became irate after he found out that she was with child. Abena's body is useless, her pregnancy a sign of a "woman in ill health and of no use whatsoever" (4), posing a burden to him. To rid himself

36. Jeanne Snitgen, "History, Identity, and the Constitution of the Female Subject: Maryse Condé's *Tituba*," 59.

of this burden and to punish Abena, he gave her to Yao, one of the Ashantis he had bought in the same batch. In contrast to the slave period, where a black woman's fertility was revered because it increased their owner's property, Abena's pregnancy was treated with derision and disdain. Davis's attempted rape of Abena evinces, first, that he was not looking for a "breeder" and, second, that Abena is more appealing and desirable when not ravaged or despoiled by pregnancy.

Tempted by the black body, Darnell gropes for Abena despite her resistance. Wanting to spare her body another act of violence, Abena attempts to kill Darnell in self-defense, an act for which she was hanged. Her execution, the swinging of her body from the branches of a silk-cotton tree, further emphasizes the worthlessness of the black female body as compared to the white body. Abena had managed only to gash Darnell's shoulder, and she was hanged for her attempts to disfigure the white body. The black body is often pierced and mutilated. For example, Yao swallowed his own tongue as if to suppress the repulsive body, and Tituba pierced John Indian's body to get some of his blood to ensure that he fell in love with her. Nonetheless, the worst form of body violation is committed on the female body. Sharing a fate similar to her mother, Abena, Tituba is raped—gang-raped at the hands of the Puritan ministers:

> The blow struck me across the mouth and drew blood. Confess that this is your doing, but that you did not act alone and denounce your accomplices. One of the men sat squarely astride me and began to hammer my face with his fists, which were as hard as stones. Another lifted up my skirt and thrust a sharpened stick into the most sensitive part of my body, taunting me: Go on, take it, it's John Indian's prick. When I was nothing more than a heap of suffering they stopped. They pounced on me again and it seemed as if the sharpened stick went right up to my throat. (91)

This rape scene, for which Tituba is eventually hanged, is revisited right before the slave uprising. Tituba dreamed that the Reverend Samuel Parris, John Indian, and Christopher, her maroon lover, "came up to [her] holding a thick, sharpened stick and [she] screamed: No, no haven't I gone through that?" (164). This memory elucidates the correlative relationship between Tituba and her mother, who had experienced similar bodily violation. The men in

Tituba's dream have all violated her body in one form or another. Though she is reduced to a "heap of suffering," all John Indian could think about as he pulled down Tituba's skirt over her violated thighs is the reproductive ability of her body. In response to her telling him that the Puritans wanted her to confess her faults even though she was not guilty, he tells her:

> Wife, my tortured wife! Once again you're making a mistake about what matters most. The important thing is to stay alive. If they ask you to denounce the others, denounce them! Give the name of half of Salem, if that's what they want! This world is not ours and if they want to set it on fire, our job is to stay away from the flames. Denounce anybody they tell you to! Guilty? Oh, yes, you are and you always will be in their eyes. The important thing is to keep yourself alive for yourself, for me . . . and for our unborn children! (92)

John Indian actively contributes to Tituba's torture, albeit psychological. His accusatory tone suggests his complicity with the patriarchy, represented by Parris, who implores Tituba to admit her guilt about her dealings in witchcraft. Earlier John Indian accuses Tituba of having black skin but wearing a white mask (32), referencing the title of Frantz Fanon's book *Black Skin, White Masks*. But in actuality, it is John Indian who is of black skin and wears a white mask. He is the stereotypical negro that Fanon talks about who is "historically steeped in [his] inessentiality of servitude, [refuses to] fight for his freedom [and] would like to be able to flee [his] blackness." An accomplice of Parris, John Indian betrays Tituba and surrenders her to the Puritans for her dealings in witchcraft. He, like the Puritans, denounces Tituba's art, witchcraft, and the essence of her being, a determinant factor in her life story and her life formation. It is the art of witchcraft that brings her and John Indian together. Paradoxically, it also stands at the root of her imprisonment and John Indian's later denouncement of her as a witch. Her being black and a woman, according to Pascale Bécel, only reinforces her stigmatization as a witch.[37]

Indeed, witchcraft is always linked to women, and being black Tituba is marked as a black witch with transgressive powers. Com-

37. Fanon, *Black Skin, White Masks*, 214, 219; Pascale Bécel, "*Moi, Tituba Sorciere . . . Noire de Salem* as a Tale of *Petite Marronne*," 611.

menting on her blackness and femaleness, the principal causes for her victimization, Tituba declares: "The color of John Indian's skin had not caused him half the trouble mine had caused me. Some of the ladies, however Puritan they might be, had not denied themselves the pleasure of flirting with him" (101). While the black female body is a site of oppression, the black male body is a site of pleasure. These injustices against women, all women, are pointedly addressed by Hester, Tituba's prison mate: "Don't talk to me about your wretched husband! He's no better than mine. Shouldn't he be here to share your sorrow? Life is too kind to men, whatever their color" (100). Like Tituba, Hester is not part of the society; she is also an outcast "locked up between the [prison] walls" (96). Hence, the women share a common bond of oppression: Hester is imprisoned for committing adultery, and Tituba is convicted and hanged for her witchcraft.

As with John Indian, Tituba's witchcraft attracted Christopher, the maroon leader and her eventual lover. From the inception of their brief relationship it is obvious that he is solely interested in self-aggrandizement as he implores Tituba to make him invincible in exchange for bodily pleasure: "[I]n exchange I'll give you everything a woman desires" (146). Unable to control her desires, she "gives in" to Christopher despite warnings of her ancestors and her own premonitions: "[H]adn't I had enough of men? Hadn't I had enough of the misfortune that goes with their affections?" (146). Tituba, having no or little control over her body, falls once again for the bait, occupying what Christopher terms her rightful place in society, not to "fight or make war, but to make love" (151). Ironically, when not violated by men, the female body is used for seductive purposes. As before, love does not bring Tituba salvation. She once again suffers betrayal at the hands of a man. Under the supervision of Christopher, she is led to the gallows, where she is hung and left to die. Her body that she repeatedly offers as a sacrifice is finally sacrificed. She becomes the sacrificial lamb.

In attempting to answer the question of why Tituba lives the kind of sexuality she does, Michelle Smith concludes that Tituba chooses "sex to avoid being forced to choose it." This might be true; however, the argument is not convincing enough and does not explain the kind of sexuality she experiences. Tituba's migration with John Indian was motivated merely by her desire to seduce him. Endeavoring to efface

the image of the black woman as sexually aggressive and promis-
cuous, Patricia Hill Collins highlights the importance of the need to
reconceptualize sexuality with an eye toward empowering African
American women.[38] This suggestion is fundamental; however, it is
seemingly apparent that this reconceptualization of female sexuality
has been widely interpreted to mean involvement in or with excessive sexual activities. Excessive sex has been employed in both novels
as a weapon for possibly restoring a nonoppressive, empowering
concept of female sexuality. While sex can be an empowering source,
it can also be disempowering. It harbors further objectification and
alienation of the subjects. Overly fond of sex, Tituba becomes a slave
to sex. The same can be said for Veronica, who willingly chooses sex
as a liberatory forum.

This medium is also alive in Condé's second novel, *A Season in
Rihata*. Sex for that novel's heroine, Marie-Hélène, is a life-giving
force: "She was tired, so tired and the only being to whom she could
stretch out her hands was him [Zek, her husband]. He leant over
her and playfully bit the nape of her neck. She pushed him away
irritably. He bit her lightly again; this time she did not object. This
pattern mirrored their relationship. At first she would refuse, and
he would insist; then she would give in, sometimes with passion."
Later, Madou, her brother-in-law and lover, questions happiness,
seeming to suggest that happiness should be attained whatever the
cost. Noticeably, it is the woman who pays: "Who had invented
such horrible words as sin and adultery? The main thing was to
be happy, and he had made Marie-Hélène happy. Thanks to him
she had stopped torturing herself; she had forgotten Zek, his nightly
absences and his infidelity. She had almost forgotten a past which
he knew was a painful one and about which he did not ask. And he
would make Sia [her daughter] happy too." Though the man is also
involved in this adulterous affair, it is the woman who suffers and
is deemed an adulterer. While Madou is freed during the sex acts,
sex only momentarily alleviates Marie-Hélène's sufferings. Enslaved
by its compelling force, she remains a victim, exiled and alienated.
Her fellow Antillean Veronica is no less a slave to sex. Her entire

38. Michelle Smith, "Reading in Circles: Sexuality and/as History in *I, Tituba,
Black Witch of Salem*," 606; P. Collins, *Black Feminist Thoughts*, 164.

life is structured around sex and sexual activity. Before her trip to Africa she broods over her previous sexual encounters: "[I]nstead of a balding wheezing white with a limp prick, I'd have myself a rich young mulatto with a permanent hard on."[39] As we observe, this sexual fantasy continues and is consummated with Sory in Africa.

Maryse Condé's protagonists choose sex as a means of belonging, to become a part of the community from which they are alienated and deemed outcasts. Sex becomes addictive, and like any other addiction the escape eventually becomes the cage. Tituba's referral to her boundless sexual acts as intoxication is apt and speaks to this addiction. As evidenced, choosing sex as a means of liberation and a means of acquiring or securing a home space is fallacious. Sex does not offer the redemptive power the protagonists seek. Tituba, in contrast to Marie-Hélène and Veronica, who seek redemption through sex, is redeemed not by her sexual activity but by her rootedness in ancestral heritage, her spirituality, her healing powers and ability to communicate with the invisible world. In spite of societal pressure (Susan Endicott and friends try to convert her to Christianity; Reverend Parris, John Indian, and Christopher try to discredit her knowledge and art), Tituba remains undaunted and rooted in her tradition and never refutes her knowledge in spite of the negative reception it receives. Tituba's witchcraft is viewed as a presumptuous act that exists outside the rules of patriarchal authority. Her witchcraft, quoting Bécel, "defines a counter discourse to the 'essence' of white presence and domination, embodied by the plantation system and the Puritan society."[40]

By fully appropriating her knowledge of witchcraft, Tituba questions the Puritans' authenticating themselves and their religious beliefs as models for all people regardless of their orientation. She also questions the discrediting and devaluing of her religion. She subverts the notion of witchcraft as evil. In her view, a sorceress is a gifted person—"not just anyone could set herself up as a witch" (17)—someone who cares and possesses clairvoyant abilities:

> It made me think. What is a witch? I noticed that when he [John Indian] said the word, it was marked with disapproval. Why should that be?

39. Condé, *A Season in Rihata*, 134, 179; Condé, *Heremakhonon*, 10.
40. Bécel, *"Moi, Tituba Sorciere,"* 611.

Why? Isn't the ability to communicate with the invisible world, to keep constant links with the dead, to care for others and heal, a superior gift of nature that inspires respect, admiration, and gratitude? Consequently, shouldn't the witch (if that's what the person who has this gift is to be called) be cherished and revered rather than feared? (17)

Tituba refuses to accept the negative connotation attached to the word *witch* or *sorceress* and claims her religion, proudly referring to herself as a witch. Contrasting colonialist beliefs, her witchcraft is geared toward doing good for all, regardless of color, class, or creed. Tituba's power benefits the community. She eases the pain of Reverend Parris's sickly wife, and before she is accused of doing devil work, she attempts to do kind things for his children. She also nurtures Benjamin Cohen d'Azevedo, a Jewish man and her eventual lover, and cares for his nine children. Tituba's story is "a counter-narrative to western historical perspectives on oppressed and colonized peoples."[41]

Tituba dismantles all misconceptions and subverts the notion of witchcraft as evil and ignominious. This concept of positive sorcery is central to the text. It is an act that reclaims and embraces the past, the African rituals and practices. Valerie Lee notes that "rather than the negative associations of witchcraft, conjuring has been an empowering concept for many black women. Conjuring pays homage to an African past, while proving a present day idiom for magic, power and ancient wisdom." Possessing conjuring powers, Tituba has access to the earthly world—the world within which the Puritans exist—and the world of the ancestors, which is inaccessible to the Puritan society. Hence, Tituba is doubly empowered. On one hand, Tituba's connection with Africa and African practices gives her legendary status, and on the other hand, her witchcraft represents her resilience, strength, and relationship with the island and her ancestors Mama Yaya and Abena. Her great conjuring ability helps her maintain a strong connection with her native island, her mother's land, Barbados, and her mothers, Mama Yaya and Abena, even while living in isolation and exile and despite the physical distance. Tituba has a unique connection with her motherlands, Africa and the Caribbean. Snitgen hints at this connection when

41. Ibid., 608.

she observes that "many Caribbean [islands], born collectively of imperialist aggression, are an offspring rejected by the aggressed—here, Africa—and the unknown by the aggressor—Europe—and misunderstood by both." Like the islands, Tituba's birth results from "imperialist" aggression. As the offspring of both the aggressed and the aggressor, she is rejected by her mother, Abena, and is ridiculed and misunderstood by the Puritan society, which is representative of her white father. She is misperceived by the Puritans and her mother for different reasons. The Puritans' misunderstanding stems from the fact that they are unable to penetrate her religion, while her mother is unable to comprehend her desire for men who repeatedly betray her. Nonetheless, Tituba eventually redirects her digressions and negotiates for maternal love, which is facilitated by her blood mother, Abena, and her "othermother," Mama Yaya. This love is manifested in the constant spiritual contact she engages with her mothers and her unwavering practice of African rituals and cultures. This ongoing engagement with the mother(lands) reinforces her subjectivity. Noting the West Indian's alienation, Snitgen concludes that "because of this is(le)olation the West Indian must search for an independent identity. [She] must establish herself as a viable subject, which looks neither to Europe, nor to Africa but to a Caribbean past for its (fictional) origins. Since this 'history' has been undocumented or lost, another must be created."[42]

Indeed, an individual Caribbean identity and history must be constructed. However, the complexities of constructing a new "invented" identity should not be overlooked. Though this identity should not be modeled after Europe or Africa, some form of historical reliance is necessary to construct this self. The past, though reconstructed, must be incorporated in this identity formation. The West Indian past is intricately linked first and foremost to the Motherland, Africa, for the inhabitants are descendants of Africans and, second, to the colonized, the mother country—England, France, or the United States—which lays claim to the peoples through colonization. As a West Indian born of an African mother and a European father, Tituba represents this link. Therefore, she embodies the complex Caribbean

---

42. Valerie Lee, *Granny Midwives and Black Women Writers: Double-Dutched Readings,* 13; Snitgen, "History," 59.

identity. She cannot completely dismiss either of her identities, nor can she absolutely divorce herself from the past, because she exemplifies the trichotomy: the mother, the motherland, and the mother country. Uniting her composite parts to create a new individualistic Caribbean identity, focused, Tituba never loses sight of who she is and from whence she came. Preserving a stable, continuous identity, Tituba is "at home" with herself. Her quest for subjectivity is completed when she returns to her native Barbados.

Upon her return "home," Tituba is bestowed with the honorary title "Mother": "[H]onor us, mother, with your presence" (142). Her confession, "[Y]es, I'm happy now. I can *understand* the past, *read* the present, and *look into* the future," speaks of her attainment of ancient knowledge and wisdom (178; emphasis added). A seasoned soothsayer, she is bestowed with seeing and visionary powers to understand, read, and penetrate. She spent her remaining days on her island, despite her confession of "how ugly [her] town was! Small. Petty. A colonial outpost of no distinction, reeking with the stench of lucre and suffering" (141). Yet, the island is alive with a soft murmur: "[S]he is back. She is here, the daughter of Abena, the daughter of Mama Yaya. She will never leave us again" (147). For Tituba, returning home to her island space, to her old cabin, is a liberatory move. Her home space is not equated with female domesticity, oppression, and subjugation, but is a site of liberation and self-expression. Home for Tituba is not a site of domination and conflict. Rather, home is liberating. It is a site of tranquillity and comfort. It is a place where she acquires visibility. Her return is not plagued with mystification because she does not have an imaginary, romanticized vision of home. Despite its dilapidation, she manages to enjoy the island's peace and freedom because she possesses a stabilized concept of home and self. For Tituba, home always was and is (pre)figured as the island of Barbados.

Home, in spite of its multiple definitions in theoretical works by other women, is a specific, concretized location in this novel and for Tituba. It is not in Carlisle Bay where she met John Indian; Mama Yaya avouches this fact as she refers to Tituba's moving there as being "dragged off to the other side" (15). It is not Farley Hill, the maroon camp where she took up residence with Christopher and the other maroons, in spite of the ancestors' displeasure. Her voicing

"I'm going home" says it all. It is on the other side, the "mysterious, and secret side, composed of passwords, whispers, and a conspiracy of silence. It is on this side that [she] lives, protected by common collusion" (156). The conspiracy of silence denies outsiders, whose agenda is to discredit her art, access to her ancestral world. This world need not be documented in the history books for it to be remembered or validated. Tituba validates it as she confesses: "I do not belong to the civilization of the Bible and Bigotry. My people will keep my memory in their hearts and have no need for the written word. It's in their heads. In their hearts and in their heads. Since I died without giving birth to a child, the spirits have allowed me to choose a descendant" (176). Here, on the other side, is where she becomes one with the island and the ancestors. As spiritual mother, mother and land merge, fostering Tituba's mothering of the land and its people. Bestowed the honorable title of "Mother," Tituba experiences the joy of motherhood. Proudly acknowledging her descendant, Samantha, she declares: "A child I didn't give birth to but whom I chose! What motherhood could be nobler!" (177). Hence, Tituba embodies the mother(land). She becomes in touch with herself through her island:

> I am never alone. There's Mama Yaya, Abena, my mother, Yao, Iphigene, and Samantha. And then there is my island. We have become one and the same. There isn't one of its footpaths I haven't trod. There isn't one of its streams I haven't bathed in. There isn't one of its silk-cotton trees in whose branches I haven't sat. This constant and extraordinary symbiosis is my revenge for my long solitude in the deserts of America. A vast, cruel land where the spirits only beget evil. (177)

In her dearly (be)loved island space, Tituba is never alone. She is always protected by the watchful eyes of her mothers, Mama Yaya and Abena.

The presence of mother figures facilitates a (re)construction of the homesite. Female elders are crucial links in this (re)construction, as strongly evidenced in *Tituba*. These ancestral figures establish and bolster that link with "home." Marie-Hélène's and Veronica's concepts of home (space) is linked to a nostalgic, romanticized notion, primarily as a result of the absence of ancestral figures. Home is a nonexistent, imaginary community. Maryse Condé actively contributes to the fostering of these romanticized, imaginary homelands by the nonnaming or fictitious naming of the African countries in *Heremakhonon* and *Rihata*. The fictitious naming of these places can also be seen as Condé's dispelling the mythic notion of a "true," concretized home in the Motherland, Africa.

Distilling the romantic vision of Africa, in *Tituba*, Condé reclaims the mother's land, Barbados. The island is named and claimed as the homesite and is indisputably figured as the homeland. Hence, *Tituba* demythologizes and dispels the mythic or imaginary creation of home space. This demythologizing is facilitated by the guidance of ancestral figures and the possession of spiritual essence. The novel restores Tituba, a black Caribbean woman, to history. Angela Davis best explains Tituba's resurgence into history in the foreword to *Tituba*: "Tituba leaps into history, shattering all the racist and misogynist misconceptions that have defined the place of black women. Tituba's revenge consists in having persuaded one of her descendants to rewrite her moment in history in her own African oral tradition. And when Tituba takes her place the history of that era—and indeed the entire history of the colonization process—is revealed to be seriously flawed" (x). Because the historical records have selectively excluded Tituba from the pages of history, she was forced to revert to her memory, to "her own African oral tradition" that fosters the inclusion of the black woman in history.

4 "An/Other Way of Knowing Things"

Ancestral Line(age), Revalidating Our Ancestral Inheritances

Read and write I don't know. Other things *I know.*

—*Jean Rhys,* Wide Sargasso Sea

We are very practical people, very down-to-earth, even shrewd people. But within that practicality we also accepted what I suppose could be called superstition and magic, which is another way of knowing things. *But to blend these two worlds together at the same time was enhancing, not limiting. And some of those* things *were "discredited knowledge" that Black people had; discredited only because Black people were discredited therefore what they knew was "discredited."*

—*Toni Morrison, "Rootedness: The Ancestor as Foundation"*
(emphasis added)

The first quote was uttered by Jean Rhys's protagonist and ancestress, Christophine, in response to Edward Rochester's suggestion that she write Bertha (Antoinette) Mason Rochester, his wife, and Christophine's surrogate daughter. The "other things" that Jean Rhys's black protagonist, Christophine, brags about knowing, on one hand, assert her sense of self, and on the other hand, speak of her unwavering acceptance of the supernatural world, a world of magic, a world discredited by white folks and embraced by blacks. Toni Morrison questions the "validity or vulnerability of a certain set of assumptions conventionally accepted among literary historians and critics and circulated as 'knowledge.'" This accepted knowledge in Morrison's observation purports its exclusivity, thus laying claim that "traditional, canonical American literature is free of, uninformed and unshaped by the four-hundred-year-old presence of, first, Africans and then African-Americans and [diasporan

136

peoples]."[1] Christophine's embrace of the supernatu
refusal to write or read or both is a denouncement of tl
that emphasizes the written and de-emphasizes the
her strong beliefs in and revalidation of "an/other wa
things." This "other [way of knowing] things," as Toni Morrison
aptly observes, is discredited and deemed inconsequential because
of the source of the knowledge—black folks. Giving credence to
the (black) supernatural world, Morrison calls for a blending and
acceptance of it, at the same time maintaining a profound rootedness
in the "real" world. However, the two worlds, the real and the
supernatural, appear to be constantly at odds with each other, and
as such, this blending and acceptance of both worlds are not easily
achieved and pose a constant struggle. The conflict between the real
and the supernatural worlds is symbolic of the struggle between the
mother country, the metropole, and the motherlands, Africa and the
Caribbean. This struggle is also an indirect war of the oral versus
the written, for the supernatural is embedded in orality and the real
world claims authenticity as a result of its literary representation.
Thus, the motherlands are engrossed in an ongoing struggle for
recognition by the colonial mother country, whose agenda is to
discredit the supernatural, rejecting the oral, the so-called undocumented, while authenticating the written. This discrediting distances
the supernatural world from the real, and often the supernatural is
seen as oppositional. It is this very distancing and rejection of the
supernatural by the so-called real by mainstream European theorists
that have perversely stimulated interest in many black women writers. One such writer is Paule Marshall who constantly juxtaposes the
two worlds in her works. This juxtaposition is ostensibly her attempt
at negotiation, a blending and acceptance of both worlds.

The struggle between the two worlds, the real and the supernatural, the mother country and the motherlands, orality versus the
written, is given full representation in Marshall's novels *Brown Girl,
Brownstones* and *Praisesong for the Widow*. The existing struggle in
these two novels lends credence to Morrison's observation that the
drive toward upward social mobility is in direct conflict with and

1. Toni Morrison, *Playing in the Dark: Whiteness and the Literary Imagination*,
4–5.

strongly opposes the supernatural world. Far from being in dialogue with each other, these two worlds are constantly, in the case of *Brown Girl, Brownstones*, and momentarily in *Praisesong for the Widow*, at war. Notwithstanding, Marshall is entirely aware of the need for the ancestors, having confessed to being an unabashed ancestor worshiper. Her novels appropriately address the importance of an ancestress or ancestral figure with a profound rootedness in the supernatural or ancestral world.[2] Morrison strongly emphasizes the ancestor as the foundation, as a life-giving source or force who guides those in need of direction and guidance (back) to and into the ancestral world. This theme is given full attention in her article quoted earlier and appropriately titled "Rootedness: The Ancestor as Foundation." Perpetuating the tradition practiced by Morrison, Marshall stresses the need for and the importance of the ancestor, who functions as the anchor of both the real and the ancestral worlds. Nonetheless, she does not propose a downright rejection of the "real" world. Instead, like Morrison, she suggests possible integration of the two worlds.

Introduced in *Brown Girl, Brownstones,* the ancestral theme–cum–ancestral worshiping comes full circle only in *Praisesong for the Widow*, a novel that exalts the widowed protagonist, Avey (Avatara) Johnson, with praisesongs, as it pays homage to the ancestors, to the "Old Time People."[3] Thematically joined, Marshall's two novels, plus her novel *The Chosen Place, the Timeless People*, celebrate the act of coming or going "home," a spiritual homecoming.

The title of Marshall's first novel, *Brown Girl, Brownstones,* suggests the struggle that exists within the novel. The juxtaposition of the physical brown girl with the material brownstones, on one hand, illuminates the existing conflict and, on the other hand, calls for a blending, a medium where the dualities can coexist. At the heart of this struggle is the brown girl, the heroine of the novel, Selina Boyce, who stands in opposition to white Eurocentric values symbolized by the brownstones. Selina is led to believe by her mother, Silla Boyce, and the Bajan community that the acquisition of brownstones will

---

2. The words *supernatural* and *ancestral* will be used interchangeably in the course of this discussion.

3. Marshall employs the term *Old Time People* to refer to the ancestors, emphasizing their ancient powers and resilience.

secure her future and grant her acceptance and easy assimilation into the white capitalist world, and thereafter her quest for subjectivity and achievement of independence will be realized. However, Selina soon realizes that obsessive acquisition of material wealth inhibits the quest for selfhood, functioning as a deterrent to self-growth and development. This inhibition is ironically manifested in the powerful mother, Silla Boyce.

Born and raised on the Caribbean island of Barbados, Silla Boyce along with many other West Indian (Barbadian) immigrants came to the United States during what is now commonly referred to as the second "wave," a period between the Great Depression and 1965. Heather Hathaway notes that this second wave was "much smaller than the first, encompassing an average of no more than three thousand Caribbeaners per year." She adds that "movement during this wave ebbed and flowed according to economic factors and immigration laws. . . . [B]y the height of the Depression . . . it was reduced to a virtual standstill."[4] The stringent economic situation in the Caribbean forced many to leave the Caribbean shores for "greener" pastures. Like many West Indians, in pursuit of a "better" life, Silla was sent to the United States by her mother on a quest for this "new and better" life. She in turn vows to perpetuate the tradition by professing to provide an even better life for her two daughters, Ina and Selina. It is with this aim in mind that Silla diligently pursues her childhood dream of attaining economic and social stability.

Leasing a brownstone apartment on Fulton Street, Brooklyn, Silla's intent, like that of the other Barbadian immigrants on this quest for upward mobility, is to eventually own one of these brownstones, a mark of status in the community, a sign that suggests one "has reached." A member of the dispossessed, the disfranchised and disempowered, Silla's claim to the city is the possession of a brownstone. However, the possession of brownstones, as is apparent,

---

4. Heather Hathaway, *Caribbean Waves: Relocating Claude McKay and Paule Marshall*, 13. Hathaway chronicles the three phases or "waves" of West Indian immigrants to the United States, "the first of which took place between 1900 and 1930 and reached its peak in the 1920s. The second fell between the Depression and 1965," and the third was "after World War II until the passage of the McCarran-Walter Act in 1952" (12–13).

comes with severe consequences. It calls for the relinquishment of the Caribbean homeland and dispossession of the (spiritual) self. Embittered by her underprivileged past, Silla in one of her many attempts to sever connection with her homeland no longer refers to it by its official name—Barbados. Her refusal to use the official name of her homeland renders it insignificant. Once a source of pride, joy, and perpetual sunlight, Barbados is now regarded as the dismal past, conveniently buried by the New York–based Bajan community. Obsessed with owning a brownstone, Silla suffers derailment and momentarily loses her sense of self, and as a result, her life soon begins to mirror the brownstones—bleak, monotonous, and void of life and color, "draped in ivy as though mourning."[5] This sorrowful image signals the imminent death of the "real" self, suggestive that Silla is forced to relinquish her "old" self, equally renouncing her soul, in order to acquire a "new" self. She seemingly has no choice but to meet the United States on its own terms. Her imminent loss of self is symbolized by her "moving away," her alienation from that "other way of knowing things," and her indirect denouncing of the ancestral world. By escaping the ancestral world, Silla simultaneously relinquishes her ancestral inheritances and her knowledge of "other things." Ensnared in this web of capitalist, colonialist values, Silla is blinded and becomes less and less sensible, eventually losing her practicality and thereafter her soul.[6]

Stripped of selfhood and zombified by capitalist values, Silla is in a trancelike state, but she is not aware of it at the time of its occurrence. She annihilates everything and everyone who crosses her path or exhibits the tiniest inclination of disrupting her quest of becoming a property owner. Ironically and tragically, her husband, Deighton Boyce, is the one that bears the brunt of her fierce anger. In contrast to his wife, Silla, Deighton is not interested in possessing brownstones. His dream is to return to the islands, a place that

5. Marshall, *Brown Girl, Brownstones,* 3. Future citations will be given parenthetically in the text.

6. Here I am suggesting that the ride to upward mobility, often mistaken for a joyride, is tumultuous and riddled with mishaps and irrecoverable losses and misfortunes. Blinded, Silla becomes subsumed by colonialist values and loses her soul, her spiritual side.

he characterizes as poverty stricken yet serene and dreamlike. He explains to his daughter Selina, who is anxious to learn about his homeland: "Barbados is poor-poor but sweet enough. That's why I going back" (11). Deighton's desire is to escape the suffocating walls of the brownstones and return to the island where he envisions "liv[ing] in style. No little board and shingle house with a shed roof to cook in" (11). His dreams are about to be realized when he receives a letter from an old aunt in the islands informing him that he has inherited property from his dead sister. This is a moment of revelation for Deighton, a moment when he can stand tall against the Barbadian community that has long ostracized him from their societal midst because he refuses to "think brownstones." Deighton views the owning of property on home soil as worthy, as a meaningful asset: "Now let those bad-minded Bajan here talk my name 'cause I only leasing this house while they buying theirs" (12). His belief stands in stark contrast to the Bajan community that places much more value on property ownership in the United States, perceiving this acquisition on foreign turf as making a statement, laying claims to the city or the country or both. Aware of the brutality of racism and discrimination, Deighton still believes that having ownership of "two acres almost [is] a lot in a place that's only 199 square miles— and a lot for a colored man to own in a place where the white man own everything" (25). Deighton's comments attest to the fact that Barbados mirrors the United States in that it is owned and controlled by whites, yet the distinction between the two places lies in the fact that Barbados is "poor-poor but sweet enough" and will always be, at least in his eyes.

In spite of his optimism, Deighton's dreams never come to fruition. After Silla finds out about his possession and unsuccessfully implores him to sell his land to purchase the brownstones, she decides to act: she forges his signature and thereby instructs his old aunt to sell the land. Silla in turn is tricked by Deighton, who retaliates by spending every cent of the money she received from the sale of the land. While Silla's act goes unnoticed by the community, Deighton is ostracized, condemned for his action, and sentenced to a lifetime of exile. Ironically, his sentencing is pronounced at a wedding ceremony, a ritual that symbolizes and commemorates new beginnings and continuities.

The wedding with its timely and arduous preparation somewhat mimics a carnival, where the participants are masked and disguised. To characterize this wedding purely as the site of communal celebration is clearly misleading and far from the truth. First, the wedding came about because a Bajan girl, 'Gatha Steed's daughter, fell in love with a boy from outside the Bajan community, an African American. Appalled by this audacity, the mother decides to marry her daughter off to "one of her own," a Bajan boy. The marriage was not one based on love; what was important to the mothers and the community was that it was a wedding to celebrate "oneness" within the Bajan community. It is rather ironic that their principle of "oneness" is based on exclusivity (excluded are Deighton and to a lesser extent his daughter Selina and the bride and the groom). Hence, this concept of "oneness" and community, while somewhat thwarted, speaks of the carnivalesque atmosphere that prevailed at the wedding. The Bajans' concept of "oneness" is their utopian vision of their community. The slogan "All o' we are one" is misleading and applies only to those who are willing to follow suit and not change or alter the course of the ride to upward mobility. In its perverse way, the Bajan community equates the acquisition of property with the acquisition of "wholeness." Having inherited land from an old aunt, Deighton is envied by Silla and the community for "making it," despite his not working hard. This "toil free" acquisition creates further distance between him and the community.

Although staged for 'Gatha Steed's daughter and her "chosen" Bajan boyfriend, the wedding was defined as " 'Gatha Steed's daughter's wedding" (134). It is rather interesting that neither the daughter nor her intended husband is referred to by name; instead, they are nameless, lacking definite identities. Robbed of identities and suffocated by the powerful mother, they go unnoticed:

> At both ends of the bridal table a pair of lovebirds carved out of ice kissed and slowly melted. Atop the six multi-tiered wedding cakes little painted bridal couples kissed under the icing trellis. *The fervor of these artificial lovers mocked the real bridal pair.* The bride sat in *wan resignation* before the cakes and lighted candles, barely smiling as the guests kissed her and wished her happiness, while the groom whom her mother had chosen twisted around in his seat to shake each guest's hand, his neck bulging out of his collar as he laughed. (138; emphasis added)

In contrast to the bride's entrance is her mother's grand entrance:

> An *impressive bustle* at the rear of the church silenced those invited. The ushers' hands described a frenzied arabesque now as a small figure draped in white appeared against the sunlight in the doorway. *The ushers hurried her and the bridal party behind a screen.* Then, in silence that was as tumid as the heat, they took down the white rope that closed off the middle aisle, and 'Gatha Steed, *vivid in green satin,* swept, *rustling mightily,* down the aisle. (137; emphasis added)

'Gatha Steed's strong, colonizing-like figure drowns out her daughter's miniature (colonized) figure. The bride's whiteness, emblematic of paleness and death, stands in stark contrast to her mother, who is bedecked in green satin: green, symbolic of youth, freshness, and vitality. Her satiny, smooth, sunlit look devours her daughter's small stature, draped in white. Like the bride, Selina Boyce is a bemused onlooker and a reluctant participant in the ceremony: "Selina averted her eyes from the bride, afraid that if she looked at her she would carry the bride's defeat and resignation as a blemish always on her mind" (138). Aware that the wedding is not for her, Selina sympathizes with the reluctant bride, but refuses to identify with her.

Far from celebrating the beginning of a love affair, this wedding celebration signals the end of a love affair and a marriage, the end of the marriage of Silla and Deighton Boyce. The participants of the Bajan community were giving Deighton a ritualized "send-off," banishing him for life from their community. While celebrating her husband's banishment, they simultaneously celebrate Silla's tenacity: her purchase of a brownstone, in spite of Deighton's so-called betrayal. Keenly observing the "spectacle," Selina determines that "the wedding was really for the mother. In her honor. The flowers and candles, the decorations. . . . [A]ll the cakes were not there for the broken bride but for the mother. Suddenly she understood that exaggerated bow the mother had given everyone in the church. She too must have sensed that the wedding was really for her" (139). Under false pretense, the Bajan community was actually celebrating the purchase of another brownstone, a subtle endorsement and worshiping of capitalist values. Silla had become an honorary member of the house owners' club, and they were celebrating her membership. Ironically, it is "the great 'Gatha Steed" (whose last name has resonance with the word *steel*), the proud owner of "many house[s] . . . three" (73), the same 'Gatha Steed who was condemned by Silla for being "nothing but a black guard [who] get on like she never christened" (73), who welcomes Silla into the community. Only the observant Selina is able to detect the falsity of the community.

Silla momentarily appears to disrupt the community's ride to social status and expose its falsity:

> The voices still clamored around them but Selina noticed that the mother was no longer listening. People still shouted their congratulations about the house but their words seemed to bring no joy now. They cried loud their condemnation of Deighton but strangely she did not join them any more. She did not, even as they called her name, make the elaborate bow. A shadow might have swept the room and crossed her face, for her elation was suddenly gone, and a sad line pulled at her mouth. Glancing up at her, Selina saw the same muted longing she had seen in the church when the mother had watched her friends with their husbands. (139)

Torn between her allegiance for her fellow Bajans and her outcast and demonized husband, Silla experiences momentary longing for her old life and the world she left behind. Her yearning is her questioning of her and the newly constructed Bajan community's motives for property acquisition: "What is the old house for wunna to make such a fuss over it, nuh? Houses! That's all the talk. Houses! When you does have to do some of everything short of murder to get them sometimes. I tell you, I tired enough hearing about them" (142–43). Silla momentarily pledges allegiance to her husband, seemingly joining arms with him in denouncing obsessive and excessive property acquisition. This loyalty is most palpable in her repeating the same words he had uttered to her when he found out she had outsmarted him of his property: "[Y]ou does have to do some of everything short of murder." This confession is suggestive of a silent agreement between Silla and her husband: excessive accumulation of material possessions bears the imprint of murderous acts. Ironically, this mutual agreement and trust between husband and wife are breached by Silla. Refusing to appear crushed and broken in front of the community, she soon regains her composure and vows "to get" Deighton: "I . . . don care if the man was to drop . . . dead . . . tonight-self. . . . Come—le'we drink" (143). Silla's premonition came true: Deighton subsequently "drop[ped] dead" by plunging to his death.

Before Deighton's physical death he had suffered a social death at the hands of the Bajan community. His exclusion precipitates his spiritual death and subsequently his physical death. Deighton had failed not only Silla but also the entire community, "for somehow their respect would mean his mastery of all of life; their contempt his failure" (135). He did not measure up to the community's expectation or, more appropriately, the mothers' expectations, because he did not acquire the necessary qualifications for communal membership—the acquisition of brownstones—and for this he was severely punished by and ostracized from the community. Deighton becomes the enemy for his refusal to "think brownstones," a refusal that in the community's eyes blurs his vision and reasoning, as it evidences his lack of (colonialist, capitalist) values and clear judgments. Deighton's ostracism equals obliteration, for he becomes invisible. It is rather ironic that his invisibility is celebrated through an extremely visual art form—dance. While everyone partakes of the dance, Deighton stands outside, alone, on the periphery of the Ring Dance:

> She [Selina] glimpsed a man standing in the doorway. She saw only his *legs, but their stillness in the midst of all the movement* arrested her, and the stance reminded her vaguely of her father. Deighton *stood uncommitted,* between the summer night filled with faces behind him and the brilliant scene in the hall. He might have been one of the *silent surging mob outside* who had been shoved by them into the light—or a guest who had purposely arrived late and *waited, poised, for his presence to be noted and his name murmured throughout the room.* His smile was ready. (149; emphasis added)

Another point of irony is the Bajan community's enactment of the Ring Dance, an African ritualized practice that celebrates togetherness and unity, to brutally exclude Deighton from their midst. Danced by the members of the Bajan community, the Ring Dance, representative of circularity and continuity, contrastingly speaks of a selective continuum rather than an unrestricted diasporic union. This selective processing is appropriately challenged by Selina, who refuses to join in the Ring Dance and instead opts to stand next to her father on the periphery of the circle. Mocked and ridiculed, Deighton is left alone to bear his sufferings:

Her [Silla's] hand half lifted as though to beckon him. . . . But even as he took the first tentative step forward, her *hand dropped and her derisive laugh drove him back.* The mother laughed, the song soared: "Small island, go back where you from. . . ." And *both sound tore his thin composure apart.* His eyes wheeled over the room in a desperate search for a single welcoming face. To the bar, but the men there had seen him, and as his eyes met theirs, as his hand lifted uncertainly, they turned away with cold nods, and *their backs formed a wall against him.* His eyes then swung in a wide arc to the dancers. . . . But they had seen him by now and they closed protectively around Silla and Ina; like the men at the bar, the *dancers turned in one body and danced with their backs to him.* (150; emphasis added)

Dance, which expresses communal life, is used as a social statement to denounce Deighton's actions, his "irregular behavior." Similar to his island characterized by its sunlight, but now standing somber, Deighton, who was always heralded by sunlight, brightness, and vivacity, now stands somber and aloof, apart from the community.[7] His aloofness is further illuminated by the timely song, and the words are undoubtedly meant for him: "Small island, go back where you from." It is extremely paradoxical that they refer to Deighton as "small island," when it is this same small island, Barbados, that binds the Bajan community. As a newly constructed community they are inferring that the acquisition of material wealth has made them larger than the island itself, yet, when others, so-called outsiders, want to join the society, they conveniently exclude them by laying claim to their small island. Not only is Deighton condemned, but so is the place from whence he came, his mother's land, Barbados: "Those eyes condemned him and their voices rushed full tilt at him, scourging him and finally driving him from their presence with their song, "Small Island, go back where you really come from!" (150). Bearing the brunt of the community's anger, Deighton and *his* island become one. His standing alone is representative of the island and contrasts the dancers "turned in one body" against him. Apparently, his "small island" mirrors his small mind, because he refuses to "think big," refuses to "think brownstones."

7. Deighton, who is defined by his vivacity, is always equated with sunlight and the island, while his wife, Silla, is equated with the coldness of the winter and the somberness of the brownstones.

Deighton's invisibility is obvious from the onset of the novel. His illegal entry into the country denies him an identity and speaks volumes of his invisibility. He is an undocumented, illegal alien, and is therefore nonexistent. Deighton's invisibility resonates with Ralph Ellison's *Invisible Man*. Leaving his mother's land for the metropole, he becomes the colonized "other," doubly othered by the United States and the Bajan community. In Deighton resides the conflict of the American Dream and the reality of American life. He, like the Invisible Man, journeys to New York only to find out that life was deceptively free. As if he had not "enough to bear" (157), shortly after his exile from the Bajan community, Deighton is injured on his job. His arm is incapacitated, crippling him further, adding insult to injury and further intensifying his invisibleness. His handicap is symbolic of emasculation. Appearing to lose his manhood, Deighton comments on his hospitalization: "I was up there in a nightgown like some woman, and all around me people hawking and spitting up their insides and crying for pain" (159). Deighton is aware of his invisibility, but is unable to capitalize on it and use it as a tool of power over those who do not see him. Instead, Deighton's invisibility renders him powerless.

Already an outcast of the Bajan community, Deighton further compounds his identity and invisibility as he foolishly joins another community, headed by the self-acclaimed religious leader Father Peace. Father Peace's kingdom does not cater to family and family needs, and upon entering his kingdom a follower is compelled to give up his identity: "[W]hen a person reached God he cannot permit an earthly wife or so-called children to lead him away. God is all!" (168–69). Noticeably, Father Peace's organization is made up solely of men, further hinting at Deighton's emasculation. Selina confirms his emasculation, questioning his inability to access power: "What was it that made her father unfit to do the same [rule]? Why was he the *seduced follower* and not the god . . . ?" (169). Deighton relinquishes not only his identity and manhood but also fatherhood. "His substance was irretrievably lost" (170), yet his emasculation is again given full attention. Upon his return home from the hospital, he refuses to enter the room and the bed he once shared with his wife, Silla: "No. That's yuh mother bed. Lemma go to the sun parlor, where I can breathe fresh air. *He lay down fully clothed*, the newspaper next to him and the bandaged arm across his chest. *His whole body seemed as limp as that arm.* All of him might have been sucked into the machine and crushed. And because he was so limp, he seemed quiet inside. A kind of dead peace hovered over him" (158; emphasis added). The room that was once a comfort zone for both husband and wife now suffocates Deighton and inhibits his manhood. He is further stripped of his manhood by the machine that has sucked and crushed his arm and his identity. This machine represents industrialization and capitalism, represented by the United States, and is indicative of the self-annihilation that the individual suffers in blind pursuit of material wealth. Without a doubt, Deighton believes that the United States is a powerful contributor to his emasculation.

Reminiscing about his dream home on the island with his daughter Selina, he vows to reclaim his masculinity and assert power over his wife: "[E]ven your mother can come [to Barbados], but she gon have to watch that mouth. I gon be firm with she 'cause it'll be my house and my land and I ain gon stand for no foolishness" (87). Deighton's comment suggests that property acquisition in the United States does not reflect self-ownership because one will always be tied to colonizing principles and be forced to compromise his or her identity. A clear indication of this compromise is characterized in the Bajan community, which has had to relinquish its past in order to exist in the present, the United States. Deighton's statement, "even your mother can come," suggests that in contrast to the United States, Barbados welcomes the individual on his or her own terms. He fantasizes about the island and considers it his port of redemption, but he later overturns his own fantasy when he recalls suffering a similar fate, rejection, in his homeland. He is brutally reminded of this when he "comes face to face" with the law, after Silla reports his illegal entry into the United States to the immigration authority:

> He studied the policeman's face and in his shattered mind it became the white faces in the stores of Bridgetown. Those faces, stippled red by the tropic sun, that had always refused his request for a clerk's job and thus turned the years at school, and his attempts to be like them in his dark wool English-cut suits, and his face clean though black—into nothing; that had utterly *unmanned him* before he was yet a man; that

had *stripped him of any possibility of self* and then hustled him out. . . . He laid his hand in resignation on the policeman's shoulder and said, "yes, officer, they did call me Deighton Boyce." (182; emphasis added)

"Unmanned" even before he was a man, Deighton is unable to regain his selfhood, his sense of self, and his self-worth. It is of great significance that Deighton's surname, Boyce, spells *boy*, the role to which he shamelessly acquiesces. His comment "they did call me Deighton Boyce" speaks of his effacement, his resignation, and ultimately his death. This comment was probably meant as foreboding, for Deighton plunges to his death in the Caribbean Sea en route to the island.

Evidently, the black man's identity is threatened and challenged in capitalist-oriented societies, namely, the United States. While the men are marginal characters in the novel, the women are at the forefront of the struggle. Their visibility stands in stark contrast to the men's invisibility. While Deighton goes unnoticed, Silla needs no introduction. She is simply referred to as "the mother," indicative of her power and her visibility. Deighton's constant referring to her, "You's God, you must know," attests to her powerful presence. Whereas the men are emasculated, the women adopt a masculine, patriarchal, colonial image. Silla embodies this colonial, patriarchal image, and her presence stifles, while it seemingly devours everything and everyone:

She [Selina] had decided to kill them [a train of ants] when she sensed the mother, and her hand paused mid-air. It was strange how Selina always sensed her. Even before she looked up and over to the park she knew that she would see the mother there striding home. . . . Silla Boyce brought the theme of winter into the park with her dark dress amid the summer green and the bright-figured dresses of the women lounging on the benches. Not only that, every line of her strong-made body seemed to reprimand the women for their idleness and the park for its senseless summer display. Her lips, set in a permanent protest against life, implied that there was no time for gaiety. And the park, the women, the sun even gave way to her dark force; the flushed summer colors ran together and faded as she passed. There was something . . . in the angle of her head that added to Selina's uneasiness. It was as though the mother knew all that had transpired in the house since morning—her father's idleness, her quarrel with Ina, the news of the land—and was coming to chastise them all. (16)

Silla's mere presence rebukes the community, sentencing every-one to death or silence as she passes judgment on friends and foes alike. She exerts power over the entire community by convincing and willing the community to join forces with her and sign a petition for the eviction of Suggie, her tenant and Selina's othermother, "as an undesirable tenant by other roomers [who] swore that they saw men visiting Suggie all day and night" (211).

Silla's drive for upward social mobility has left her indifferent to life itself. Chasing after capitalist values with great intensity, she has begun to mirror the colonizer. Her desire to acquire property is equally matched by her desire to control and to "colonize" others, including her daughter Selina. Significantly, the people whom she sentenced to death, either literally or figuratively, function in one way or another as surrogate mothers to Selina. It is when "the mother" thinks that she has Selina all to herself (Deighton is dead, and her tenant Suggie is evicted) that Selina asserts her self and is most rebellious. This moment of self-assertion is a moment of both rejection and identification.

The moment of identification with the women comes earlier than Selina expected. In the face of racial stereotypes, when she experiences a racial confrontation with her white friend's, Margaret's, mother, she is forced to acknowledge her kinship with her mother and the Bajan women:

> She was one with Miss Thompson, she knew. One with the whores, the flashy men, and the blues. . . . She was one with them: the mother and the Bajan women, who had lived each day what she had come to know. How had the mother endured, she who had not chosen death by water? She remembered the mother striding home through Fulton Park each late afternoon, bearing the throw-offs under her arm as she must have borne the day's humiliation inside. How had the mother contained her swift rage?—and then she remembered those sudden, uncalled-for outbursts that would so stun them and split the serenity of the house. The mother might have killed them. For they were the ones who drove her to that abuse each day, whose small faces reflected her own despised color. (293)

Selina "acknowledges [diasporic] unity vis-à-vis common oppression."[8] She identifies not only with the Bajan women but also with

8. Martin Japtok, "Paule Marshall's *Brown Girl, Brownstones*: Reconciling Ethnicity and Individualism," 311.

the entire community, which in spite of its claim to fame through the acquisition of brownstones remains an outsider in the eyes of white America. The community's "outsideness" is vocalized by Margaret's mother, who ignorantly chides Selina about her black West Indian heritage:

> We once had a *girl who did our cleaning* who was *from there* [West Indies]. *She wasn't a girl, of course. We just call them that.* She was so honest. I could leave my purse lying around and never worry. You don't find help like that every day, you know. *Some of them are . . . well . . .* just impossible. Oh, it's not their fault, of course, *poor things! You can't help your color. It's just a lack of the proper training and education.* I have to keep telling some of my friends that. Oh, *I'm a real fighter* when I get started! I wish they were here tonight to meet you. You . . . well, dear . . . you *don't even act colored.* I mean, *you speak so well and have such poise.* And it's just wonderful how you've taken your *race's natural talent for dancing and music* and developed it. *Your race needs more smart young people like you.* (287–88; emphasis added)

Selina realizes and for the first time accepts that the Bajans' notion of easy assimilation into the white metropolitan city through the acquisition of brownstones is a misconception, as she is made brutally aware. She comes to the cruel realization that she is just another black face to the white world, a Bajan, triply othered: Bajan, woman, and black. This condemnation signals a moment of truth for Selina: "She looked up and saw her reflection in those pale eyes [her friend's mother], she knew that the woman saw one thing above all else. For the first time, Selina truly saw—with a sharp and shattering clarity—the full meaning of her black skin" (289). While both ridiculing and condemning the black race, Margaret's mother yet attempts to identify with them through Selina, whom she holds accountable for her entire race, for their "barbarism." This "girl," referred to condescendingly and made mention of in a trite manner, could have been Selina's mother or the other Bajan women who scrubbed the floors of the whites.[9]

9. Margaret's mother, like most racists, has no idea that she is condescending and derogative. Her singling out of Selina from the black race is seen (by her) as doing justice to Selina; little does she know that in criticizing the black race, she is indirectly ridiculing and condemning Selina. Selina is part of the community and race that she decries. Marshall illuminates this racist gesture with the mother's choice of noncapitalized "dear" when referring to Selina.

"The girl" also embodies the woman who had "not chosen death by water," in spite of the humiliation they face day in and day out.[10] Yet, these women remain unblemished on the surface, while carrying their rage and pent-up anger within. Selina acknowledges that only a strong black (West Indian) woman, like her mother, could "contain her swift rage" (293) and bear such humiliation and abuse of their race yet continue to thrive. In her young eyes, the resilience of these Bajan women is unmatched, with the representative of the matriarch, Silla, leading them on, becoming "the collective voice of all the Bajan women, the vehicle through which their former [and present] suffering[s] found utterance" (45).

In spite of their strength and resilience and her identification with the women, Selina is confronted by a lack and experiences a sense of unbelonging, a sense of loss, thus disabling her to fully identify with and unquestionably accept these women. Because the Bajan community is founded on exclusivity, this loss that Selina feels can be interpreted as a lack of connectedness with other black diasporic peoples. By excluding other blacks from their midst, the Bajan community is mimicking the colonials. In spite of the community's presumed formidableness, it exhibits tolerance only for its own and those who are willing to follow their rules and adopt their agenda. The members wished not to be identified with those who "ain got nothing and ain looking to get nothing" (24).

Claremont Sealy, a fellow Barbadian, sees through the cracks and crevices of the community and the Bajan association, and he aptly calls for a change, a needed change that will include all black diasporic peoples:

> Stabbing out at the banners on the walls. "They need changing," he was shouting. "You need to strike out that word Barbadian and put Negro. That's my proposal. *We got to stop thinking about just Bajan. We ain't home no more. It don matter if we don know a person mother or his mother mother.* Our doors got to be open to every colored person that qualify. . . . I know it gon take time. Wunna gon have to ruminate long, but I ain gon

10. The woman who remains or lives to fight the cause is contrasted, to a greater extent, with Deighton, who suffers defeat by jumping to his death and, to a lesser extent, the other men in the community, who are secondary, marginal characters but duly represented by Deighton Boyce.

return till I see that word Barbadian strike out and Negro put in its place." (222; emphasis added)

Claremont Sealy illuminates the paradoxical nature of their cause: the members of the community have abandoned their homeland and have come to the metropole with the hope of being accepted and treated as equals, yet their motto is one that promotes inequality and discrimination. Claremont's proposal for the integration of all blacks is based on the all-inclusive African notion of kinship and community, and to qualify one just has to be black. Being black is not a choice, but a state of being. His proposal enraged the Association of Barbadian Homeowners and Businessmen, and Selina concludes that their "furor was but another dimension of their force, which would sweep aside all like Claremont Sealy from their sure way" (222–23). It was this force that Claremont sees as destructive, and Selina later comes to see how destructive it was that it alienated her from the community, rather than enabling her to establish a communal bond: "What was it that made them so unreal? Why should she feel such loneliness and alienation among them when after all, they were her people? Where was her place if not with them?" (227).

Unable to find her place among her people, Selina, similar to Claremont Sealy, relinquishes her membership of this monolithic and artificial community and shortly thereafter makes plans to visit her parents' past, their homeland, Barbados, arguably with the hope of finding a solution for their present state. Selina's "rejection" of the community is interpreted as "a rejection of her own people" by Gavin Jones.[11] In actuality, Selina rejects not "her own people" but what they had become and what they now represent. Her journey into the past is a journey into self and awareness. It intended to bridge the gap between the past and the present; symbolic of diasporic connections and continuities, it further supports and validates Selina's need to connect to, rather than reject, her people.

She openly voices her disapproval of the community's course of advancement. When asked her opinion about the society by one of the young members of the association, Selina angrily responds:

11. Gavin Jones, " 'The Sea Ain' Got No Back Door': The Problem of Black Consciousness in Paule Marshall's *Brown Girl, Brownstones*," 599.

"I think it stinks." She wished that her father could witness it. "And why does it stink? Because it's the result of living by the most shameful codes possible—dog eat dog, exploitation, the strong over the weak, the end justifies the means—the whole kit and caboodle. Your Association? It's a band of small frightened people. Clannish. Narrow-minded. Selfish. . . . Prejudiced. Pitiful—because who out there in that white world you're so feverishly courting gives one damn whether you change the word Barbadian to Negro? Provincial. That's your Association." (227)

Exposing the clannish, colonialist, predator-like nature of the society, Selina has exacted revenge for her father—"[I] wished that [he] could witness it"—on the community that has brutally extradited him, extinguishing him from their midst. She finally laid her father to rest after stunning and silencing the Barbadian association with her renouncement of them, pronouncing finally to her mother: "He's dead. And I want to forget him" (306). She has apparently taken Suggie's advice, and in renouncing the society is "do[ing] the living for [her father]" (209). Nonetheless, she wished he had lived to see the falsity of this community that he desperately wanted to accept him and become a part of, but the members whose motto resonates, "It is not the depths from which we come but the heights to which we ascend" (220), would not let him in on his own terms. The motto speaks of the members' quest for upward mobility, a pursuit that often forces one "to do some of everything short of murder," a quest that is for the moment, temporal, that rejects the past ("It is not the depths from which we come"), while it purports to construct a new and bright future. This community that prides itself on communal relations and on kinship and collective exploits shamefully endorses separatist values. In so doing, it perpetuates the crime of the white colonial world, the "white world," which, according to Selina, they are "so feverishly courting" (227). Selina sees this intolerant community as a threat to her because it stifles the self, the individual (growth). It drowns and suffocates the individual if given that chance.

Weakened by the community, Deighton drowns; he suffers a cruel fate by sea. Tragically, it is the Caribbean Sea that engulfs him within its waters as if also rejecting him from returning to and entering his island home. This (suffocating) waterlike image appears yet again in the novel when Selina is announced the winner of the scholarship by the association: "The applause burst afresh and she gazed wonderingly over the smiling faces, which had resembled a *dark sea*—alive under the sun with endless mutations of the one color. They no longer puzzled or offended her. Instead, their purposefulness—charging the air like a *strong current*—suddenly *charged her strength and underpinned her* purpose. The tightness in her chest eased and her heart calmed" (302–3; emphasis added). The faces of the assembled associates are the faces of the bottomless dark sea that took Deighton below its depths. Selina is stifled, suffocated within their presence. Their company drowns her and deprives her of identity. Accepting the scholarship equals death or suffocation. By rejecting the scholarship, she asserts her self, her individuality, and as a result expresses her desire to be her own person. She refuses to die or drown like Deighton and refuses the life her mother has chosen for her, and instead chooses her own path, thereby asserting her selfhood. Selina's rejection of the community, like her father's ostracism, takes place at a dance, the masquerade of ritual.

Commenting on Deighton's ostracism, Barbara Christian observes that "the scene in which the community ostracizes Deighton is, as it must be, one of ritual and form, a moment when it is present in its totality and in its essence." Christian further contends that "such occasions occur for a community when it is celebrating life, death, or renewal."[12] Selina is celebrating her new self. Consequentially, before her departure for Barbados, Selina dances solo, a ritual that symbolizes her impending freedom. This solo performance contrasts the ritualized collective dance the community enacted during her father's excommunication. Here, the community is noticeably excluded as Selina dances alone; hence, the novel's dance ritual is enacted to celebrate both community and self, life and death. Selina dances a birth-to-death cycle, symbolic of renewal: her birth, her new self, and the death cycle as a tribute to her dead father. The dance celebrates Selina's first steps into "wholeness," and her eventually laying her father to rest. Only after she dances solo is she finally able to admit and enunciate that her father is dead. She willingly dances alone, privately celebrating her father's life and death, as she relives his memories through dance. She concurrently celebrates her

12. Barbara Christian, *Black Women Novelists: The Development of a Tradition, 1892–1976*, 92.

coming into being by embracing her self, her body, and her inner being, which "must speak for her," through dance, yet simultaneously "giv[e] [others] something of herself" (281). Dance merges the past and the present. It is symbolic of diasporic unity and continuity, linking the past with the present, the old with the new. Significantly, dance, categorized by limitless boundaries, transcends barriers—economical, gender, and evidently racial—because Selina dances for a predominantly white audience. In a way, she continues the tradition of her father, whose love for traditional music and dance remains unwavering, despite severe condemnation and ridicule from the community. Dancing keeps her in touch with herself, as well as with the past, the "other" world and other ways.

A sizable distance is established from this "other" world, which is noticeably rejected by not only Silla but also the Bajan community as a whole. Hesitant about dancing with a longtime friend and culture bearer, Seon Brathwaite, Silla is cautioned by him:

> But what wrong with you, Silla, that you change up so since you come to these people New York? You don does dance! You must think I forget how you used to be wucking up yourself every Sat'day night when the Brumlee Band played on the pasture. You must think I forget how I see you dance once till you fall out for dead right there on the grass. You must think I forget, I ain forget. *How you can forget the past, mahn? You does try but it's here today and there waiting for you tomorrow.* In the midst of all this—we's in death. (145; emphasis added)

Seon Brathwaite's cautionary message, although addressed to Silla, is meant for the entire Bajan community. They, the members, have lost themselves on their way to "freedom." This so-called search for freedom is reminiscent of Jamaica Kincaid's protagonist Lucy's comment that on their way to freedom some people find riches, while some people find death. Silla has found both: riches in the form of the brownstone and spiritual death, a loss of selfhood. Silla has selectively forgotten and relinquished her past in search of "freedom," and herein lies her tragic mistake. Marshall admonishes that for black people to define themselves on their own terms they must engage their past. Silla, on the contrary, has mistakenly disengaged her past. Her obsession with property has caused her to become uncompassionate, and sexually, physically, and spiritually disembodied, creating distance not only from her husband but also from her family. Before Silla's obsession with the brownstones, she and Deighton once had a meaningful and loving relationship. Looking at his older daughter, Ina, Deighton reminisces that "she had been conceived in love, in the first year of their marriage, and she seemed to reflect the love they had lost" (26). Her daughter Selina cannot envision the young, spiritually and culturally moored Silla dancing on the pasture because "there was nothing to form the image. She could imagine the pasture" (145). Silla has suffered spiritual death by giving up her traditions and neglecting to answer the call of her ancestors. As Trudier Harris observes, the things that once culturally and spiritually defined her have vanished, as she readily gives up her old life and self: "[T]he sooner the traces of home are wiped away, as soon as the traces of cutting cane and the smell of salt fish (which Suggie loves and cooks) have been cleaned from the brownstones of Brooklyn, the better." Silla has also surrendered her traditional African values and culture. When advised by her friend Florrie to "put down something outside her tenants' doors to make them move," she laughs derisively, saying, "What you pretending for? You know Florrie *does still* believe in obeah and does walk 'bout with piece of coal tie round she waist and carrying finny and goat for luck" (71). The phrase "does still" suggests that Silla had once believed in and practiced such rituals, but her newfound "religion," the acquiring of brownstones, leaves her little or no time for ancestral worshiping. Deighton, in contrast, had not given up his cultural or ancestral blessings, and his love for sunlight, traditional music and dance, and sexual passion attests to this fact. Keith Byerman correctly observes that "the husband-father is the bearer of the old culture."[13] Despite his being the culture-bearer, Deighton's mistake lies in his mythical, dreamlike (re)creation of the island. Barbados was always "sweet, sweet," a safe haven to which he plans to return as "soon as [he] catch [his] hand" (11). Contrastingly, Silla views the island as a place of chaos and perpetual havoc. Entrapped in his dreams, Deighton had no way out. Silla correctly observes that he

13. Kincaid, *Lucy*, 129; Marshall, "Shaping the World of My Art," 97–112; Trudier Harris, "No Outlet for the Blues: Silla Boyce's Plight in *Brown Girl, Brownstones*," 61; Keith Byerman, "Gender, Culture, and Identity in Paule Marshall's *Brown Girl, Brownstones*," 137.

"was always looking for something big and praying hard not to find it" (174). His dream crumbled before his eyes even before it came to fruition:

> He was watching the slow dissolution of his dream: the white house with Grecian columns and stained-glass bathroom windows crumbling before it was even built, the flamboyant tree withering before it could take root. He moaned, breaking inside as the dream broke. Yet, as the moon tapered into a sigh, something else emerged. That sigh expressed a profound relief. It was as though Silla by selling the land, had unwittingly spared him the terrible onus of wresting a place in life. The pretense was over. He was broken, stripped, but delivered. . . . Perhaps he sensed that, like his defeat then [refusal of an accounting job], his loss of the land now was simply his due. (115)

Noticeably, Deighton has a European-inspired dream: "white house with Grecian columns." Like his dream, Deighton is rootless and accordingly crumbles.

When his lifelong dream and supposed freedom were taken from him, Deighton did the only possible thing. He took his own life. Returning to his island home meant freedom for Deighton; it was the "landscape on which his manhood [could have been] realized."[14] His inheritance was his passport back to the island; with that gone, the walls, meaning his dreams, that he built around himself and within which he sought refuge crumble, leaving him no purpose in life. In their final moment before Deighton's deportation, husband and wife seriously question their motives: "Silently they asked each other what had gone wrong, what it was that had ruined them for each other, and their mutual bewilderment confessed they did not know" (182). Both blinded, Deighton by his dreams and Silla by her obsession with material wealth, the Boyces have staged their own deaths and are unable to diagnose the cause. Fortunately, their daughter Selina, an "outsider," still keen and ardent, is the one who diagnoses the cause of their physical and spiritual deaths. Privy to both worlds, the extreme romantic, idealized world of her father and the excessively materialistic, harsh world of her mother, Selina will, ones hopes, not fall prey to either.

14. Byerman, "Gender, Culture, and Identity," 141.

Ostensibly, Selina's connection to both worlds is through dance, which bridges the two worlds. Incorporating modern dance steps or moves (she dances ballet also) into African Ring Dances, Selina connects with her present, physical side and her past, spiritual side. Dance affords her a sense of freedom, and with her newfound freedom Selina departs to the island of Barbados, where she hopes to perfect her dancing. Hence, Selina is well on her way to the acquisition of selfhood.

Judiciously not repeating the mistakes of her parents, Selina confronts the past, deprived her, on one hand, by her father's nostalgic creation of home space and, on the other hand, by her mother's rejection and condemnation of it. In spite of their vast variation of and reconstruction of this past, "her mother's and hence, her father's past," notes Barbara Christian, "cannot stand by itself. Her father had given her the gift of wonder, of imagination. An artist without a form, he had bestowed his sensibility on his daughter in images so lucid, so indelible, that she would never forget them." It is her father's "gift of wonder and of imagination" that Selina desperately wants to explore. Fortunately, she will be able to do so in and through dance. Selina's mother has equally contributed to her growth and development. Illuminating the mother's contribution, Hélène Christol contends, "Selina is going back to her father's land, supported by her mother's strength that she inherited and her mother's experience that taught her how to construct her identity and her freedom."[15] The tension between mother and daughter arises from the simple fact that Selina has inherited her mother's strong will and determination, and Silla herself acknowledges this as she confesses that "two head-bulls can't reign in a flock" (307). Their sameness is most tangible in the text when Selina, like Silla who outsmarted Deighton of his inheritance, almost outsmarted the Bajan community of its scholarship money. Fortunately, though, Selina quickly realizes that she has to make a choice between freedom and commitment, and she prudently chooses freedom, refusing to be bound to the society and its thwarted principles like her mother.

15. Christian, *Black Women Novelists*, 84, 99; Hélène Christol, " 'The Black Woman's Burden': *Black Women and Work in the Street* (Ann Petry) and *Brown Girl, Brownstones* (Paule Marshall)," 158.

Selina equally acknowledges her mother, the part of her mother that resides within her. Perversely, this moment of recognition comes by and through rejection: "separating from her while acknowledging that part of herself which is truly her mother's child." Mary Helen Washington parallels this rejection of the mother with the rejection of the Bajan community, which she deems necessary because the community needs to reorder itself. This renunciation of mother by daughter is an integral part of Selina's self-fashioning. Washington argues: "[I]t is this rebellion against her mother that has nurtured this self-ownership." "Selfhood," she continues, "is not defined negatively as separateness from others, nor is it defined narrowly by the individual dyad—the child and its mother—but on the larger scale as the ability to recognize one's continuity with the larger community."[16]

Acknowledging this continuity between herself and her mother, Selina notes that she is not Deighton's Selina as she was previously referred to, but her mother's daughter: "I have to disappoint you. Maybe it's as you once said: that in making your way you always hurt someone. Everybody used to call me Deighton's Selina but they were wrong. Because you see I'm truly your child. Remember how you used to talk about how you left home and came here alone as a girl of eighteen and was your own woman? I used to love hearing that. And that's what I want. I want it" (307). Selina is aware that she has to establish and recognize this continuity with her mother first and foremost because she is the connection to the Bajan community and the mother's land, Barbados. Acceptance and identification with the mother, in turn, facilitate acceptance and identification with the mother's land.

Hearing her own words—"in making your way you always hurt someone"—repeated to her by her daughter, Silla now fully understands the implications of those words as her daughter enacts a similar separation from her that she herself enacted from her mother several years ago. "Glimps[ing] in Selina the girl she had once been . . . her hands lay open like a girl's on her lap, she became the girl, who had stood alone and innocent, at the ship's rail" (307).

16. Mary Helen Washington, "I Sign My Mother's Name: Alice Walker, Dorothy West, Paule Marshall," 158–59.

As the mother, Silla, is transformed into a girl, her daughter Selina celebrates her entrance into womanhood. Unable to conceal her hurt, Silla reluctantly sets her daughter free as she bestows upon her motherly blessings: "G'long. G'long! You was always too much woman for me anyway, soul. And my own mother did say two head-bulls can't reign in a flock. G'long!" Her hand sketched a sign that was both a dismissal and a benediction. "If I din dead yet, you and your foolishness cant kill muh now" (307). Setting her daughter free, Silla identifies with her own mother, repeating her mother's words, "two head-bulls can't reign in a flock," to her daughter, as she continues the mother-daughter tradition of separation, a separation, though wrenching, that is necessary.

As a final acknowledgment of mother and daughter sameness, Selina reenacts her mother's departure, except she leaves for her mother's land, the island of Barbados, and not the metropole. Paying final tribute to her mother and the community, Selina walks down Fulton Street, reliving memories, memories that will always sustain her, as "[the varied] faces [of the community] hung like portraits in her mind. Those faces, those voices, those lives touching hers had ruined her, yet, she sensed—letting her gown trail on the sidewalk— they had bequeathed her a small strength" (306–7). Fulton Park, which had once accommodated the mothers, now lay bare and ruined as Selina browsed its four corners. Seemingly, she is "the sole survivor amid the wreckage" (310). Her embrace of her spiritual, emotional essence and physical presence keeps her in touch with her self. The disparate selves in her mother and father have merged in Selina, constituting her construction of "wholeness." Wanting to leave something with the Bajan community in her memory, Selina hurled one of her two bangles "high over her shoulder. [It] rose be- hind her, a bit of sliver against the moon, then curved swiftly down- ward and struck a stone. A frail sound in that utter silence" (310).

Tossing one of her bangles into "a vast waste—an area where blocks of brownstones had been blasted" (309), while keeping the other, speaks of and for Selina's acceptance of her dual heritage: African American and Afro-Caribbean. It is also suggestive of a possible dialogue and reconciliation between the two peoples and their cultures and acceptance of the real world and the supernatural. The vast waste where blocks of brownstones once stood speaks of renewal and change. By throwing one of her bangles to and into the wasteland, Selina acknowledges the need for change and renewal. This acknowledgment coupled with her departure might prompt her mother and the Bajan community to restructure its course to accommodate both peoples: African Americans and Afro-Caribbeans. It should be underscored that after Selina's rejection of the scholarship and Claremont Sealy's condemnation of the society that the members of the Bajan community began to take a serious inner look at their agenda and at themselves. Though this is a hopeful and promising gesture, we are yet to witness the community's "progression from a national to a transnational, diasporic organization."[17] Selina's departure to Barbados is a marker of transatlantic connections.

This selfish preoccupation that characterizes the Bajan community is noticeably absent in the community of Bournehills of *The Chosen Place, the Timeless People.* Marching under the banner of their hero and ancestor, Cuffee, whose motto resonates "all o' we is one," the Bournehills inhabitants exhibit their deep communal kinship. This strong connection speaks of a people who had not only lived together but also worked together. For them, living selfishly is symbolic of not having lived at all:

> *They had worked together!*—and as if, in their eyes, this had been the greatest achievement, the thing of which they were proudest, the voice rose to a stunning crescendo. . . . Under Cuffee, they sang, a man had not lived for himself alone, but for his neighbor also. If we had lived selfish, we couldn't have lived at all. They half-spoke, half-sung the words. They had trusted one another, had set aside their differences and stood as one against their enemies. *They had been a People!*[18]

Wisely setting aside their differences, the Bournehills people, in contrast to the Bajan community, join hands, standing "as one against their enemies," refusing to be contaminated by the neocolonial intervention that threatens the island. Aware that the acceptance of this intervention will annihilate their selfhood and subjectivity, the Bournehills inhabitants cautiously limit the influence of Westernization, as they proudly embrace their culture, resisting and renouncing colonial intervention, and instead opt for the acceptance of self and

17. Jones, "'The Sea Ain' Got No Back Door,'" 599.
18. Marshall, *Chosen Place*, 287; emphasis added.

roots. Renowned for their resistance to colonial intervention, they are honored by being the chosen people, and their island, in spite of its poverty-stricken status, is the chosen place. Their timelessness speaks to their ability to transcend time and place. They are the chosen ones, and they are timeless. Invoking the past in the present, the inhabitants make a powerful statement, revalidating the past while insinuating that the past and the present are intricately bound together. The past is invoked and employed for the needs of the present.

Taking her first steps to self-fashioning, Selina is fully aware that in order to achieve "wholeness," she has to confront her past. Thus, Selina is about to live that phenomenal experience of "going back" that Saul Amron, Jewish American anthropologist in *Chosen Place*, acknowledges as vital in the construction of subjectivity, a return that is necessary in enabling the individual to "come into her own":

> If they [those who have been deprived of their past] mean to come into their own, start using their history to their advantage. Turn it to their own good. You begin . . . by first acknowledging it, all of it, the bad as well as the good, those things you can be proud of such as, for instance, Cuffee's brilliant coup, and the ones most people would rather forget, like the shame and ignominy of that long forced march. But that's part of it too. . . . [Y]ou have to try and learn from all that's gone before—and again from both the good and the bad—especially that! Use your history as a guide, in other words. Many times what one needs to know for the present—the action that must be taken if a people are to win their right to live, the methods to be used: some of them unpalatable, true, but again, there's usually no other way—has been spelled out in past events. . . .
>
> [One must] go back and understand. More of us should try it. It's usually so painful though: looking back and into yourself; most people run from it. . . . But sometimes it's necessary to go back before you can go forward, really forward.[19]

19. Saul Amron, a U.S. anthropologist, had a mission to "modernize" Bournehills and its inhabitants, who were labeled as backward and underdeveloped. After living among the inhabitants and participating in their yearly reenactment of the slave revolt conducted by their physically dead hero, Cuffee Ned, he questions his motives for being on the island. Thereafter, he openly admits that the reenactment is surely not a mark of insanity or illness, as they are diagnosed, but an acceptance of their past, an embrace of their African Caribbean cultures and their "oneness" with their spiritual self. Marshall, *Chosen Place*, 315, 359.

By returning to her mother's land, Barbados, Selina is negotiating her right to be, as she refuses to be influenced by her parents' perceptions of the past.

Saul Amron's powerful idea of "going back" is enacted by the Carriacou residents, the island community of Marshall's *Praisesong for the Widow*. The "out-islanders," as the Carriacou residents are often referred to, literally "go back" to their native land, Carriacou, on a yearly basis on a two- to three-day excursion, the Carriacou Excursion, in spite of the fact that they work and live on the island of Grenada. The Excursion, like the carnival for the Bournehills folks, is "serious business" for the residents of Carriacou: "The Carriacou Excursion! Is a serious business, oui! Every year this time every man, woman and child that's from the place does pick up themself and go. They don't miss a year. No matter how long they been living over this side, even when they's born here, come time for the excursion they gone."[20]

In contrast to the inhabitants of Carriacou, Avatara (Avey) Johnson, the protagonist for whom the novel is named and the praisesong is sung, has embarked on a different route, traveling in the opposite direction, away from "home." In spite of geographic location, Avey once identified spiritually with the Carriacouan residents, for she also returned "home" (to South Carolina) to offer libations to the ancestors. Now she finds herself quite by accident on the island and alienated not only from "home" but also from the people and the culture. Clueless, the history of the Carriacou Excursion is "passed on" to her by a local taxi driver with whom she shares a similar fate: neither can fathom the islanders' obsession with the Excursion. Similar to the inhabitants of other surrounding communities, who are baffled by the Bournehills residents' dauntless worshiping of their ancestors, Avey and other outsiders are also amazed by the Carriacou residents' enthusiasm. The "out-islanders" are faithful to their culture and roots in every sense of the word, not only returning annually for the Carriacou Excursion, but also refusing to use the language of the "oppressor," "standard" English, when paying

20. Marshall, *Praisesong for the Widow*, 75. Future citations will be given parenthetically in the text.

homage to the ancestors, and instead use the ancestral language, patois or, rather, "African mix-up something," to borrow the taxi driver's words:

> Is just some African mix-up something. You used to hear the old people 'bout here speaking it when I was a boy, but no more. Only the out-islanders still bother. That's another thing about them. They can speak the King's English good as me and you, but the minute they set foot on the wharf for the excursion is only Patois crossing their lips. Don' ask me why. And the nice nice way they dress! The way they stepping! I tell you, you would think they was taking a boat—a decent boat—to go to America or England or someplace that's someplace instead of just to a little two-by-four island up the way. The Carriacou Excursion! Is a thing I don' understand, oui. . . . Why waste my time going to visit someplace that's even smaller than here. That's so small scarcely anybody has ever heard of it. (75–76, 77)

Thus, by paying homage to the ancestors, the Carriacou residents preserve the oral history, culture, and tradition, an act for which they are viewed as "mad, strange people." This so-called strangeness is echoed by the taxi driver, who confesses: "Only the out-islanders still bother. . . . The Carriacou Excursion! Is a thing I don' understand." Their refusal to speak the King's English is a deliberate act of resistance, one that lends validity to their cultural heritage and language, "African mix-up something," and their "way of knowing things." Tarnished by colonial indoctrination, the taxi driver equates the "nice nice way they dress" with going abroad, to the metropole, "America or England or someplace that's someplace"; to him only such a journey elicits such arduous and timely preparation, and not a "little [insignificant] two-by-four island." Obviously, the taxi driver has discarded his Old World culture and is steadfast in mimicking the metropolitan culture, tangible in his way of dress: his cowboy boots and the "country-and-western music coming from the [car's] tape deck" (75). His mimicking of the mother country parallels the so-called modernization of Grenada, he openly admits to Avey: "Hotels. That's all we got in Grenada now" (75). This admittance speaks to the colonization of the island in the form of a booming tourist industry. Adopting the metropolitan culture, the taxi driver has no time for ancestral worshiping. He relates to Avey: "I was liking a girl from Carriacou once. Months before the time she would be busy making more dresses and buying more presents to take to her family over there. All her talk was 'bout the excursion. And she was always after me to go, saying it would do me good. But not me, oui! Why waste my time going to visit someplace that's even smaller than here" (76–77). His refusal to identify with the islanders, and with his ancestry, has cost him the relationship, and apparently his sense of self.

Similar to the taxi driver's experience, Avey "used to hear people talk" about African cultural practices. This history was "passed on" to her by her great-aunt Cuney, who in turn was told by her grandmother Gran. This generation of women kept the Ibo myth alive. Great-aunt Cuney repeatedly recounts the story "word for word" of the "stepping" Ibos, who could "see in more ways than one," and of Ibo Landing, a county in Tatem, South Carolina, where the Ibos landed. The Ibos were "pure-born" African soothsayers brought to Tatem by white slave masters. Being soothsayers they saw everything and envisioned their fate; they "can tell you 'bout things happened long before they was born and things to come long after they's dead" (37–38). Seeing "what was to come," the Ibos, instead of enduring the hardships to which they were destined,

> [w]alked on back down to the edge of the river. Every las' man, woman and chile. They had seen what they had seen and those Ibos was stepping! And they didn't bother getting back into the small boats drawed up here—boats take too much time. They just kept walking right on out over the river. Now you wouldna thought they'd of got very far seeing as it was water they was walking on. Besides they had all that iron on 'em. But chains didn't stop those Ibos none. . . . They just kept on walking like the water was solid ground. (38–39)

When told this story of the "stepping Ibos," young Avey asked, "But how come they didn't drown, Aunt Cuney?" who accordingly responds, "[D]id it say that Jesus drowned when he went walking on the water in that Sunday school book you momma always send with you?" (39). While questioning the biblical scripture, Great-aunt Cuney simultaneously instills in Avey "an other way of knowing things." Great-aunt Cuney's unwritten story parallels the biblical story documented in the Sunday-school book. Marshall's incorporation of the biblical scripture is her questioning of this script as the ultimate truth, and in so doing, she simultaneously renders authenticity to the untold and unwritten story of slavery. Dorothy Hamer

Denniston states that "by making reference to biblical scripture and by using the oral storytelling form, Marshall allows us to overhear the sacred, unwritten history of the Ibo people."[21] Gran sustained the oral (unwritten) story by "passing it on" to the women of her family. For believing and upholding this myth, this "discredited knowledge," Gran was accused of being crazy, for "the way my gran' tol' it (other folks in Tatem said it wasn't so and that she was crazy but she never paid 'em no mind) 'cording to her they just kept on walking like the water was solid ground" (39).

Gran, like the inhabitants of Bournehills, exhibits unwavering alliance to her ancestors. In her eyes, they had accomplished a heroic deed, which need not be forgotten. Refusing to have the "stepping Ibos" written out of history and forgotten, Gran appoints herself as the disseminator of their heroic feats, their "way of knowing things," cherishing their memories as she passes on their story. Her story, according to Karla Holloway, "serves as the living embodiment of the myth of the Africans who came to Tatem Island and who, in rejecting its isolation and system of slavery, turned back toward the sea and walked across it back home." Holloway further adds, "Cuney's grandmother, whose 'mind was with the [re]turned Ibos,' was the spiritual presence that maintained the past in the present and that obliterated the distinction between them." Confessing that her "body . . . might be in Tatem but her mind, her mind was long gone with the Ibos" (39), Gran acknowledges her link and physical presence in the "real" world and her spiritual presence in the supernatural world of the ancestors and the world of the spirits. By walking back home, the Ibos had resisted subjugation; they had resisted the New World culture, and further enslavement. Such resistance signifies the denunciation of European and metropolitan cultures and ways of life. Identifying with the Ibos, "those pure-born Africans" (37), and keeping their memory alive, Gran repeatedly tells their heroic story. Although physically dead like the Ibos, Gran is kept alive by the myth of the "stepping Ibos." Therefore, says Peter Paris, Gran's transition from the "real" world to the supernatural, "her departure from physical life marks a transition of the human

---

21. Dorothy Hamer Denniston, *The Fiction of Paule Marshall: Reconstructions of History, Culture, and Gender*, 128.

spirit from the state of mortality to that of ancestral immortality." Hence, Gran had long entered the realm of the ancestors, dutifully functioning as the intermediary between the two worlds: the real and the supernatural. Paris further contends that "interestingly, the ancestral spirits are thought to continue life in much the same way as they lived it in history. That is to say, they retain their moral character, social, and familial consciousness."[22]

Apart from retaining her familial consciousness, Gran has also retained her spiritual consciousness. Like the Ibos, she had vision, "the power to see in more ways than one" (37). Even before Avey's birth, she knew she was coming and had demanded rights to her: "She had laid claim to her for a month each summer from the time she was seven. Before she was seven! Before she had been born even! There was the story of how she had sent word months before her birth that it would be a girl and she was to be called after her grandmother who had come to her in a dream with the news: 'it's my gran' done sent her. She's her little girl!' " (42). This claiming of Avey even before her birth speaks to her being the chosen one, the one who would maintain the continuity of the ancestral lineage. By instilling the story of the Ibos in Avey's mind, "the old woman had entrusted her with a mission" (42). Assigned the dutiful role of ancestress, Avey, named Avatara in honor of Gran, was "saddled with the name of someone people had sworn was crazy" (42). On the contrary, Avatara in Sanskrit translates as the incarnation of a deity whose mission is to counteract some particular evil in the world. The evil that Gran counteracts, as Avey is expected to, is the effacement of history and the historical past, the discrediting of the ancestral world, and the deeming of this "other way of knowing things" inconsequential and insignificant.

Thus, introduced to the Old World culture at a tender age, Avey is expected to uphold and promote this "other way of knowing things." Unfortunately, she had "believed till the age of ten, [after which] she rid herself of the notion [of being the chosen one]" (42). Similar to the taxi driver, she rejects the teachings of the Old World for materialistic values. Like the driver who is obsessed with city life, Avey's ideal

22. Karla Holloway, *Moorings and Metaphors: Figures of Culture and Gender in Black Women's Literature*, 89; Peter J. Paris, *The Spirituality of African Peoples*, 52.

city was no "two-by-four" unknown, small, underdeveloped island "that scarcely anybody has ever heard of," but the sheltered, secure suburban town of North White Plains.

Avey and her husband, Jerome (Jay) Johnson, were Brooklyn natives before taking up residence in the suburbs of North White Plains. As evidenced, Avey is no stranger to African culture; she and Jay were once ardent practitioners of this culture, as unabashed ancestor worshipers. "Jay and Avey Johnson of Halsey Street," observes Ebele Eko, "present a rare and refreshing picture in Black literature of a happy, loving couple and strong family unit."[23] Small rituals and private pleasures were the order of the day. The Jay of Halsey is an avid and faithful listener of blues singers such as Ida Cox, Ma Rainey, and Mamie Smith, among others:

> Some days called for the blues. Those evenings coming in he didn't even stop to take off his coat or hat before going to the closet in their bedroom, where at the back of the top shelf he kept the old blues records in an album that was almost falling apart. The records, all collector's items, had been left him by his father, who had been a scout for Okeh Records in the twenties. . . . In his hands the worn-out album with its many leaves became a sacred object, and each record inside an icon. So as not to risk harming them he never stacked them together on the machine, but played them individually, using the short spindle. A careful ritual went into dusting each one off, then gently lowering it onto the turntable. (94)

This tradition of listening to the blues had been handed down to Jay by his father, who was also a practitioner of the African oral culture. Perpetuating this tradition, Jay practiced this ritual daily, and "no matter how exhausted he was, [he] never sat down when listening to the blues record" (94). Blues are sacred to him, and they "administer healing and strength at the end of each day to his tense and work-worn body" (94). It is symbolic that Jay listens to blues music, music influenced by work songs and "field hollers" that address quotidian trials and tribulations of life. Employing the blues as a vehicle of and for self-expression, Jay accordingly vents his anger and displeasure with life. At the same time, by listening to this

---

23. Ebele Eko, "Oral Traditions: The Bridge to Africa in Paule Marshall's *Praisesong for the Widow,*" 145.

music he also asserts and exerts power, control, and independence over his life. By listening to and dancing to the blues, Jay experiences and achieves a kind of transcendence:

> The Jay who emerged from the music of an evening, the self that would never be seen down at the store, was open, witty, playful, even outrageous at times: he might suddenly stage an impromptu dance just for the two of them in the living room. . . . And affectionate: his arms folding around her from behind when she least expected them, the needful way he spoke her name even when they quarreled—"Avey . . . Avey, would you just shut up a minute!" And passionate: a lover who knew how to talk to a woman in bed. (95)

In addition to relieving tension, the blues music revitalizes Jay after a hard day's work; he experiences spiritual "wholeness" listening to this music. The Johnsons' entire lives are imbedded and engraved in rituals—even their lovemaking is categorized as ritual, "another kind of poetry":

> There was his scandalous talk, and then, when she finally drew him into her, his abrupt, awestruck silence. His stillness. He would lie within her like a man who has suddenly found himself inside a temple of some kind, and hangs back, overcome by the magnificence of the place, and sensing around him the invisible forms of the deities who reside there. . . . Jay might have felt himself surrounded by a pantheon of the most ancient deities who had made their temple the tunneled darkness of his wife's flesh. (127)

Jay and Avey Johnson lived for rituals. When told about the Ibos who had walked on water back to their homeland, Jay never questioned the myth, but undeniably believed and accepted it as the gospel: "I'm with your aunt Cuney and the old woman you were named for. I believe it, Avey. Every word" (115). Jay and Avey continued the tradition, initiated by Gran, of paying homage to the ancestors by organizing ritualized visits to Ibo Landing every summer. The landing reminded Jay of "home," of Leona, Kansas, where he was born. This tradition was religiously practiced until they fell prey to capitalist values. Unfortunately, the loving couple's obsession with material gain and upward mobility heralds the dissolution of their marriage. The quest precipitates their "fall," the neglecting of their spiritual side and their not adhering to or answering the call of their ancestors.

Apart from the spiritual deaths that the Johnsons' suffer, the disregard and repudiation of their spirituality also herald the death of their marriage:

> The yearly trip south became a thing of the past. . . . So did the trips they used to regularly make over to Harlem to see their old friends, and the occasional dance they would treat themselves to. All such was soon supplanted by the study manuals, the self-improvement books, the heavy sample case containing the vacuum cleaner. And the man Jay used to become at home, who was given to his wry jokes and banter, whose arms used to surprise her as they circled her from behind, gradually went into eclipse during the years following that near-fatal day. (116)

The "near-fatal day" referred to is one Tuesday when the Johnsons became engaged in a heated argument, an argument that mirrored their neighbors', the "half-crazed woman" and her drunken, "derelict, delinquent husband," the people they definitely did not want to be compared or identified with. But "it seemed that they had changed places with the two down in the street; had even become them" (110). The Johnsons naively thought that acquiring status and wealth would shield them from the evils of society. However, Mr. and Mrs. Johnson "gradually fell victim to the strains, to the sense of the downward slide which had brought on that Tuesday night . . . and to the punishing years that followed. Jay's touch increasingly became that of a man whose thoughts were elsewhere, and whose body, even while merged with hers, felt impatient to leave and join them" (129). The playfulness that once characterized Jay vanished, and in its place stood a zombified being, stripped of his former self and identity, now a new, strange, and alien man, obsessed with material gain and social status. Jay's loss of "self" not only is spiritual, but also becomes evident even in his physical appearance:

> Not long after the move to North White Plains, Jay Johnson shaved off his mustache. A small thing, Avey quickly told herself as he emerged from the bathroom that morning with it gone; nothing to get upset about. Why then did the sight of that suddenly naked space above his lips fill her with such dismay, and even fear? After a while it was if he had always been clean-shaven. Nevertheless, at a deeper level, she remained unreconciled to the change. (130)

Jay's beard that once defined him, which was once a sign of his cultural mooring, for it was modeled after his father's own beard, was now gone, and in its place was nakedness, "naked space." The once treasured moustache, had, in Jay's words, now become a nuisance. "With the moustache [gone, the last] trace of everything that was distinctive and special about him had vanished also. With it shaved off he had lost a necessary shield. He was exposed and vulnerable suddenly as a prizefighter who had foolishly let drop his guard" (130–31).

Jay foolishly discards his beard, his shield of protection, thereby dangerously exposing himself to the ills of society, epitomized in the capitalist values he seeks, with the intent to conquer. "Guard down," Jay allows himself easy victimization, permitting the riches he feverishly craves and chases to define him. Not only had he become estranged from himself, but also in place of his former self or face, "another face [was] superimposed on his." Someone else had "taken up residency behind his dark skin" (131), but he had also become a stranger to his wife, Avey, who found it increasingly difficult to refer to him lovingly as Jay, and instead found herself referring to him unintentionally as Jerome Johnson. The nakedness of Jerome Johnson's beard symbolizes his own spiritual nakedness, the loss of his "self."

The loss of his beard was the first sign of Jerome's loss of spiritual and cultural moorings. Migrating to the suburbs of North White Plains, Jerome had also left behind "the little private rituals and pleasures [he and his wife, Avey, once shared]. . . . The playfulness and wit of those early years, the host of feelings and passion that had defined them in a special way back then, and the music which had been nourishment [had vanished]. All these had departed with him that Tuesday night" (136). The voice that once sang praises to his kin(d), black people, his ancestry, now curses them: "That's the trouble with half these Negroes you see out here. Always waiting for the white man to give them something instead of getting out and doing for themselves. . . . Just look at 'em! Not a thing on their minds but cutting up and having a good time. If it was left to me I'd close down every dance-hall in Harlem and burn every drum! That's the only way these Negroes out here'll begin making any progress" (131–32). Black music and dance had now become "devil" music for

Jay, and he refers to them deferentially as merely "cutting up and having a good time."

Expounding on his transition from rootedness to rootlessness, Karla Holloway contends that "Jay begins to lose things that are spiritually important to him, like music and his old blues records, at the same time he begins to value the *materia* of the Western world and its ethic." Holloway further concludes that "Jerome shelves the songs and telling voices by which black women learn to manage their beings. He abandoned them on the sidelines, out of his *line of vision*."[24] In so doing, Jay inadvertently abandons his wife as well, and the private rituals that once fashioned their lives are also condemned and thoughtlessly cast aside. All that remain of those memorable moments husband and wife once shared are memories, memories that speak of what they once had, memories of the not too distant past. Even before Jerome's actual (physical) death, Avey mourned the death of Jay Johnson of Halsey Street, who had died long before Jerome Johnson. Little did Jay know that the casting away of the African dance rituals and music, these seemingly insignificant acts that had possessed transcendent qualities, signaled the simultaneous casting away of the self, the killing of the spirit and spiritual self. These rituals-cum–ancestral inheritances "had reached back beyond her life and beyond Jay's to join them to the vast unknown *lineage* that had made their being possible. And this *link, these connections*, heard in the music and in the praisesongs of a Sunday, had both protected them and put them in possession of a kind of power" (137; emphasis added). These rituals were the Johnsons' connection and link to the "other" supernatural world, and to the "other ways of knowing things and seeing."

Hence, the Johnsons are deprived of this vision and knowledge because they foolishly relinquish their ancestral inheritances, thereby becoming vulnerable and powerless, both spiritually and physically. They had bared their souls for material gains. "What kind of bargain had they struck?" (139) What had the Johnsons gotten in exchange for their souls? For what is a man profited, if he shall gain the whole world, and lose his own soul? "How much had the [Johnsons] foolishly handed over in exchange for the things they had gained?—

24. Holloway, *Moorings and Metaphors*, 127. Emphasis in original.

an exchange they could have avoided altogether had they been on their guard!" (140) While secretly referring to her husband as Jerome Johnson and mourning not so much Jay's death but instead the latter stage of his life, Avey begins to admit that she was an accomplice in this betrayal of the spirits and as a result found it increasingly difficult to refer to herself as Avatara, and in the same formal way had "started to call herself Avey Johnson. The woman to whom those names had belonged had gone away, had been banished along with her feelings and passions to some far-off place" (141). Like Jay, who obfuscates the past by severing the ancestral link, Avey's compliance is altogether noticeable. Ebele O. Eko notes that the "yearly trip south to their heritage is soon forgotten, so are old friends and old tested values. Their new links are with the Masons and the Elks, with snobbish upward-bound Blacks like the Moores, with white folks of North White Plains who tour the Laurentians of the Arctic Circle rather than Africa."[25] These new links are discernible detours from the Johnsons' former lives and as such are devoid of any kind of spirituality or spiritual consciousness.

The ruination of Avey Johnson is further demonstrated when she remains clueless as to what Lebert Joseph, the griot and ancestor who eventually plays a leading and vital role in redirecting her wanderings, meant when he poses to her these questions: "And what you is? . . . What's your nation?" (166–67). Abena Busia correctly observes that in the answers to these questions "lies the key to [Avey's] self-understanding." Spiritually broken, Avey, of course, was unable to provide an answer to the sage's crucial questions. After being informed by Avey that she had no nation because she was a visitor from the United States, Lebert Joseph becomes bereaved, mourning the loss of Africa's children. In his eyes, Avey Johnson is just another "loser," one of the many who in Lebert Joseph's words "can't call their nation" (175) and "who don' know nothing 'bout the nation dance" (168). The losers are the ones spiritually unmoored and alienated from their cultural heritage. To this list we may add the taxi driver, Jerome Johnson, and the grandchildren and great-grandchildren of Lebert Joseph, lost to him and their rich heritage, faraway in the metropolitan countries of Canada and the United

25. Eko, "Oral Traditions," 146.

States: " 'I has grand and great-grand born in that place I has seen. Josephs who has never gone on the excursion! Who has been to a Big Drum! Who don' know nothing 'bout the nation dance!' He fell silent, but the angry bereavement in his voice hung on in the room, troubling the air and darkening the almost sacred light that filled the place. Avey was at a loss as to how to take the sudden sadness that had come over him" (168). This cultural and spiritual loss is traumatic, and Lebert Joseph attests to this grave fact as he silently grieves and rages "over the loss of the grandchildren and great-grandchildren he had never seen" (169), who in his words had "gone up to live that way long ago," referring to Canada, England, and the United States, but refusing to "mention the names" (183). Busia accordingly documents the traumatic experience when she notes, "Marshall articulates the scattering of the African peoples as a trauma—a trauma that is constantly repeated anew in the lives of her lost children."[26] She diagnoses the traumatic experiences that African Americans live predicated on the sacrifices they have to make, often not on their own terms but on the terms of U.S. society, terms that often entail the severance from the past, from their cultural roots. Similar to Avey and Jerome Johnson, the new generations of blacks, Lebert Joseph's grand- and great-grandchildren included, are busy pursuing the "American Dream," busy chasing status and identity in the white community, symbolically represented by North White Plains, thus leaving no time for ancestral worshiping. However, this chase for position and selfhood clandestinely dispossesses the individual of identity, forcing the subject to offer up herself as a sacrificial lamb.

On the verge of becoming the ultimate sacrifice, Avey Johnson is redeemed by the ancestor Lebert Joseph, who is assigned the task of returning Avey to her spiritual moorings. Eugenia Collier determines that Lebert Joseph is the liaison between man and the gods. As a crossroad character, Lebert Joseph links the spiritual and physical worlds, the ancestors with the living and the unborn.[27] He

26. Abena Busia, "What Is Your Nation? Reconnecting Africa and Her Diaspora through Paule Marshall's *Praisesong for the Widow*," 196, 197.
27. Eugenia Collier, "The Closing of the Circle: Movement from Division to Wholeness in Paule Marshall's Fiction," 313.

is seer and shaman to the people of Carriacou, the intermediary between them and the ancient gods, between the "real" world and the supernatural world. He further functions as the embodiment of Aunt Cuney, connecting Avey's past with her present, her physical world with the spiritual world of her ancestors. Like the Ibos, Lebert possesses double vision:

> [Lebert] already knew of the Gethsemane [Avey] had undergone last night, knew about it in the same detailed and anguished way as Avey Johnson, although she had not spoken a word. His penetrating look said as much. *It marked him as someone who possessed* ways of seeing *that went beyond mere sight and* ways of knowing *that outstripped ordinary intelligence (Li gain connaissance) and thus had no need for words.* (172; emphasis added)

Similar to Aunt Cuney and, before her, Gran, who possessed extraordinary "ways of seeing" and "ways of knowing," Lebert Joseph is the embodiment of spiritual consciousness and has the ability to foresee and foretell the experiences of others, particularly those about to be initiated into the ancestral realm.

Bound for what her youngest daughter, Marion, refers to as a "meaningless cruise with a bunch of white folks" on a cruise ship, the *Bianca Pride*, Avey's holiday cruise is brutally halted when she is confronted in a dream by Aunt Cuney. There she was, larger than life, "standing waiting for [Avey] on the road that led over to the Landing" (32). Reluctantly, Avey found herself "being dragged forward in the direction of the Landing" (43). Engaged in a tug-of-war, which escalated into a "bruising fist fight" (45), Avey eventually suffers defeat. Haunted by the dream, Avey is unable to continue her holiday cruise, and instead "abandons ship" with the intention of returning home to North White Plains. Unable to get a flight to New York, Avey is forced to stay overnight on the island of Carriacou. This one-night stay extends into a memorable journey down memory lane to the ancestral world she had ruthlessly abandoned.

Accompanying her on this pilgrimage to ensure her safe deliverance is the sage Lebert Joseph, whose noble task entails redirecting her wandering steps. Unable to continue the battle she had begun with Aunt Cuney and with Lebert Joseph, Avey eventually accepts that "for all his appearance of frailty he had proven the stronger of the two" (184), and succumbs to his wishes, accompanying him to the Carriacou Tramp (also known as the Carriacou Excursion), an event that commemorates the ancestors with African rituals: the Ring Shout, the Big Drum, and the Nation Dance.

Thus, Lebert Joseph redirects Avey's wandering steps, introducing her to the Ring Shout and the Nation Dance, thereby empowering her to know and, subsequently, call her nation. In so doing, he emphasizes the importance of staying connected to one's roots and offering libations or paying homage to the ancestors, the "Long-time People." Stressing the importance and need for familial relationships, family, and community, Lebert Joseph relates: "A man lives in this place all year he must go look for his family. His old father and mother if they's still in life, and the rest of his people. Sometimes he has a wife or a woman who has children for him back in Carriacou. He must go look for them" (164). Lebert Joseph unremittingly accentuates the necessity of staying connected with those "still in life" as well as those who have passed on to the "other" world. His advocacy speaks to Paris's earlier comment that the death of the ancestor is a celebration of the human spirit from a state of mortality to one of immortality. Paris concludes that "the ancestor is thought to live on in the realm of the spirit world in a state of existence that Mbiti calls 'the living dead,' a term he prefers to ancestor because of the tendency of Westerners to associate the latter with the state of death. The term living dead conveys both continuity with and transition from temporal life."[28]

In addition to familial connection, Lebert Joseph talks about the importance of maintaining connection to the home(land) as well: "He's [a man] sure to have a piece of ground there he has to see to. Or he might be building a house for when he goes home for good" (164). Therefore, Avey, with her earthly ancestor Lebert Joseph, embarks on a spiritual journey where she will pay homage to the "living dead," Aunt Cuney and the other ancestors, and to the mother(land). In addition to paying homage to the Long-time People and connecting with the mother(land), Lebert Joseph confirms that the Carriacou

---

28. Paris, *Spirituality*, 52. John Mbiti specializes in African religions and cultures. Paris constantly refers to Mbiti's *African Religions and Philosophy* in his own work.

Excursion is also a time for celebration and relaxation. Notwith-standing, this spiritually filled event is also cataloged as one of the many "special reasons" for the Excursion. Ironically, Lebert Joseph validates and endorses the same ritualized festivities that Jay had come to despise and reject:

> A man goes to relax hisself. To bathe in Carriacou water and visit 'bout with friends. And to fete—dance, drink rum, run 'bout after women. A little sport, oui. The excursion ain' all business. But it have another reason. Is the Old Parents, oui. The Long-time People. Each year this time they does look for us to come and give them their remembrance. I tell you, you best remember them. If not they'll get vex and cause you nothing but trouble. They can turn your life around in a minute, you know. All of a sudden everything start gon' wrong and you don' know why the reason. You can't figger it out all you try. Is the Old Parents, oui. They's vex with you over something. Oh, they can be disagreeable, you see them there. Is their age, oui, and the lot of suffering they had to put up with in their day. We has to understand and try our best to please them. (165)

Lebert Joseph's commentary is seemingly directed at Avey, as it offers a diagnosis of her spiritual unmooring and her wanderings, for she has indeed vexed Aunt Cuney, and as a result, Aunt Cuney, to borrow his words, has caused her "nothing but trouble . . . turn[ing] [her] life around in a minute." Blessed with double vision, Lebert Joseph foresees that "everything start gon' wrong" with Avey, and she "don' know why the reason [and] can't figger it out all [she] try." Unable to decode her dream, Lebert has given Avey an apt interpre-tation of it: Aunt Cuney is angered by Avey for neglecting her and not giving her "remembrance." "Only at this point," observes Karla Holloway, "is Avey able to understand the idea of ancestry embodied in the 'Old Parents' and the 'Long-time People' whom Lebert Joseph tells her are due the ritual of the yearly remembrance."[29] The Long-time People should be honored for their resilience, their longevity, their timelessness and age. Accordingly, to appease Aunt Cuney and the other ancestors, Avey must now pay them homage and beg forgiveness. Similar to the Carriacou residents who pay tribute annually to their ancestors, the "Long-time People," Avey must join

29. Holloway, *Moorings and Metaphors*, 133.

in the sanctified ancestral worshiping. In celebration of this yearly ritual, "every year God send [Lebert Joseph] holds a Big Drum for them" (165), where the Beg Pardon is sung. Complete participation in the rituals of drumming, dancing, and celebrations is an affirmation of their African roots, and by extension their "selves." Saddled with her duty to her ancestors, Avey Johnson must join in and immerse herself in these ritualistic dances and songs if she is to be saved or forgiven. She must literally beg pardon.

In order to enter into the sacred realm of her ancestry, Avey must relinquish some of the values of the New World she has come to idolize. She must shed material possession (her old self) that has consumed and zombified her very being. Aunt Cuney makes this clear when, in the fistfight with Avey, she rips off her expensive clothing, leaving her bare. This bareness is reminiscent of what Jerome experienced after he had shaved off his coat of protection: his beard. While Jerome willingly gives up his armor of protection and his self in exchange for material possession, Avey is now reluctant to give up the material wealth that she and her husband had fought so hard to attain, and it is with great and noticeable pain that she eventually gives in to Aunt Cuney, as she watches "the fur stole like her hard won life of the past thirty years being trampled into the dirt underfoot. And the clothes being torn from her body" (45). Avey's imposed bareness is, on one hand, emblematic of her childlike state—her expensive clothing becomes burdensome as she struggles to take them off "slow and clumsy as a two-year old" (151)—and, on the other hand, her implied rebirth. Aunt Cuney's gesture speaks of the need for Avey to be reborn, to be cleansed in order to enter into the realm of the ancestors and assume the task that Gran had assigned her long before her birth. Ironically, assigned this role before her actual birth, Avey now has to be reborn to assume this role. She has to return to her past, to her childhood, to assume this role and thereby become one of the ancestors. Under the guidance of Aunt Cuney, Avey wanders into Lebert Joseph's rum shop, but her wandering is no longer aimless, for she is ready to beg pardon and "return home." It is the elder, Lebert Joseph, assigned this noble task, who takes Avey by the hand and leads her home.

Symbolically, Avey's rebirth is staged aboard a schooner, the *Emanuel C.* This schooner, packed with bodies, is reminiscent of the

Middle Passage journey that Avey's ancestors had endured. Once aboard the schooner, task accomplished, Lebert Joseph "led [Avey] across to the oldest among the women" (193), indicative that the rebirth process is an exclusively female task. In addition, the fact that Lebert Joseph "hands Avey over" to the oldest of the women suggests that the task should be completed by someone, namely, a woman who through her age and resilience has acquired and possessed "ways of seeing and knowing," attributed solely to her status as ancestress. Immediately, Avey experiences spiritual kinship and recognition:

> The moment she saw them sitting there in their long somber dresses, their black hands folded in their laps and their filmy *eyes overseeing everything on deck,* she experienced a shock of recognition that for a moment made her forget her desire to bolt. They were—she could have sworn it!—the presiding mothers of Mount Olivet Baptist (her own mother's church long ago)—the Mother Caldwells, and Mother Powes and Mother Greens, all *those whose great age and long service . . . had earned them a title even more distinguished than "sister"* and a place of honor in the pews up front. (193–94; emphasis added)

This kinship, now certified, is established even before the boat ride: Avey is not perceived as a stranger and is often mistaken for an islander. In a case of mistaken identity, a man addresses her, "Ida, doux-doux, qu'est-ce qu'il y a? Ma'ché! Ma'ché!" Realizing his mistake, he adds apologetically, "Don' ever let anybody tell you, my lady, that you ain' got a twin in this world!" (72). Similarly, Lebert Joseph mistook her for a member of his tribe, the Chamba, and he also recognizes in her traits and characteristics of other tribes.

Not only does Avey seemingly have a twin, but the Carriacou women are also replicas of her mother, her aunt, and the "presiding mothers of Mount Olivet." For their longevity and service, they have earned the titles *Ancestress* and *Mother.* Earning the distinguished titles, these women will stage Avey's rebirth and, "waving Lebert Joseph aside, they took charge" (194). Thus, Avey's rebirth begins with a cleansing, the *Lavé Tête*, a literal purging of the self:

> She vomited in long loud agonizing gushes. As each seizure began her head reared back and her body became stiff and upright on the bench. She would remain like this for a second or two. . . . Then as her stomach

heaved up she would drop forward and the old women holding her would have to tighten their grip as the force of the vomiting sent her straining out over the railing, dangerously close to the water. The paroxysms repeated themselves with almost no time in between for her to breathe. Hanging limp and barely conscious over the side of the boat after each one, she would try clearing her head, try catching her breath. But before she could do either the nausea would seize her again, bringing her body stiffly upright and her head wrenching back. . . . And then she would be hawking, crying collapsing as her stomach convulsed and the half-digested food came gushing from her with such violence. . . . After what in her agony seemed to be hours, the contractions changed direction. Instead of passing up through her emptied stomach into her throat, they reversed themselves and began . . . moving down into the well of her body. Because with the sudden shift in direction, the bloated mass that couldn't be—whatever was left of it—was being propelled down also. Down past her navel. Down through the maze of her intestines. Down into her bowel. (204–5, 207)

Avey's illness or, rather, her purging of self lasted the entire boat ride across the sea from Grenada to the off-island of Carriacou. This illness can be perceived as a reliving of the Middle Passage. Trapped and enslaved between her vomit and bowels, like her ancestors were trapped and enslaved by chains, Avey somewhat experiences what they, her ancestors, had many years ago:

She had the impression as her mind flickered on briefly other bodies lying crowded in with her in the hot, airless dark. A multitude it felt like lay packed around her in the filth and stench of themselves, just as she was. Their moans, rising and falling with each rise and plunge of the schooner, enlarged upon the one filling her head. Their suffering—the depth of it, the weight of it in the cramped space—made hers of no consequence. (209)

For the first time Avey understood and partially experienced what Lebert Joseph was referring to when he spoke of the magnitude of the suffering her ancestors "had to put up with" (165). The schooner in which Avey lay has a dual function: first, it is reminiscent of the slave ship that her ancestors forcibly boarded centuries ago, and second, it functions as the womb within which she is contained, awaiting to be (re)born.

At the end of the "Middle Passage" journey, we witness Avey's return to self and presence mediated by Rosalie Parvay, Lebert Joseph's daughter, who shares a common bond with Avey: widowhood. Rosalie Parvay, appropriating an air of transcendence that Avey hopes to attain upon her rebirth, is the embodiment of strength and resilience in Avey's eyes, surviving not only the death of her husband but also life's trials and tribulations. Like her father, Rosalie Parvay possesses special "powers of seeing and knowing" (218). Standing beside Avey's bed and tending to her every need and want, Rosalie Parvay is transformed into Avey's mothers, personifying Aunt Cuney and her own mother: "In her confused state, the figure had been any number of different people over the course of the night: her mother holding in her hands a bottle of medicine and a spoon, the nurse in the hospital where she had had her children leaning over her spent body to announce that it was healthy and a girl; the figure had grown to twice its height at one point to become her great-aunt beckoning to her in the dream" (217).

Reassured by Aunt Cuney's beckoning, as if to complete the rebirth, Rosalie Parvay gives Avey her first bath: "[I]s time now to have your skin bathe. And this time I gon' give you a proper wash-down" (217). As Ann Armstrong Scarboro observes, a "rite of purification is present in the physical care Avey receives from Rosalie Parvay."[30] Receiving this "rite of purification," Avey is cleansed and hence transformed into the innocent and trusting child she once was: "The hands, small and deft and with a slightly rough feel to the palms, had immediately stripped her of everything she had on, hastily washed her off and then slipping on her the nightgown from her suitcase had put her to bed. A baby that had soiled itself. And shame once again brought her body heaving up with a strangled sob" (217). Once again Avey is stripped of her clothing, but now this dispossession is complete, for she is washed and cleansed of all impurities. Similar to a newborn baby whose presence into the world is recorded by "strangled sob[s]," Avey also sobbed uncontrollably upon her rebirth, and she accordingly required "a laying on of hands" to be calmed (217).

This first bath, the birth bath, is followed by another bath, a ritualized, spiritual bath:

---

30. Ann Armstrong Scarboro, "The Healing Process: A Paradigm for Self-Renewal in Paule Marshall's *Praisesong for the Widow* and Camara Laye's *Le Regard du roi*," 31.

She washed a hand, an arm, a shoulder, a breast, bathing only one side of her at a time which made it easier to keep her covered. When . . . she reached the emptied-out plain of her stomach and her pelvis below she did not turn or fold back the sheet, but simply held it up slightly with one hand so that it formed a low canopy as she thoroughly washed her there. . . . As if the bath was an office they performed every day for some stranger passing through, Rosalie Parvay and the maid smoothly exchanged the washcloth, towels and soap between them without uttering a word. (220)

This bath was indeed "an office," distinguished by the tub used by Rosalie that is a replica of the one in which Avey took many special baths during frequent, arranged visits to her aunt in Tatem. Upon noticing the bathtub, memories overflowed in Avey, and she was the "child in the washtub again" (221). The entire ritual evoked memories that Avey thought had long been dead, ones that she thought she had safely buried. These memories are now cherished as she reminisces. Inundated in her now treasured past, Avey "hadn't realized what had happened, that a connection had been made" (196).

This bond is finally sealed by Avey's participation in the Big Drum. Avey's total rebirth culminates in the Big Drum celebration. After being an ardent onlooker of the celebrations, Avey's "feet of their own accord began to glide forward. She moved cautiously at first, each foot edging forward as if the ground under her *was really water—muddy river water*" (248; emphasis added). The muddy river water is suggestive of the river, the water that the Ibos walked over as though it was solid ground. Avey has begun to identify with the Ibos like Gran identifies with them, surrendering her mind to the all-powerful, all-seeing Ibos for guidance and protection. Without intending to, Avey of her own accord joined in the Creole dance, the Carriacou Tramp, a dance of which she earlier had no memory:

And under cover she was performing the dance that wasn't supposed to be dancing, in imitation of the old folk shuffling in a loose ring inside the church. And she was singing along with them under her breath: "Who's that ridin' the chariot." . . . The Ring Shout. She had finally after all these decades made it across. The early Shouters in the person of the out-islanders had reached out their arms like one great arm and drawn her into their midst. And for the first time since she was a girl she felt the threads, which were thin to the point of invisibility yet as strong as the ropes at Coney Island. Now, suddenly, as if she were that girl again, with her entire life yet to live, she felt the threads streaming out from the old people around her. From their seared eyes. From their navels and their cast-iron hearts. And their brightness as they entered her spoke of possibilities and becoming even in the face of the bare bones and the burnt-out ends. She began to dance then. Just as her feet of their own accord had discovered the old steps, her hips under the linen shirtdress slowly began to weave from side to side on their own. . . . All of her moving suddenly with a vigor and passion she hadn't felt in years, and with something of the stylishness and sass she had once been known for. (249)

Like her Aunt Cuney, Avey surreptitiously performs the dance that was not supposed to be dancing, for the flailing bodies are allowed every liberty, but their feet are not supposed to leave the floor or cross each other in a dance step (33). Adhering to the rules, Avey engages in this dance that not only connects her with Aunt Cuney and the ancestors, but also connects the people of Tatem, South Carolina, with the people of the Caribbean island of Carriacou, illuminating kinship and connections in spite of geographical distance between the two peoples.

The dance characterized by the shuffling of feet is indicative of the ancestors whose movements were limited because of the chains that restrained them, yet in spite of these chains they danced and celebrated life. Noticeably, dance here has similar connotations to the dance that Selina of *Brown Girl, Brownstones* performs. Avey, like Selina, is renewed and figuratively reborn through dance and rituals. Paulette Brown-Hinds observes that "dance becomes an expression which builds bridges to connect seemingly unconnectable spaces." In dancing, Avey proclaims her kinship and ancestry with all blacks, bridging the gap between Mother Africa, duly represented by the stepping Ibos, and the black diaspora: Tatem and Carriacou. "The ritual of drumming, song and especially dance," according to Eugenia Collier, "is a celebration of African roots. The ritual draws together Black people from throughout time and space and declares their commonality." Performing the Creole dance and singing the Beg Pardon, Avey literally begs pardon. Absolved, she is accepted into the Ring Dance, "the out-islanders had reached out their arms like one great arm and drawn her into their midst," and can now seemingly walk on water like the Ibos. The thread that Avey feels is the umbilical cord that unites and weaves all the lost children of the diaspora and Mother Africa. Validating this claim, Velma Pollard concludes that "cultural unity joins the black people of the Sea Islands of the southern United States to the black people of the Caribbean and by implication to all diaspora people."[31] The Carriacou Tramp had indeed stayed the course of history, uniting all, "including these strangers who had become one and the same with people in Tatem" (250).

No longer a stranger, Avey, the once lost and wandering soul, has finally returned "home," fulfilling her earlier desire when she confesses: "All I knew was that I wanted to go home" (171). Ironically, she does not return to her home in North White Plains, but instead enacts a significant, spiritual return to her ancestral home. Hers is a smile of triumph. When asked "And who you is?" she recalls Aunt Cuney's words and jubilantly responds: "Avey, short for Avatara" (251). This self-invocation and self-reclamation return Avey to her self. Her return is complete. She has been spiritually renewed. She has achieved spiritual "wholeness." Barbara Christian notes that recognizing herself as Avatara "is also essential to the ritual, for in African cosmology it is through *nommo*, through the correct naming of a thing, that it comes into existence." Being able to name herself and "call her nation," Avey fully comes into existence. Thus, she has come into being through spiritual healing and acceptance. Her individual healing offers hope as it unites communities. Hence, declares Abena Busia, "through the healing of one of Africa's lost daughters, a scattered people are made whole again." Avey has endured the course of this ride. She has endured the "physical and psychical memories of slavery," thereby qualifying her as a "true" ancestress, appropriately earning the respect of this title.[32]

The first to welcome her into the ancestral realm is the sage and aged Lebert Joseph, who "bowed, a profound, solemn bow that was

31. Paulette Brown-Hinds, "In the Spirit: Dance as Healing Ritual in Paule Marshall's *Praisesong for the Widow*," 108; Collier, "Closing the Circle," 313; Velma Pollard, "Cultural Connections in Paule Marshall's *Praisesong for the Widow*," 286.
32. Christian, *Black Women Novelists*, 83; Busia, "What Is Your Nation?" 199; Holloway, *Moorings and Metaphors*, 89.

like a genuflection" (250). His daughter Rosalie Parvay followed suit, and "others in the crowd of aged dancers, taking their cue from him also, began doing the same. One after another of the men and women trudging past, who were her senior by years, would pause as they reached her and, turning briefly in her direction, tender her the deep almost reverential bow" (250). It is of utmost significance that all those who offer her reverence are elderly, indicative of one of the many requirements of the ancestral line(age). At the age of sixty-five, Avey is a qualified member who will take over and take on the honored role of storyteller, becoming a griot like her Aunt Cuney. Thus, Avey arrives at an ensured awakening, for she now knows what has to be done in order to stay the course. Like Lebert Joseph who confesses, "When you see me down on my knees at the Big Drum singing the Beg Pardon, I don' be singing just for me one. Oh, no! Is for tout moun" (175), Avey also neither speaks nor sings for herself but for communities and for future generations. Her voice is the communal voice.

Bestowed with spiritual blessings, Avey answers her ancestral calling, vowing to convert all those who have strayed and suffered cultural unmooring. Her first self-assigned task is to convert the taxi driver:

> [S]he would quote him the line from the story that had been drilled into her as a child, which had been handed down from the woman whose name she bore. "Her body she always usta say might be in Tatem but her mind, her mind was long gone with the Ibos . . ." Nor would she stop with the taxi driver, but would take it upon herself to speak of the excursion to others elsewhere. Her territory would be the street corners and front lawns in their small section of North White Plains. And the shopping mall and train station. As well as the canyon streets and office buildings of Manhattan. (254–55)

The spreading of the gospel holds no limits or boundaries. Avatara, as Karla Holloway observes, "is indeed the embodiment of the deities that Jay senses reside in her. They are ancient spirits who bridge the geographic and cultural diaspora and they are all women. These are deities whom Avey will eventually come to honor through her choice to become a teller and to pass on her ancestors' story."[33]

33. Holloway, *Moorings and Metaphors*, 134.

Upon her return to North White Plains, Avey will unite with her daughter Marion, who is already an avid ancestral worshiper, to spread the word. Thus joining with Marion, Avey will continue the lineage enacted by Aunt Cuney by having her grandsons come to visit her at the Ibo Landing each summer. Recapturing her lineage, Avey not only dances the Juba, a dance practiced mainly by women in pairs, and the Nation Dance, but also vows to narrate the history of these African rituals, thereby ensuring their continuance. Her storytelling, like her ancestors before her, qualifies her as ancestress and griot. Avey has successfully traveled the distance and has made the Carriacou Tramp, the Ring Shouts and Dance, her newfound religion.

5 "Call[ing] Your Nation"

A Journey Completed

Lebert Joseph's cautionary message about the importance of being able to "call your nation" is of crucial importance to black diasporic peoples, because in calling their nation, they, on one hand, disclaim the history that has rendered them and their knowledge insignificant and, on the other hand, reclaim their historical past and validate African oral traditions, that "other way of knowing things." In calling one's nation the individual not only claims her self, but also claims an entire family and generational history. This tracing of the family lineage has nationalistic (diasporic) capabilities, and Lebert Joseph confirms that the lineage is boundless. Avey, an African American woman, is able to call her nation on a Caribbean island, unknown to her before this journey, and reestablish kinship with her long-lost mothers and sisters. The scattered peoples of the diaspora have a dire need to trace their family line to unite that which was disrupted and those who were separated by the Middle Passage journey, and also those who are derailed by encroaching Western values. The claiming of one's lineage is of such colossal significance that the Carriacouan folks celebrate this national ritual with a Big Drum each year to remember the ancestors and offer them libations.

In addition to this "name claiming," another hallmark of identifying with and being able to call your nation is through dance. Avey, initially unable to call her nation, eventually dances it, after which she is able to partake in the Beg Pardon and other Nation Dances. The various dances and accompanying songs not only disclose to which tribe an individual belongs, but also relate the historical past, the lives of the ancestors during slavery and before the slave trade. Many of the dances and songs are also linked to historical places, but the memories are not buried in the historical archives; they are remembered as they "had come down in the blood" (178). By partaking in these rituals, the past is invoked and relived in the present.

Though this invocation of an African past is of an oral nature, the endorsement of oral histories does not negate or denounce mainstream literary tradition; rather, we witness a blending of the oral and written in black women's writings. Accentuating this mutually enriching blend, Marshall observes that the past "figures prominently in [my] work, but not to the exclusion of the present or the future." In order to be able to call her nation, the black woman has to journey back into her historical past, whether symbolically, physically, or spiritually. Giving precedence to the spiritual, Marshall contends that "the spiritual return is a metaphor for the psychological and spiritual return back over history, which I am convinced Black people in this part of the world must undertake if we are to have a sense of our total experience and to mold for ourselves a more truthful identity. Moreover, I believe this exploration of the past is vital in the work of constructing our future."[1] The "Black people in this part of the world" that Marshall talks about are the people who constitute the diaspora, those who share a common history of oppression: slavery and now colonization. In spite of the oppressive atmosphere assimilated with these forms of enslavement, this past has to be confronted to foster creation of the self, for knowledge of one's cultural and historical past is the key to understanding the self.

Faced with the arduous task of creating another art form that will adequately and competently document black women and their lives and experiences, the black woman writer is faced with a monumental responsibility, as Marshall summarizes: "The main responsibility falls to the Black writer. [She has] the greatest part in establishing the cultural base. And [her] task is two-fold: on one hand to make use of the rich body of folk and historical material that is there; and on the other to interpret that past in heroic terms, in recognition of the fact that our history . . . is one of the greatest triumphs of the human spirit in modern times."[2]

Marshall's call for the incorporation of "folk and historical material" in present works is indicative of her struggle to maintain an African dimension in diasporic literature in spite of strong, imposing Western influences. She also suggests that black people need to over-

1. Marshall, "Shaping the World," 108, 107.
2. Ibid., 108.

look the foul deeds of the slave and colonial masters and, instead, celebrate the past heroically, though the enforced subjugation was far from heroic. But, as Marshall correctly contends, celebrating that history in heroic terms is a moment of triumph, triumph of a people who had endured so much yet are able to claim victory.

Commenting on the incorporation and recapturing of the past in women's works, Karla Holloway argues that memory and myth are key components in black women's writings. In a close reading of Marshall's *Praisesong for the Widow*, she contends:

> [The] presence of mythologies in black women writers' texts points toward the elements of myth—metaphor, spirituality, and memory— as they appear in the system of literature, rather than toward individual myths of West Africa. The cultural presence within literature acknowledges spoken language as its source. The potential to reformulate story, not into constituent patterns but into frames that reconstruct more ancient patterns of memory and telling— mythologies—is of interpretive significance. . . . Texts by black women writers privilege an older understanding of literature. Because their structures acknowledge the mythic traditions that have generated them, these works are not distinguished from their ancestry.[3]

In spite of the privileging of an older understanding of literature, orality, this advantage does not come at the expense of the written word. While this orality validates African religious practices and cultures, it simultaneously acknowledges the written as a constituent. Nonetheless, this acknowledgment of the written does not in the least prevent the exposing of the flaws of the so-called historical facts or records. These defects are shamelessly uncovered in Condé's rewriting of the history of Tituba.

In calling for a celebration of the past, Marshall underscores the importance of both oral and print literature. Nevertheless, as a result of misrepresentation of the black woman's history in print, the so-called original word has been tailored and transformed by black (Caribbean) women writers to suit their needs.[4] We, therefore, witness consistent engagement of the past with the present in black

---

3. Holloway, *Moorings and Metaphors*, 89.
4. By the "original" word, I am referring to the Queen's English, the colonial mother tongue.

women's narratives, as the works of Jamaica Kincaid, Paule Marshall, and Maryse Condé testify. While Marshall is tenaciously and incomparably entrenched in the distant past, namely, the reenactment of the Middle Passage and slavery, Condé and Kincaid are more preoccupied with what I refer to as the present past: colonization and its effect. Notwithstanding, the past figures prominently in their writings.

In celebration of the black woman's resurgence into history, the novels map the journeys, whether physical or spiritual, of both the writers and their protagonists. Purposefully enacted, these journeys facilitate the acquisition of spiritual wholeness or consciousness. Reenacting the Atlantic crossing, history is relived, and Africa is revisited through the Caribbean, and a new self is born or re-created.[5] This historical self is conceived on respective Caribbean islands. Noted for its insularity and suggestive of containment and isolation, the Caribbean simultaneously possesses transcendent qualities, for it is depicted in the novels as a safe haven, the chosen ancestral land, a place where African culture is religiously preserved and practiced. The insular nature of the Caribbean connotes a villagelike atmosphere, conducive for the survival of the ancestor and ancestral worshiping. By positing the Caribbean as the chosen ancestral land, Condé, Marshall, and Kincaid seemingly promote the concept of "city limits, [and] village values" addressed by Morrison in an article that bears the same title. Offering a comparative analysis between mainstream writers and black writers, Morrison contends that unlike black writers, the village, distinct from the city, for white writers seemingly has "no moral life or manners." Identifying probable causes for black writers' affinity for the village or village values, Morrison maintains that because they are "generally viewed as victims, wards, and pathologies in urban settings [and] not participants," black people, unlike whites, do not experience any sense of belonging to the city. They are unable to lay claim to the city like the "poorest white factory worker or white welfare recipient."[6]

5. I view Avey's spiritual return to the Motherland via the Caribbean as the reenactment of the Atlantic crossing.
6. Toni Morrison, "City Limits, Village Values: Concepts of the Neighborhood in Black Fiction," 37.

Morrison's observation holds true in the case of Marshall's novel *Brown Girl, Brownstones,* for we witness the Bajan community's obsession with land and property ownership as a means of claiming the city of New York, yet they remain outsiders and are distinguished from the white inhabitants of the city. Margaret's mother, who undermines the efforts of the Bajan women as she relegates them to the margins of society with her condescending comments, parallels Morrison's observation about white mainstream writers' undermining of black writers who exhibit a propensity for village values in their works: "[S]uch critics tend not to trust or respect a hero who prefers the village and its tribal values to heroic loneliness and alienation. When a character defies a village law or shows contempt for its values, it may be seen as a triumph to white readers, while Blacks may see it as an outrage."[7]

It is such an outrage that Lebert Joseph in *Praisesong for the Widow* expresses when he finds out that Avey Johnson is unable to "call her nation" because of her prior obsession with material values and city life. It is the same outrage that he expresses over his grand- and great-grandchildren's monumental loss: their migration to the metropolitan cities in North America, a move that seemingly comes at the expense of village values. It is the relinquishing of ancestral values and, in turn, the past, that outrages the ancestors. Reiterating Lebert Joseph's earlier comment, the ancestors are angered when they are not offered libations or, worse, when they are totally disregarded or ignored. Morrison sees this disregard for the ancestors as the missing quality in city fiction, and a palpable presence in village fiction. She asserts that the "advising, benevolent, protective, wise Black ancestor is imagined as surviving in the village but not in the city." She, however, contends that the reason for that depiction is not simply a hatred for city life on the writer's part, but her longing for the ancestor, for the city is depicted as wholesome and loved when there is an ancestral presence. She concludes that disregard or absence of the ancestor is the main reason for black writers that "the city has huge limits and the village profound values."[8]

7. Ibid., 38.
8. Ibid., 39.

Unparalleled, the ancestral presence is omniscient in all of Marshall's novels. He is the shopkeeper, the tribal African chief, who sits behind his counter and offers libations to the gods; she is Merle Kinbona, who keeps the Bournehills community together and alive. She is also Leesy, the protector and consultant to Merle, in *The Chosen Place, the Timeless People;* he is Lebert Joseph, who redirects the wanderings of the widowed protagonist, Avey; she is Great-aunt Cuney, the protector, nurturer, and spiritual guide of her niece, Avey. She is also Mama Yaya of Condé's *I, Tituba, Black Witch of Salem,* who bestows upon her surrogate daughter the gift of witchcraft; she is also her birth mother, Abena. The ancestress is also Ma Chess of Kincaid's *Annie John.*

It is no mere coincidence that the ancestors are predominantly women. They are the ones who facilitate the lineage and generational continuity. In analyzing a few texts by black women writers, Marshall's *Praisesong* included, Karla Holloway notes that the texts "make it clear that these ancestral women's lineage is inhabited by women of the African diaspora."[9] The absence of women or mother figures signals the fracture of the generational lineage, because they are the ones who maintain and preserve the continuance of the lineage.

The absence of the ancestor speaks to the devastation and loss of the characters. Morrison notes that "if we don't keep in touch with the ancestor then we are, in fact, lost. When you kill the ancestor you kill yourself." Kincaid's Xuela and Condé's Veronica reject all ancestral presence, which accounts for their wanderings. In a similar manner, Marshall's Silla, even after realizing her dreams of acquiring a brownstone, remains deflated and unregenerated. Her disillusionment is a result of the absence of the ancestor. Although she is regarded as "the mother," a title that possesses ancestral qualities and potentials, Silla "becomes merely an adult and is thereby seen as a betrayer—one who has abandoned [her] traditional role of advisor with a strong connection to the past."[10] Her daughter Selina will seemingly recapture this ancestral presence that she has negated, leaving it behind with her past in Barbados. The heroine, Avatara

9. Holloway, *Moorings and Metaphors,* 139.
10. Morrison, "Rootedness," 344, 340.

Johnson, who wanders fleetingly, is brought back to spiritual consciousness with the aid of the ancestors. Loneliness and alienation are condemned by the ancestors and as such are not viewed as acts of heroism, as they are in city fictions, but rather are categorized as selfish, unheroic deeds that work against communal relationships, community, and kinship.

Morrison argues that the presence of the ancestor, whether in the village or the city, is the determining factor in the success of the protagonist's life. The village is predominantly represented as conducive for the survival of the ancestor and the practicing of ancestral values and culture. In all the novels discussed, the ancestors inhabit the rural areas. In addition, the ancestors are noted for their limited travels or journeys. Aimless journeys or wanderings are signs of physical and cultural displacements within the African diaspora. Nonetheless, the characters have to journey and experience life's trials and tribulations, or symbolically experience slavery, like Avey and to some extent Tituba, who follows her husband into slavery, in order to be bestowed the honor of ancestress.

These early wanderings stand in stark contrast to the rootedness of those who have already been bestowed the honorary title. Lebert Joseph refuses to leave the island and go abroad to the United States, where his unknown grandchildren reside. Mama Yaya refuses to cross water and repeatedly tells Tituba that she will be unable to protect her while in Massachusetts, away from the island, and across the sea, with her husband, John Indian. Ma Chess refuses to board the steamer that transports travelers from one island to the next and instead opts for the African traditional means of transportation, flying.

The island, in spite of its suffocating, womblike image, is a place of refuge, a place of significant value because of the ensured presence of the ancestors. The island, "villagelike" in nature, cut off from "civilization and modernization," becomes the ideal place for ancestor worshiping. Free from contamination of city life in the village, the ancestors, when faced with semblance of capitalist ideologies, occasionally exhibit fear of "fast life," fear of urbanization and industrialization. Leesy Walkes, the old aunt of Vere, exhibits compelling fear of machinery and technology in *Chosen Place*. In her eyes, Vere died because of his strong craving for city life, his love for machinery.

He goes to the United States and becomes entrapped in the web of capitalist values and as such renounces his village values.

This "fight" for upward mobility prohibits as well as inhibits ancestral worshiping. In a similar manner, Silla Boyce is consumed by materialism and "taken in" by the bright lights of New York. Her migration from the rural Bimshire, as she condescendingly refers to Barbados, is a relinquishment and renouncement of her village values. Noticeably, in all the novels the ancestors are village inhabitants. Renouncing the "dog eat dog" capitalist system and placing less emphasis on material possessions, the ancestors maintain and sustain the generational lineage in the village. The Caribbean, a site where African oral traditions are recaptured, qualifies as a new site, a newfound homeland. As such, we witness reverse migration, where the inhabitants of the metropole journey to the Caribbean in search not of material wealth but of spiritual wholeness.

In search of this home, Selina Boyce leaves the United States for her mother's land, Barbados. In *Praisesong*, Avey Johnson forcibly reroutes her holiday cruise, transforming it into a spiritual journey and homecoming as she finds herself on the Caribbean island of Carriacou. In Marshall's *Chosen Place*, Bournehills, a Caribbean island, is recaptured as a homesite.

These novels celebrate ancestry and the ancestral presence. Marshall confirms that together her three books—*Brown Girl*, *Chosen Place*, and *Praisesong*—describe in reverse the "slave trade's triangular route back to the motherland, the source."[11] She emphasizes that she is not talking about an actual return, though it is couched in those terms. The inability to return to or embrace the past is catastrophic because it severs the generational lineage or matrilineage. Deprived of the womb, the mother's and the island, Xuela is unable to call her nation. She is culturally and spiritually vacuous. Although the island does not provide Xuela with the support and love she craves, it is a source of spirituality for Avatara Johnson and Tituba, who are conferred the status of ancestress after they have unequivocally claimed the island and the island's (African) culture.

Success of the characters is determined by the ancestral presence, that spiritual, conjuring woman who practices her religion, her craft,

11. Marshall, "Shaping the World," 107.

and her art. Spiritually blessed, she not only knows "other things," but also possesses the ability to see and validate "other ways of knowing things." She is Ma Chess in *Annie John*, Merle and Vere's aunt Leesy in *Chosen Place*, Aunt Cuney and subsequently Avey in *Praisesong*, Miss Thompson in *Brown Girl*, and Mama Yaya, Abena, and subsequently Tituba in *Tituba*.

No longer silenced by the historical records, women reclaim their herstories. By giving their protagonists voices, the writers empower them to reclaim their history and selfhood. They, the protagonists, in turn rewrite (or reright) themselves back into history. The titles of the novels—*Brown Girl, Brownstones; Praisesong for the Widow; Annie John;* and *I, Tituba, Black Witch of Salem*—speak of this writing or righting back into history these women who were once dispossessed, disrobed metaphorically and literally, and stripped of their identities. The titles of the novels are also celebratory; at once empowering and self-affirming, they connote presence and self-definition *(Tituba, Brown Girl,* and *Annie John),* sing praises for the women *(Praisesong for the Widow,* and *Tituba),* and pay tribute to the mothers *(Autobiography of My Mother).*

Making up for the injustices done and the pain inflicted, Marshall determinedly asserts that her reason for writing is "to make women—especially black women—important characters in [my] stories. . . . To make up for the neglect, the disregard, the distortions, and untruths, [I] wanted them to be center-stage."[12] Women are certainly at the center of the stories of these novels. Without a doubt, these works have offered young black women a more truthful image of themselves in literature. Condé, Marshall, and Kincaid have created a space, a female space, a mother's land, wherein history and myth coalesce, where fiction and reality are conflated, and where the black woman is at home with herself. They have successfully captured and depicted the complexities of the black female being.

Having successfully accomplished the tasks set out before them, Marshall, Kincaid, and Condé have accomplished not only a literary journey but also a spiritual journey, and are therefore able to triumphantly "call their nation."

12. Paule Marshall, "An Interview with Paule Marshall," 20.

Bibliography

Anderson, Benjamin. *Imagined Communities: Reflection on the Origin and Spread of Nationalism*. London: Verso, 1983.

Andrade, Susan Z. "The Nigger of the Narcissist: History, Sexuality, and Intertextuality in Maryse Condé's *Heremakhonon*." *Callaloo* 16:1 (winter 1993): 213–26.

Bakhtin, Mikhail. *Rabelais and His World*. Bloomington: Indiana University Press, 1984.

———. *Speech Genres and Other Late Essays*. Ed. Caryl Emerson and Michael Holquist. Trans. Vern W. McGee. Austin: University of Texas Press, 1970.

Baugh, Edward. *Critics on Caribbean Literature*. New York: St. Martin's Press, 1978.

Bécel, Pascale. "*Moi, Tituba Sorciere . . . Noire de Salem* as a Tale of *Petite Marronne*." *Callaloo* 18:3 (1995): 608–15.

Bell, Roseann P., Bettye J. Parker, and Beverly Guy-Sheftall, eds. *Sturdy Black Bridges: Visions of Black Women in Literature*. Garden City, N.Y.: Doubleday, Anchor Press, 1979.

Bennett, Louise. *Jamaica Labrish*. Kingston, Jamaica: Sangster's Book Store, 1966.

Benstock, Shari, ed. *The Private Self: Theory and Practice of Women's Autobiographical Writings*. Chapel Hill: University of North Carolina Press, 1988.

Berrian, Brenda F. *Bibliography of Women Writers from the Caribbean*. Washington, D.C.: Three Continents Press, 1988.

———. "Masculine Roles and Triangular Relationships in Maryse Condé's *Une Saison à Rihata*." *Bridges* 3 (1991): 5–20.

Blackburn, Regina. "In Search of the Black Female Self: African-American Women's Autobiographies and Ethnicity." In *Women's Autobiography: Essays in Criticism*, ed. Estelle C. Jelinek, 133–48. Bloomington: Indiana University Press, 1980.

Bobo, Jacqueline. *Black Women as Cultural Readers*. New York: Columbia University Press, 1995.

Brathwaite, Edward Kamau. *Contradictory Omens: Cultural Diversity and Integration in the Caribbean*. Mona, Jamaica: Savacou Publications, 1974.

————. *History of the Voice*. London: New Beacon Books, 1984.

————. *Roots*. Ann Arbor: University of Michigan Press, 1993.

Braxton, Joanne M. *Black Women Writing Autobiography*. Philadelphia: Temple University Press, 1989.

Breslaw, Elaine G. *Tituba, Reluctant Witch of Salem*. New York: New York University Press, 1996.

Brock, Sabine. "Transcending the 'Loophole of Retreat': Paule Marshall's Placing of Female Generations." *Callaloo* 10:1 (winter 1987): 79–90.

Brodber, Erna. *Myal*. London: New Beacon Books, 1988.

Brown-Guillory, Elizabeth, ed. *Women of Color: Mother-Daughter Relationships in Twentieth-Century Literature*. Austin: University of Texas Press, 1996.

Brown-Hinds, Paulette. "In the Spirit: Dance as Healing Ritual in Paule Marshall's *Praisesong for the Widow*." *Religion and Literature* 27:1 (spring 1995): 107–17.

Bruner, Charlotte, and David Bruner. "Buchi Emecheta and Maryse Condé: Contemporary Writing from Africa and the Caribbean." *World Literature Today* 59:1 (winter 1985): 9–13.

Busia, Abena. "What Is Your Nation? Reconnecting Africa and Her Diaspora through Paule Marshall's *Praisesong for the Widow*." In *Changing Our Own Words: Essays on Criticism, Theory, and Writing by Black Women*, ed. Cheryl A. Wall, 196–211. New Brunswick: Rutgers University Press, 1989.

————. "Words Whispered over Voids: A Context for Black Women's Rebellious Voices in the Novel of the African Diaspora." In *Black Feminist Criticism and Critical Theory*, ed. Joe Weixlmann and Houston A. Baker Jr., 1–41. Studies in Black American Literature, no. 3. Greenwood: Penkevill Publishing, 1988.

Byerman, Keith. "Gender, Culture, and Identity in Paule Marshall's *Brown Girl, Brownstones*." In *Redefining Autobiography in Twentieth-Century Women's Fiction: An Essay Collection*, ed. Janice Morgan, 135–47. New York: Garland, 1991.

Cabral, Amilcar. "National Liberation and Culture." In *Colonial Discourse and Post-colonial Theory*, ed. Patrick Williams and Laura Chrisman, 53–65. New York: Columbia University Press, 1994.

Christian, Barbara. *Black Women Novelists: The Development of a Tradition, 1892–1976.* Westport, Conn.: Greenwood Press, 1980.

———. "Ritualistic Process and the Structure of Paule Marshall's *Praisesong for the Widow.*" *Callaloo* 6:2 (1983): 74–84.

Christol, Hélène. " 'The Black Woman's Burden': *Black Women and Work in the Street* (Ann Petry) and *Brown Girl, Brownstones* (Paule Marshall)." In *Les États Unis: Images du travail et des loisirs,* ed. Serge Ricard, 145–58. Aix-en-Provence: Univ. de Provence, 1989.

Clark, Vévè A. "Developing Diaspora Literacy: Allusion in Maryse Condé's *Heremakhonon.*" In *Out of the Kumbla,* ed. Carole Boyce Davies and Elaine Savory Fido, 303–19. Trenton, N.J.: Africa World Press, 1990.

———. "Developing Diaspora Literacy and Marasa Consciousness." In *Comparative American Identities: Race, Sex, and Nationality in the Modern Text, Essays from the English Institute,* ed. Hortense Spillers, 40–61. New York: Routledge, 1991.

Cobham, Rhonda. "Revisioning Our Kumblas: Transforming Feminist and Nationalist Agendas in Three Caribbean Women's Texts." *Callaloo* 16:1 (winter 1993): 44–64.

Cobham, Rhonda, and Merle Collins. *Watchers and Seekers: Creative Writing by Black Women.* New York: Peter Bedrick Books, 1987.

Collier, Eugenia. "The Closing of the Circle: Movement from Division to Wholeness in Paule Marshall's Fiction." In *Black Women Writers, 1950–1980,* ed. Mari Evans, 295–315. Garden City, N.Y.: Doubleday, 1984.

Collins, Merle. *Rain Darling.* London: Women's Press, 1990.

———. *Rotten Pomerack.* London: Karia Press, 1985.

Collins, Patricia Hill. *Black Feminist Thoughts: Knowledge, Consciousness, and the Politics of Empowerment.* New York: Routledge, 1991.

Condé, Maryse. "L'Afrique, un continent difficile: Entretien avec Maryse Condé." Interview by Marie-Clotilde Jacquey and Monique Hugon. *Notre Librairie* 74 (1984): 21–25.

———. *Heremakhonon.* Boulder, Colo.: Lynne Rienner Publishers, 1985.

———. *I, Tituba, Black Witch of Salem.* New York: Ballantine Books, 1992.

———. "An Interview with Maryse Condé and Rita Dove." By Mohamed B. Taleb-Khyar. *Callaloo* 14:2 (spring 1991): 347–66.

———. "Je me suis reconcilié avec mon île (I have made peace with my island): An Interview with Maryse Condé." By Vévè Clark and Cecile Daheny. *Callaloo* 12:1 (winter 1989): 95–133.

———. "No Silence: An Interview with Maryse Condé." By Barbara Lewis. *Callaloo* 18:3 (summer 1995): 543–50.

———. "Pan-Africanism, Feminism, and Culture." In *Imagining Home: Class, Culture, and Nationalism in the African Diaspora*, ed. Sidney J. Lemelle and Robin D. G. Kelley, 55–65. New York: Verso, 1994.

———. *A Season in Rihata.* London: Heinemann Educational Books, 1988.

Cudjoe, Selwyn R. *Resistance and Caribbean Literature.* Athens: Ohio University Press, 1980.

———, ed. *Caribbean Women Writers: Essays from the First International Conference.* Wellesley, Mass.: Calaloux Publications, 1990.

Dance, Daryl Cumber. *Fifty Caribbean Writers: A Bio-bibliographical Critical Sourcebook.* Westport, Conn.: Greenwood Press, 1986.

Danticat, Edwidge. *Breath, Eyes, Memory.* New York: Soho Press, 1994.

Davies, Carole Boyce. *Black Women, Writings, and Identity: Migrations of the Subject.* London: Routledge, 1994.

———. "Collaboration and the Ordering Imperative in Life Story Production." In *De/Colonizing the Subject: The Politics of Gender in Women's Autobiography*, ed. Sidonie Smith and Julia Watson, 3–19. Minneapolis: University of Minnesota Press, 1992.

Davies, Carole Boyce, and Elaine Savory Fido. "Black Woman's Journey into Self: A Womanist Reading of Paule Marshall's *Praisesong for the Widow.*" *Matatu* 1:1 (1987): 19–34.

———, eds. *Out of the Kumbla.* Trenton, N.J.: Africa World Press, 1990.

de Abruña, Laura Niesen. "The Ambivalence of Mirroring and Female Bonding in Paule Marshall's *Brown Girl, Brownstones.*" In *International Women's Writing: New Landscape of Identity*, ed. Anne E. Brown and Marjanne E. Goozé, 245–52. Westport, Conn.: Greenwood Press, 1995.

———. "Family Connections: Mother and Mother Country in the Fiction of Jean Rhys and Jamaica Kincaid." In *Motherlands: Black Women's Writing from Africa, the Caribbean, and South Asia*, ed. Susheila Nasta, 257–89. New Brunswick: Rutgers University Press, 1992.

Denniston, Dorothy Hamer. *The Fiction of Paule Marshall: Reconstructions of History, Culture, and Gender.* Knoxville: University of Tennessee Press, 1983.

de Weever, Jacqueline. *Mythmaking and Metaphor in Black Women's Fiction.* New York: St. Martin's Press, 1991.

Dingledine, Donald. "Woman Can Walk on Water: Island, Myth, and Community in Kate Chopin's *The Awakening* and Paule Marshall's *Praisesong for the Widow.*" *Women's Studies* 22:2 (1993): 197–216.

Donnell, Alison. "Dreaming of Daffodils: Cultural Resistance in the Narrative of Theory." *Kunapipi* 14:2 (1992): 45–52.

———. "When Daughters Defy: Jamaica Kincaid's Fiction." *Women: A Cultural Review* 4:1 (spring 1993): 18–26.

Dutton, Wendy. "Merge and Separate: Jamaica Kincaid's Fiction." *World Literature Today* 63:3 (summer 1989): 406–10.

Eko, Ebele. "Oral Traditions: The Bridge to Africa in Paule Marshall's *Praisesong for the Widow.*" *Western Journal of Black Studies* 10:3 (1986): 143–47.

Ellison, Ralph. *Invisible Man.* New York: Vintage, 1995.

Evans, Mari, ed. *Black Women Writers, 1950–1980.* Garden City, N.Y.: Doubleday, Anchor Press, 1984.

Fanon, Frantz. *Black Skin, White Masks.* New York: Grove Press, 1967.

Ferguson, Moira. *Colonialism and Gender Relations from Mary Wollstonecraft to Jamaica Kincaid: East Caribbean Connections.* New York: Columbia University Press, 1993.

———. *Jamaica Kincaid: Where the Land Meets the Body.* Charlottesville: University Press of Virginia, 1994.

———. "Lucy and the Mark of the Colonizer." *Modern Fiction Studies* 39:2 (1993): 242.

Flannigan, Arthur. "Reading below the Belt: Sex and Sexuality in Françoise Ega and Maryse Condé." *French Review* 62:2 (1988): 300–312.

Fox-Genovese, Elizabeth. "My Statue, My Self: Autobiographical Writings of Afro-American Women." In *Reading Black, Reading Feminist: A Critical Anthology,* ed. Henry Louis Gates Jr., 179–203. New York: Meridian Books, 1990.

Friedman, Susan Stanford. "Women's Autobiographical Selves: Theory and Practice." In *The Private Self: The Theory and Practice of Women's Autobiographical Writings,* ed. Shari Benstock, 34–62. Chapel Hill: University of North Carolina Press, 1988.

Gates, Henry Louis, Jr. *Race, Writing, and Difference.* Chicago: University of Chicago Press, 1986.

———, ed. *Reading Black, Reading Feminist: A Critical Anthology.* New York: Meridian Books, 1990.

Gilbert, Sandra, and Susan Gubar. *Madwoman in the Attic: The Woman Writer and the Nineteenth-Century Literary Imagination.* New Haven: Yale University Press, 1979.

Glissant, Edouard. *Caribbean Discourse.* Charlottesville: University Press of Virginia, 1989.

Green, Mary J. *Postcolonial Subjects: Francophone Women Writers.* Minneapolis: University of Minnesota Press, 1996.

Harkins, Patricia. "Family Magic: Invisibility in Jamaica Kincaid's *Lucy." Journal of the Fantastic in the Arts* 4:3 (1991): 53–68.

Harris, Trudier. "No Outlet for the Blues: Silla Boyce's Plight in *Brown Girl, Brownstones." Callaloo* 6:2 (1993): 57–67.

Hathaway, Heather. *Caribbean Waves: Relocating Claude McKay and Paule Marshall.* Bloomington: Indiana University Press, 1999.

Hearne, John. *Carifesta Forum: An Anthology of Twenty Caribbean Voices.* Kingston, Jamaica: Carifesta '76, 1976.

Hirsch, Marianne. "Maternal Narratives: 'Cruel Enough to Stop the Blood.' " In *Reading Black, Reading Feminist: A Critical Anthology,* ed. Henry Louis Gates Jr., 415–30. New York: Meridian Books, 1990.

Holloway, Karla. *Moorings and Metaphors: Figures of Culture and Gender in Black Women's Literature.* New Brunswick: Rutgers University Press, 1992.

Hooks, bell. *Talking Back: Thinking Feminist, Thinking Black.* Boston: South End Press, 1989.

Japtok, Martin. "Paule Marshall's *Brown Girl, Brownstones:* Reconciling Ethnicity and Individualism" *African American Review* 32:4 (winter 1998): 305–15.

Johnson, Lemuel. "A-beng: (Re)Calling the Body in(to) Question." In *Out of the Kumbla,* ed. Carole Boyce Davies and Elaine Savory Fido, 111–42. Trenton, N.J.: Africa World Press, 1990.

———. "Sisters of Anarcha: Speculum in a New World? Caribbean Literature and a Feminist Hermeneutics." In *African Literature Studies: The Present State,* ed. Stephen Arnold, 229–44. Washington, D.C.: Three Continents Press, 1996.

Jones, Gavin. " 'The Sea Ain' Got No Back Door': The Problem of Black Consciousness in Paule Marshall's *Brown Girl, Brownstones.*" *African American Review* 32:4 (winter 1998): 597–606.

Kaplan, Caren. "Deterritorializations: The Rewriting of Home and Exile in Western Feminist Discourse." *Cultural Critique* 6 (spring 1987): 187–98.

Kincaid, Jamaica. *Annie John.* New York: Penguin Books, 1986.

———. *At the Bottom of the River.* New York: Penguin Books, 1992.

———. *The Autobiography of My Mother.* New York: Penguin Books, 1996.

———. " 'I Come from a Place That's Very Unreal': An Interview with Jamaica Kincaid." By Allan Vorda. In *Face-to-Face: Interviews with Contemporary Novelists,* ed. Allan Vorda and Daniel Stern, 77–106. Houston: Rice University Press, 1993.

———. "An Interview with Jamaica Kincaid." By Allan Vorda. *Mississippi Review* 20:1–2 (1991): 7–26.

———. "An Interview with Jamaica Kincaid." By Kay Bonetti. *Missouri Review* 15:2 (1992): 124–42.

———. "An Interview with Jamaica Kincaid." In *Backtalk: Women Writers Speak Out,* ed. Donna Perry, 127–41. New Brunswick: Rutgers University Press, 1993.

———. "A Lot of Memory: An Interview with Jamaica Kincaid." By Moira Ferguson. *Kenyon Review* 16:1 (1994): 163–88.

———. *Lucy.* New York: Penguin Books, 1991.

———. *A Small Place.* New York: Penguin Books, 1988.

Knight, Frank, and Colin Palmer. *The Modern Caribbean.* Chapel Hill: University of North Carolina Press, 1989.

Ledent, Benedicte. "Voyage into Otherness: Cambridge and *Lucy.*" *Kunapipi* 14:2 (1992): 52–53.

Lee, Valerie. *Granny Midwives and Black Women Writers: Double-Dutched Readings.* New York: Routledge, 1996.

Lionnet, Françoise. *Autobiographical Voices: Race, Gender, Self-Portraiture.* Ithaca: Cornell University Press, 1989.

Loncke, Joycelynn. "The Image of the Woman in Caribbean Literature with Special Response to *Pan Beat* and *Heremakhonon.*" *Bim* 64 (1978): 272–81.

Lorde, Audre. *Zami: A New Spelling of My Name.* Freedom, Calif.: Crossing Press, 1982.

Marshall, Paule. *Brown Girl, Brownstones*. New York: Feminist Press, 1981.

——. *The Chosen Place, the Timeless People*. New York: Vintage Books, 1992.

——. "An Interview with Paule Marshall." By Daryl Cumber Dance. *Southern Review* 28:7 (1992): 1–20.

——. "Meditations on Language and the Self: A Conversation with Paule Marshall." By Melody Graulich and Lisa Sisco. *NWSA Journal* 4:3 (1992): 282–302.

——. *Praisesong for the Widow*. New York: Penguin Books, 1983.

——. *Reena and Other Stories*. New York: Feminist Press, 1983.

——. "Return of a Native Daughter: An Interview with Paule Marshall and Maryse Condé." By John Williams. *Sage* 3:2 (fall 1986): 52–53.

——. "Shaping the World of My Art." *New Letters* 40:1 (autumn 1973): 97–112.

McDonald, Ian, and Stewart Brown. *The Heinemann Book of Caribbean Poetry*. London: Heinemann Educational Books, 1992.

Minh-ha, Trinh T. *Woman, Native, Other*. Bloomington: Indiana University Press, 1989.

Mordecai, Pamela, and Betty Wilson. *Her True-True Name: An Anthology of Women's Writing from the Caribbean*. Portsmouth, N.H.: Heinemann Educational Books, 1990.

Morris, Ann R., and Margaret M. Dunn. " 'The Bloodstream of Our Inheritance': Female Identity and the Caribbean Mothers'-Land." In *Motherlands: Black Women's Writing from Africa, the Caribbean, and South Asia*, ed. Susheila Nasta, 219–37. New Brunswick: Rutgers University Press, 1992.

Morrison, Toni. "City Limits, Village Values: Concepts of the Neighborhood in Black Fiction." In *Literature and the Urban Experience: Essays on the City and Literature*, ed. Michael C. Taye and Ann Chalmers Watts, 35–43. New Brunswick: Rutgers University Press, 1981.

——. *Playing in the Dark: Whiteness and the Literary Imagination*. New York: Vintage Books, 1993.

——. "Rootedness: The Ancestor as Foundation." In *Black Women Writers, 1950–1980*, ed. Mari Evans, 339–45. Garden City, N.Y.: Doubleday, Anchor Press, 1984.

———. "The Site of Memory." In *Inventing the Truth: The Art and Craft of Memoir*, ed. William Zinsser, 103–24. Boston: Houghton Mifflin, 1987.

———. *Sula*. New York: Penguin Books, 1982.

———. *Tar Baby*. New York: Penguin Books, 1981.

Mudimbe, Elisabeth Boyi. "Giving a Voice to Tituba: The Death of the Author?" *World Literature Today* 67:4 (fall 1993): 751–56.

Murdoch, Adlai H. "Divided Desire: Biculturality and the Representation of Identity in *En attendant le bonheur*." *Callaloo* 18:3 (summer 1995): 579–92.

———. "The Novels of Jamaica Kincaid: Figures of Exile, Narratives of Dreams." *Clockwatch Review* 9:1–2 (1994–1995): 141–54.

———. "Severing the (M)other Connection: The Representation of Cultural Identity in Jamaica Kincaid's *Annie John*." *Callaloo* 13:2 (spring 1990): 325–40.

Myers, Eunice, and Ginette Adamso, eds. *Continental, Latin American, and Francophone Women Writers*. Lanham, Md.: University Presses of America, 1987.

Nasta, Susheila, ed. *Motherlands: Black Women's Writing from Africa, the Caribbean, and South Asia*. New Brunswick: Rutgers University Press, 1992.

Natov, Roni. "Mothers and Daughters: Jamaica Kincaid's Pre-Oedipal Narrative." *Children's Literature* 18 (1990): 1–6.

Ngate, Jonathan. "Maryse Condé and Africa: The Making of a Recalcitrant Daughter?" *Current Bibliography on African Affairs* 19:1 (1986–1987): 5–20.

Nichols, Grace. *I Is a Long Memoried Woman*. London: Karnak House, 1983.

Nyatetu-Waigwa, Wangari wa. "From Liminality to a Home of Her Own? The Quest Motif in Maryse Condé's Fiction." *Callaloo* 18:3 (summer 1995): 551–64.

O'Callaghan, Evelyn. *Woman Version: Theoretical Approaches to West Indian Fiction by Women*. New York: St. Martin's Press, 1993.

Paravisini, Lizabeth, and Barbara Webb. "On the Threshold of Becoming: Contemporary Caribbean Women Writers." *Cimarron* 1:3 (1988): 106–32.

Paris, Peter J. *The Spirituality of African Peoples*. Minneapolis: Fortress Press, 1995.

Perret, Delphine. "Dialogue with the Ancestors." *Callaloo* 18:3 (summer 1995): 652–67.

Perry, Donna. "Initiation in Jamaica Kincaid's *Annie John.*" In *Caribbean Women Writers: Essays from the First International Conference,* ed. Selwyn R. Cudjoe, 245–53. Wellesley, Mass.: Calaloux Publications, 1990.

———, ed. *Backtalk: Women Writers Speak Out.* New Brunswick: Rutgers University Press, 1993.

Perry, Ruth, and Martine Watson Brownley, eds. *Mothering the Mind: Twelve Studies of Writers and Their Silent Partners.* New York: Holmes and Meier Publishers, 1984.

Pettis, Joyce. "Self-Definition and Redefinition in Paule Marshall's *Praisesong for the Widow.*" In *Perspectives of Black Popular Culture,* ed. Harry B. Shaw, 93–100. Bowling Green: Ohio University Press, 1990.

———. *Toward Wholeness in Paule Marshall's Fiction.* Charlottesville: University Press of Virginia, 1995.

Pfaff, Françoise. *Conversations with Maryse Condé.* Lincoln: University of Nebraska Press, 1996.

Pollard, Velma. *Considering Woman.* London: Women's Press, 1989.

———. "Cultural Connections in Paule Marshall's *Praisesong for the Widow.*" *World Literature Written in English* 25:2 (autumn 1985): 285–98.

Pryse, Marjorie, and Hortense Spillers, eds. *Conjuring: Black Women Fiction and the Literary Tradition.* Bloomington: Indiana University Press, 1985.

Rahming, Melvin. "Toward a Caribbean Mythology: The Function of Africa in Paule Marshall's *The Chosen Place, the Timeless People.*" *Studies in the Literary Imagination* 26:2 (1993): 77–87.

Reyes, Angelita. "Politics and Metaphors of Materialism in Paule Marshall's *Praisesong for the Widow* and Toni Morrison's *Tar Baby.*" In *Politics and the Muse: Studies in the Politics of Recent American Literature,* ed. Adam J. Sorkin, 179–205. Bowling Green, Ohio: Popular, 1989.

———. "Reading Carnival as an Archaeological Site for Memory in Paule Marshall's *The Chosen Place, the Timeless People,* and *Praisesong for the Widow.*" In *Memory, Narrative, and Identity: New Essays in Ethnic American Literatures,* ed. Amritjit Singh, Joseph Skerrett, and Robert Hogan, 179–97. Boston: Northeastern University Press, 1994.

Rhys, Jean. *Wide Sargasso Sea*. New York: W. W. Norton, 1982.

Rich, Adrienne. *Of Woman Born: Motherhood as Experience and Institution*. New York: W. W. Norton, 1976.

Said, Edward. *Orientalism*. New York: Vintage Books, 1979.

Sandiford, Keith A. "Paule Marshall's *Praisesong for the Widow*: The Reluctant Heiress; or, Whose Life Is It Anyway?" *Black American Literature Forum* 20:4 (winter 1986): 371–92.

Scarboro, Ann Armstrong. "The Healing Process: A Paradigm for Self-Renewal in Paule Marshall's *Praisesong for the Widow* and Camara Laye's *Le Regard du roi*." *Modern Language Studies* 19:1 (1989): 28–36.

Scharfman, Ronnie. "Mirroring and Mothering in Simone Schwarz-Bart's *Pluie et vent sur Télumée Miracle* and Jean Rhys' *Wide Sargasso Sea*." *Yale French Studies* 62 (1981): 88–106.

Schipper, Mineke. *Unheard Words: Women and Literature in Africa, the Arab World, Asia, the Caribbean, and Latin America*. London: Allison and Busby, 1985.

Schneider, Deborah. "A Search for Selfhood: Paule Marshall's *Brown Girl, Brownstones*." In *The Afro-American Novel since 1960*, ed. Peter Bruck and Wolfgang Karrer, 53–73. Amsterdam: B. R. Grüner Publishing, 1982.

Schwarz-Bart, Simone. *The Bridge of Beyond*. London: Heinemann Educational Books, 1982.

Simmons, Diane. *Jamaica Kincaid*. New York: Twayne Publishers, 1994.

Smith, Arlette M. "Maryse Condé's *Heremakhonon*: A Triangular Structure of Alienation." In *International Women's Writing: New Landscape of Identity*, ed. Anne E. Brown and Marjanne E. Goozé, 63–69. Westport, Conn.: Greenwood Press, 1995.

———. "The Semiotics of Exile in Maryse Condé's Fictional Work." *Callaloo* 14:2 (spring 1991): 381–88.

Smith, Michelle. "Reading in Circles: Sexuality and/as History in *I, Tituba, Black Witch of Salem*." *Callaloo* 18:3 (summer 1995): 602–7.

Smith, Sidonie. *A Poetics of Women's Autobiography: Marginality and the Fictions of Self-Representation*. Bloomington: Indiana University Press, 1987.

Smith, Sidonie, and Julia Watson, eds. *De/Colonizing the Subject: The Politics of Gender in Women's Autobiography.* Minneapolis: University of Minnesota Press, 1992.

Snitgen, Jeanne. "History, Identity, and the Constitution of the Female Subject: Maryse Condé's *Tituba.*" *Matatu* 3:6 (1989): 55–73.

Soestwohner, Bettina. "Uprooting Antillean Identity: Maryse Condé's *La Colonie de nouveau monde.*" *Callaloo* 18:3 (summer 1995): 690–706.

Spillers, Hortense. "Mama's Baby, Papa's Maybe: An American Grammar Book." *Diacritics: A Review of Contemporary Criticism* 17:2 (summer 1987): 65–81.

———, ed. *Comparative American Identities: Race, Sex, and Nationality in the Modern Text, Essays from the English Institute.* New York: Routledge, 1991.

Spivak, Gayatri. "Can the Subaltern Speak?" In *Colonial Discourse and Post-colonial Theory,* ed. Patrick Williams and Laura Chrisman, 66–111. New York: Columbia University Press, 1994.

Suárez, Isabel Carrera. "Absent Mother(land)s: Joan Riley's Fiction." In *Motherlands: Black Women's Writing from Africa, the Caribbean, and South Asia,* ed. Susheila Nasta, 290–309. New Brunswick: Rutgers University Press, 1992.

Tate, Claudia, ed. *Black Women Writers at Work.* New York: Continuum Publishing, 1983.

Tiffin, Helen. "Cold Hearts and (Foreign) Tongues: Recitation and the Reclamation of the Female Body in the Works of Erna Brodber and Jamaica Kincaid." *Callaloo* 16:4 (fall 1993): 909–21.

Timothy, Helen Pyne. "Adolescent Rebellion and Gender Relations in *At the Bottom of the River* and *Annie John.*" In *Caribbean Women Writers: Essays from the First International Conference,* ed. Selwyn R. Cudjoe, 233–42. Wellesley, Mass.: Calaloux Publications, 1990.

Troester, Rosalie Riegle. "Turbulence and Tenderness: Mothers, Daughters, and 'Othermothers' in Paule Marshall's *Brown Girl, Brownstones.*" *Sage* 1:2 (fall 1981): 13–16.

Ty, Eleanor. "Struggling with the Powerful (M) Other: Identity and Sexuality in Kogawa's *Obasan* and Kincaid's *Lucy.*" *International Fiction Review* 20:2 (1993): 120–26.

Vološinov, V. *Marxism and the Philosophy of Language.* Trans. I. R. Titunik. New York: Seminar Press, 1973.

Wade-Gayles, Gloria. "The Truths of Our Mothers' Lives: Mother-Daughter Relationships in Black Women's Fiction." *Sage* 1:2 (fall 1984): 8–12.

Washington, Mary Helen. "I Sign My Mother's Name: Alice Walker, Dorothy West, Paule Marshall." In *Mothering the Mind: Twelve Studies of Writers and Their Silent Partners,* ed. Ruth Perry and Martine Watson Brownley, 142–63. New York: Holmes and Meier Publishers, 1984.

Waxman, Barbara Frey. "The Widow's Journey to Self and Roots: Aging and Society in Paule Marshall's *Praisesong for the Widow.*" *Frontiers* 9:3 (1987): 94–99.

Wilentz, Gay. *Binding Cultures: Black Women Writers in Africa and the Diaspora.* Bloomington: Indiana University Press, 1992.

———. "Toward a Spiritual Middle Passage Back: Paule Marshall's Diasporic Vision in *Praisesong for the Widow.*" *Obsidian II* 5:3 (winter 1990): 1–21.

Willis, Susan. *Specifying: Black Women Writing, the American Experience.* Madison: University of Wisconsin Press, 1987.

Wilson, Elizabeth. "Le Voyage et l'espace clos (Island and journey as metaphor): Aspects of Woman's Experience in the Works of Francophone Caribbean Women Novelists." In *Out of the Kumbla,* ed. Carole Boyce Davies and Elaine Savory Fido, 45–57. Trenton, N.J.: Africa World Press, 1990.

Wilson, Lucy. "Aging and Ageism in Paule Marshall's *Praisesong for the Widow* and Beryl Gilroy's *Frangipani House.*" *Journal of Caribbean Studies* 7:2–3 (spring 1990): 189–99.

Wisker, Gina. *Black Women's Writing.* New York: St. Martin's Press, 1993.

Index

of Memory, 28; At the Bottom of the River, 54–55
Kitchen women, 24

Lamming, George, 103
Language, 24; imposition and infusion of, 40–41, 64; as mark of new identity, 44; colonial, 57, 60, 65, 89–90
Lee, Valerie, 131
Lionnet, Françoise, 15, 100, 110, 117–18

Marshall, Paule, 1, 3–4, 16–17, 21–23, 26–27, 31–32, 35–41, 61, 66, 137–38, 156, 164, 166–67, 175, 189–93, 195–96; *Praisesong for the Widow,* 16, 23, 26–27, 43, 137–38, 164, 190, 192, 195–96; *Brown Girl, Brownstones,* 22, 23, 26, 36, 43, 66–67, 137–38, 184, 192, 195–96; *The Chosen Place, The Timeless People,* 138, 162–63, 193, 194–96
Master narrative, 2
Matrilineage, 121, 195
Matrophobia, 25
Memory, 38, 74
Métis, 15
Middle passage, 9, 104, 117, 180–81, 188, 191
Minh-ha, Trinh, 55–56
Monologic discourse, 43
Morris, Ann, 17, 82
Morrison, Toni, 31, 42, 136–38, 191–92, 194; *Rootedness: The Ancestor as Foundation,* 136, 138
Mother Africa, 13, 103, 107, 111, 121, 184–85
Mother country, 3–4, 6–8, 10, 12, 16–21, 25–26, 41, 72, 74, 87, 101, 132–33, 137
Mother culture, 26
Mother-daughter relationship, 18–20, 22, 24, 45–46, 48–49, 62, 65, 68, 76; estrangement/separation in, 54, 67, 94
Motherland(s), 3–4, 6–8, 10, 12, 16–21, 25–26, 41, 98–99, 100–101, 103,

106–7, 112, 116, 118, 122, 132, 135, 137, 177
Mother/mothering/motherhood, 17, 22, 24, 68, 86, 94, 116, 134; as form of colonization, 68; as mirror, 78–79, 83, 134
Mother poets, 24, 35, 38, 40–41
Mother's land, 43–44, 72, 78, 90, 93, 122, 131, 133–35, 161, 164, 196
Mother tongue, 44
Murdoch, Adlai, 108

Nasta, Susheila, 3, 7, 8, 19, 22; *Motherlands,* 3
Nation, 11, 12, 13, 21
Nationalism, 13, 19; black, 30
Nationality, 5
Négritude, 9–10, 14–15, 98
Negroes, 103
Negroization, 117
Neocolonial intervention, 162
Ngate, Jonathan, 112, 114, 118, 121
Nichols, Grace, 98
Niggerfies, 113
Niggerish, 116
Niggerize, 117
Nyatetu-Waigwa, Wangari wa, 118–19, 122

Orality, 36, 137, 190
Other(ness), 7, 20, 55, 99, 121, 125, 156, 177
Othermother(s), 7, 23, 48, 69, 122, 132
Outsideness, 151

Padmore, George, 9, 30
Pan-Africanism, 9, 13–14, 15, 98
Paris, Peter, 167, 177
Patriarchy, 24, 27, 64, 120; conventions of, 64; dominion of, 91; authority of, 130
Pfaff, Françoise, 101
Phallocentricity, ancestral, 107
Pollard, Velma, 67, 185
Power/powerful/powerless, 19, 20, 45, 49, 57, 61, 107, 142
Preverbal bonding, 47
Promised Land, 101

Race, 5; polarization of races, 6

Permissions

Reprinted by permission of Farrar, Straus and Giroux, LLC and the Random House Group Ltd./Jonathan Cape: Excerpts from *Annie John* by Jamaica Kincaid. Copyright © 1985 by Jamaica Kincaid. Excerpts from *A Small Place* by Jamaica Kincaid. Copyright © 1988 by Jamaica Kincaid. Excerpts from *Lucy* by Jamaica Kincaid. Copyright © 1990 by Jamaica Kincaid. Excerpts from *The Autobiography of My Mother* by Jamaica Kincaid. Copyright © 1996 by Jamaica Kincaid.

Reprinted by permission of the Feminist Press: Excerpts from *Brown Girl, Brownstones* by Paule Marshall, 1981.

Reprinted by permission of Putnam Berkley, a division of Penguin Putnam Inc. and Writer's House: Excerpts from *Praisesong for the Widow* by Paule Marshall, copyright © 1983 by Paule Marshall.

Reprinted by permission of Merle Collins: Excerpts from *Rotten Pomerack*.

Reprinted by permission of Louise Bennett: "Back to Africa," from *Jamaica Labrish*. 1966.